THE AMERICAN SUPREME COURT

THE CHICAGO HISTORY OF
AMERICAN CIVILIZATION

DANIEL J. BOORSTIN, EDITOR

Robert G. McCloskey

The
American
Supreme
Court

Second Edition

Revised by Sanford Levinson

The University of Chicago Press
Chicago & London

ROBERT G. McCLOSKEY was professor of government at Harvard University.
He is the author of *American Conservatism in the Age of Enterprise* (1951)
and editor of *Essays in Constitutional Law* (1957).
SANFORD LEVINSON is the W. St. John Garwood and
W. St. John Garwood Jr., Regents Chair in Law at the
University of Texas Law School. He is the author of *Constitutional Faith* (1988).

The University of Chicago Press, Chicago 60637
The University of Chicago Press, Ltd., London
© 1960, 1994 by The University of Chicago
All rights reserved. Published 1994
Second edition 1994
Printed in the United States of America
03 02 01 00 99 98 97 96 95 94   1 2 3 4 5

ISBN: 0-226-55677-8 (cloth)
0-226-55678-6 (paper)

Library of Congress Cataloging-in-Publication Data

McCloskey, Robert G. (Robert Green)
    The American Supreme Court / by Robert G. McCloskey.—2nd ed. /
revised by Sanford Levinson.
    p. cm.
Includes bibliographical references and index.
    1. United States. Supreme Court. I. Levinson, Sanford, 1941–
II. Title.
KF8742.Z9M3   1994
347.73'26—dc20
[347.30735]   94-10905
                                                              CIP

To My Wife

R. G. McC.

*To Meira and Rachel and
to the memory of their grandfather, Fred Yenkin*

S. L.

Contents

EDITOR'S FOREWORD TO THE SECOND EDITION

RARELY DOES A BOOK about a controversial contemporary institution survive the decades and continue to command an admiring general and scholarly audience. Robert G. McCloskey's *American Supreme Court,* published in 1960, has done just that. When an updated edition of the book was called for, we therefore decided that it was important, while adding new facts and cases, emphatically to preserve the point of view and elegance of style that have given this book its high reputation. Professor Sanford Levinson has accomplished this difficult task.

The reader will find the entire text of the original edition. At the same time, Professor Levinson has acutely extended McCloskey's analytic framework into the 1990's and has provided his own preface, two new concluding chapters, his coda on the role of the Supreme Court in the most recent decades of American History, an updated chronology, and a new bibliographic essay. By this sensitive revision, he has given renewed life to McCloskey's work, and has helped it serve the large purpose of our series: to provide readable and up-to-date interpretations of our dynamic American civilization.

Daniel J. Boorstin

Editor's Foreword to the First Edition

Today the strength of the Supreme Court of the United States seems the best proof that our political system is capable of firmness and dignity. Yet President Washington had difficulty finding men of national stature willing to sit on so inconsequential a court. Historians still disagree over what powers the Founding Fathers intended to give these judges. Certainly the Founding Fathers had no blueprint for such a court. Many of them would be astonished and most might be shocked that any branch of the central government had attained such power. Of all the achievements of American civilization none is more the accidental by-product of our past.

The history of the Supreme Court, and especially the story of judicial review to which this volume is mainly devoted, is the surprising account of how a few men have used powers of dubious legality to uphold the rule of law in American life. There is no more ironic aspect of our history.

Every generation, while finding its own uses for the Court, has preserved the Court as a symbol of the need for limits and for continuity in a nation of novelties. The Supreme Court has thus become the American political conscience, a kind of secular papacy, a new search in every generation for what the more large-minded and more foresighted of the Founders might have meant if they were alive. It is the Great Remembrancer of our foundations.

Actually the Court has become a monument both to our need to search for historical consistency and to the limits of such consistency. Through the history of the Court we see that men can serve a traditional purpose only by changing instruments and by shifting ground. And we discover how great judges make the cautionary wisdom of the past speak in the technical language of the common law.

In the present volume, Mr. McCloskey gives us a concise and dramatic account of that part of the Court's work which has been closest to the mainstream of American politics. All the crises in our political history have sooner or later been stated in legal terms. Mr. McCloskey shows us how the major changes in our political and economic life have been moderated and justified by the Supreme Court.

The importance of the Supreme Court has come not only from the Court's insistence on measuring the present against the past, "needs" against "rights," opinion against law, but also from the desire of the American people to take the Court's decisions seriously. From time to time it has been said that the Court—by its decisions about slavery, about the New Deal, or about educational equality—has made trouble for the nation. It would be more accurate to say that the American people have made trouble for themselves by listening reverently and obediently to men who remind them of their past, who prefer legality to popularity. The uncanny American reverence for law has made possible the uncanny power and dignity of the American Supreme Court.

By relating the history of the Supreme Court to other aspects of American civilization, Mr. McCloskey serves the purposes of the "Chicago History of American Civilization." This series aims to make each aspect of our culture a window to all our history. The series contains two kinds of books: a *chronological* group, which provides a coherent narrative of American history from its beginning to the present day; and a *topical* group, which deals with the history of varied and significant aspects of American life. This book is one of the topical group. Sixteen titles in the series have now been published, and twenty-odd are in preparation.

Daniel J. Boorstin

PREFACE TO THE SECOND EDITION

THIS IS LITERALLY a labor of love. Robert G. McCloskey was my faculty adviser some thirty years ago when I was a graduate student at Harvard, and I prepared my Ph.D. dissertation under his supervision. As a teaching assistant in his courses on the American Supreme Court and on civil liberties, I heard him lecture many times; more importantly, I spent hundreds of hours with him in conversation over postclass coffee discussing not only these matters but life in general. He was everything a mentor should be.

It is, though, not only my respect for the memory of a wonderful man that has led me to revise his book in the specific manner that I have. *The American Supreme Court* is justifiably regarded as a classic. It has remained in print since its publication in 1960 and continues to be assigned in courses. It not only presents a remarkably concise overview of the history of the Supreme Court, it also articulates with almost matchless clarity a particular view of the role best played by the Court within the American political system. Though McCloskey may be a voice from the past, he spoke to concerns that certainly remain present today.

This accounts, then, for the basic decision to *add to*, rather than genuinely *revise*, his book. The first seven chapters are exactly as he wrote them at the end of the 1950's, save for the silent correction of a very few factual errors and, more importantly, different titles for chapters 6 and 7. I argue in my own final chapter that the term "welfare state," used in the original title for chapter 6, is better used for the regime that emerged in the United States following Lyndon B. Johnson's "Great Society" and its consolidation by Richard Nixon. I thus substitute the term "regulatory state" for "welfare state" in the original title. It also seemed obviously desirable to find a new title for chapter 7 insofar as McCloskey's "modern court and modern America" are now a full generation old.

I certainly do not want to suggest that I would argue for no changes in McCloskey's own arguments were this a genuinely co-authored work. Inevitably, both developments in disciplinary scholarship and generational shifts in overarching ideological perceptions would lead to differences in argument. I do not, for example, share McCloskey's awe for John Marshall; I substantially agree with one critic who describes McCloskey's treatment of *Marbury* v. *Madison* as entirely too "romantic." More importantly, I would probably focus more on slavery as a dominating issue of the first seventy years, rather than treat it simply as one aspect of the controversies about federalism that McCloskey emphasizes. And so on. However, for the reasons indicated above, I view this, in significant measure, as *his* book rather than my own. My task is to try to update it and make it useful even for another third of a century.

This being said, I gladly accept full responsibility for the two chapters that I have added, though I have tried to write them in a McCloskean spirit. In the new chapter 8, I try primarily to bring up to date the story that he began telling in terms of the Court's role as protector of the civil rights and liberties of vulnerable, often unpopular, minorities. I draw at least in part on several essays that McCloskey wrote during the 1960's, before his dreadfully premature death in 1969. Chapter 9, on the other hand, represents something potentially quite new, for there I argue that this role has in significant ways been supplemented, and perhaps supplanted, by a distinctively new role as monitor of the "welfare state" that I identify with developments that occurred in the decade after the publication of *The American Supreme Court*.

It is only after these two new chapters that the reader will find the original Epilogue: "The Supreme Court and the Lessons of History." In keeping with what I hope is the spirit of this book, I am reprinting it too as it was published in 1960, though I have added a coda that continues a conversation that began more than a quarter-century ago in Cambridge and will, I hope, initiate new conversations with the readers of this edition.

Sanford Levinson

Acknowledgments

AS NOTED IN my preface, my deepest acknowledgment is indeed to Robert McCloskey. It is no coincidence at all that McCloskey is a dedicatee of *Processes of Constitutional Decisionmaking,* a casebook that I co-edit with Paul Brest. And Brest himself amply deserves tribute, for his invitation to me in 1979 to collaborate with him on the second edition of his path-breaking casebook provided the occasion not only for deepened friendship, but also the opportunity (and necessity) to reflect at length about developments in recent American constitutionalism and how they can best be organized for pedagogical purposes. Chapter nine of this book could never have been written had I not struggled over several summers to organize a new chapter in the 1992 edition of *Processes* on the Constitution and the modern welfare state.

Co-dedicatees of my portion of the casebook, along with McCloskey, are my colleagues at the University of Texas Law School, who have always proved willing to read my drafts and discuss my ideas. Especially helpful in regard to this manuscript were Jack Balkin, Sam Issacharoff, Scot Powe, and Mike Sharlot. Gerry Rosenberg, of the University of Chicago, also provided invaluable help on the bibliography as well as helpful suggestions in regard to my general argument. That I did not accept all of them leaves him (and many others) the opportunity to question and challenge my own views on the complex events of the past thirty years.

Finally, I am grateful to John Tryneski of the University of Chicago Press for his encouragement, over the years, regarding the possibility of bringing out a new edition of *The American Supreme Court.* Once it seemed, finally, appropriate to go ahead with the project, he and his colleagues at the Press could not have been more accommodating.

Sanford Levinson

PREFACE TO THE FIRST EDITION

THIS BOOK DEALS with the work of the Supreme Court of the United States as a constitutional tribunal, exercising the power of judicial review. It does not purport to describe the activity of the Court as a whole; much less is it a history of constitutional law in the widest possible sense, treating of constitutional developments that have been brought about by legislative and executive action, or by the more subtle process we call custom. Finally, because it is a brief book, I cannot of course even claim that it covers the story of judicial review comprehensively. The chapters are interpretive essays in the history of judicial review. They deal with aspects of that history that seem to me important and interesting, but they omit material that might legitimately seem equally important or interesting to another.

My aim has been, within this compass, to understand the way the Supreme Court has conducted itself to achieve its results, the role it has played in American life. I have been most concerned, as the text will reveal, to see the Court as an agency in the American governing process, an agency with a mind and a will and an influence of its own. Greatly as we may respect John Marshall, not many sophisticated persons would now take these words of his very seriously: "Judicial power, as contradistinguished from the power of the laws, has no existence. Courts are the mere instruments of the law, and can will nothing."

Yet there has been too little effort, I believe, to project a contrary view back into judicial history in order to see what the Court *was,* if it was not what Marshall asserted. And because this has not been done, as I am at pains to suggest in the epilogue to this volume, we are not prepared as we should be to evaluate the Court of today, either as critics or as defenders.

One

The Genesis and Nature of
Judicial Power

On June 21, 1788, when the convention of New Hampshire voted 57 to 46 to approve the proposed national constitution, the requirement of nine ratifying states was fulfilled and the United States of America sprang into legal being. Opportunity for instant creation of this magnitude occurs only in fiction and law, and the delegates did not underrate their historic moment. They were careful to specify that it came at one o'clock in the afternoon, for they feared that Virginia might act that very evening and claim a share in the honor. They need not have worried. The Virginians were in for three more days of oratory, mostly by Patrick Henry, before their state's proud name could be added to the list.

Fifteen months later, President Washington accomplished another of these portentous juridical feats by signing the Judiciary Act of 1789, which was to be called many years afterward "probably the most important and the most satisfactory Act ever passed by Congress." The latter-day eulogist was himself a Supreme Court justice, and his good opinion of a law that made him one of the most august figures in the nation is not surprising; a long roll of eminent statesmen since 1789 could be called to testify on the other side. But hardly one of them would dispute his opinion that the Act was extremely important, for it not only established the far-flung system of federal courts but boldly defined their jurisdiction, and especially that of the Supreme Court, in such a way that the states, Congress, and the President could be held subject to judicial authority.

Finally, on February 2, 1790, some of the men who had received these high commissions and whose duty it therefore was to give living force to these paper enactments, assembled in the Royal Exchange building in New York and organized as the Supreme Court of the United States. The occasion was solemn, and the newspapers followed it closely, passing on to the people every crumb of detail about this third great department of their young national republic. Yet neither the press nor the people nor the justices themselves could quite know how momentous the day was, and there is good evidence that they did not. Only four of the six men Washington had chosen to adorn the Supreme Court turned up for that first official meeting. Robert H. Harrison declined appointment, apparently because he thought his judicial post as chancellor of Maryland was more important; and John Rutledge, though officially a member of the Court in its first three terms, never attended a session and soon resigned to accept the chief justiceship of South Carolina. Looking back, we can see that the first meeting of the Supreme Court of the United States was one of the mileposts in the history of jurisprudence. We can see that the ratifying of the Constitution and the signing of the Judiciary Act had, when taken together, opened great wells of judicial power, and that the four justices who sat together in the Royal Exchange that winter were inaugurating a governmental enterprise of vast and unprecedented dimensions. But the principals were looking forward, not back, and the future must have seemed cloudy.

In the nature of the case they would not have known much about the prospects of their Court and the Constitution, for the very good reason that so little about either had been firmly decided. The delegates who framed the Constitution have been traditionally and deservedly praised for producing a document that could earn the approval of such diverse states as Massachusetts and Georgia and such diverse men as John Adams and Thomas Jefferson (neither of whom, by the way, attended the Federal Convention). But this congenial result had been achieved not only by compromise but by forbearance. The Constitution clearly established a few principles about which there was no serious colonial disagreement, for example, the representative system for choosing officials and the separation of powers between the departments of the national government. It compromised a few more troublesome issues like the question of equal state representation versus representation based on population, and the question of the slave trade. But still weightier difficulties that might have prevented ratification were either left severely alone by the Founding Fathers or treated in ambiguous clauses that passed the problems on to posterity.

No one quite knew, for example, what was meant when the Constitution endowed Congress with power "to regulate commerce among foreign nations, and among the several states"; or to make all laws "necessary and proper" for carrying out the national government's other powers; or when it was asserted that the Constitution as well as laws and treaties made by the nation were "the supreme law of the land." No one was sure how the "ex post facto" clause or the "contract clause" would restrict state inroads on the rights of property-holders. Some had hopes and others had suspicions about the meaning of these and other enigmatic phrases in the document. But if either the hopes or the suspicions had been fully warranted by clear language in the Constitution itself, it seems most unlikely that ratification would have been possible. The issue underlying these uncertainties was no less than this: whether a nation or a league of sovereign states was created by the Constitution. That was the question still awaiting decision in 1790, and until America began answering it, the full significance of New Hampshire's historic vote was a matter for guess work. If a true nation emerged as the future unfolded, then New Hampshire's action was unforgettable. If not, ratification would be seen as a comparatively minor incident in modern world history.

As for the Supreme Court, its future was even more uncertain. The Constitution has comparatively little to say about the Court or the federal judiciary in general. The "judicial power of the United States," whatever it may be, is vested in the Supreme Court and in such other courts as Congress may establish. But the composition of the Court, including the number of its members, is left for congressional decision; and, while federal judges cannot be removed except by impeachment, there is nothing to prevent Congress from creating additional judgeships whenever it chooses. Furthermore, although the judicial power "extends" to a variety of cases described in Article III, section 2, the second paragraph of that section significantly qualifies what the first seems to have granted, and gives Congress power to control the Supreme Court's jurisdiction over appeals from lower courts. Since the cases that reach the Court directly without first being heard in other courts are comparatively minor in quantity or importance, this legislative authority over appeals (over the "appellate jurisdiction") is a license for Congress to decide whether the Supreme Court will be a significant or a peripheral factor in American government.

Most important of all, the Constitution makes no explicit statement about the nature of the Court's power even when a case admittedly falls within its jurisdiction. Some of the uncertainties outlined above were resolved, temporarily at any rate, by the passage of the Judiciary Act. Its famous Section 25 gave the Supreme Court power to reverse or affirm state court decisions which had denied claims based on the federal Constitution, treaties, or laws. This meant that such cases could be reached by the Supreme Court through its appellate jurisdiction. But suppose a state court had denied such a claim under the federal Constitution and the Supreme Court of the United States reversed on the ground that the state court's interpretation of the Constitution was in error. And suppose further that the state court obstinately continued to insist upon its own interpretation. Was there anything in the Constitution to guarantee that the Supreme Court's opinion would prevail, that the Supreme Court's authority was superior to state courts? Or suppose, to carry the matter a step further, that the state court had held a federal law invalid as conflicting with the *national* Constitution and the Supreme Court *agreed* with this holding, thus asserting its authority to overthrow an act of Congress. Does the Constitution make it *clear* that the Court has this final authority of "judicial review" over national legislative enactments?

The answer to both questions is a fairly solid "no." As for state decisions it has been argued that the "supreme law of the land" clause and the clause extending the judicial power to cases arising under the Constitution do make it clear that the Supreme Court was intended to be preeminent on questions of constitutional interpretation. If the Constitution is supreme and the Supreme Court has jurisdiction over cases involving the Constitution, then it follows that the Court's word on such matters is paramount over all others—so the argument runs. But in the first place this reasoning is not unassailable, for as defenders of states' rights were later passionately to insist, the fact that the Constitution is supreme does not settle the question of who decides what the Constitution means. And in the second place enthusiasts for judicial review have never quite been able to explain why so formidable a power was granted by implication rather than by flat statement. As for judicial review of congressional acts, the support in the language of the Constitution was even more supposititious, and arguments for the authority derived solely from that language seem inevitably to beg the question.

None of this is to say that the framers of the Constitution would have been surprised to see the Supreme Court exercising the power of judicial review in some form, both as against the states and as against Congress. Indeed there is ample evidence that most of them who had thought about it expected that the Court would do so, however distressing it is that they failed to make their expectations explicit. But neither the framers nor the ratifying state conventions (whose views are in some ways more relevant to the issue) had any general understanding about the particular form that the judicial review would take and the role that the Supreme Court would therefore assume.

Some, like Alexander Hamilton, certainly hoped that the justices would act as general monitors, broadly supervising the other branches of government and holding them to the path of constitutional duty, though even he seems to have conceived this exalted notion only after the Convention's adjournment. Others, like Robert Yates, also of New York, feared that the Court would so regard its function. But James Madison, the highest possible authority on the Constitution's intent, though apparently expecting the Supreme Court to disallow laws that *clearly* contravened the Constitution, by no means conceded that the Court could apply its negative judgment to more debatable points or that the judicial pronouncements were intended to be final and binding on the other branches of government. And the evidence of both the Convention and the ratification controversy suggests that other participants were equally doubtful about these questions and that many more had simply not considered the matter at all.

In short, neither the words of the Constitution nor the provable intent of those who framed and ratified it justified in 1790 any certitude about the scope or finality of the Court's power to superintend either the states or Congress. The most that can be said is that language and intent did not *preclude* the Court from becoming the puissant tribunal of later history.

GREAT EXPECTATIONS

Nevertheless those four men in the Royal Exchange, though without any ironclad assurances, might well have had a strong hunch that destiny sat beside them, that the Constitution would be transfigured from a bitterly debated paper enactment into a venerated symbol of Americanism, and that the Court would emerge as the chief expounder of its mysteries and a beneficiary of its prestige. They must have realized that by tradition and temperament the new nation was ripe for such developments.

For the Constitution was potentially the convergence point for all the ideas about fundamental law that had been current in America since the colonization period. Of course the notion of a law-above-government, a "higher" law, was well known throughout the Western world, but the colonists had given it a special domestic cast, infusing it with interpretations drawn from their own unique experience. While most Europeans thought of higher law as exercising a moral restraint on government, they did not argue that this moral limit was legally enforceable, that it was positive law, practically binding the governors. Even before the Revolutionary controversy, Americans had found it easy to assume that it was just that, for their own legislatures had long been literally bound by "higher law" in such forms as the colonial charters and decisions of the British Privy Council. But the struggle with England turned assumption into fiery conviction as the colonists argued that Parliament was forbidden, not only morally but literally, to transgress the rights Americans claimed under their charters and under the British Constitution. And after the break with England this now very American idea of a written, tangible higher law was further embodied in the new state constitutions and in the Articles of Confederation. The document of 1789 then could draw on this enormous fund of prestige that the higher-law idea had assimilated in America.

Such circumstances might help explain, at least initially, why the Constitution won such ready devotion. But the question remains, it might be said, why the Court should be chosen to share in and perpetuate the Constitution's glory. We have seen that the language of the Constitution is inconclusive on this matter and that the intentions of the framers were ambiguous. Jefferson, Madison and many other almost equally illustrious statesmen were later to argue that the Congress, the President, and even the individual states were, no less than the courts, guardians of the Constitution and coequal interpreters of its meaning. What warrant then had our four new judges for hoping that history would reject these rival claimants and confirm the Supreme Court's constitutional prerogative? To put the question somewhat differently, what made it likely, though perhaps not certain, that the Court would play the great part it has played in American life?

THE HIGHER-LAW BACKGROUND AND POPULAR SOVEREIGNTY

With the benefit of hindsight, it is not hard to find a number of answers to these questions. The common law traditions deriving from the great seventeenth-century English jurist, Sir Edward Coke, exalted judges above other folk, and that tradition was cherished by Americans with peculiar tenacity. The Federalists, who enjoyed political ascendancy during the first decade of the Republic's history, tried to use their temporary prestige to implant in the popular mind a respect for judges, so that Federalism might find a haven against the adversity of a Jeffersonian political victory. The very fact that the concept of judicial review was, at the outset, imperfectly understood was a point in its favor, for it enabled judges to build up the Court's power gradually and almost imperceptibly and its opponents thus found themselves in the frustrating position of those who fight shadows. These factors, among others, are surely relevant to the problem. But they are not sufficient to explain the Court's impending future; they seem to rest on a broader, underlying causal condition whose roots drive deeper into the subsoil of American political life.

To understand that condition it is necessary to look again at the climate of political opinion in eighteenth-century America and particularly at the quarter-century that preceded the Constitution. We have seen that the old doctrine of fundamental law was stimulated by the events and idea currents of the Revolutionary era. Now it must be observed that the movement for revolution also supplied a vital impetus for another, and in some ways, contradictory, notion—the theory of popular sovereignty. American pamphleteers had insisted on the principle of home rule; the Declaration of Independence had founded just government on the "consent of the governed"; the next and natural step was to regard the people as not only a consenting but a willing entity and to declare, as Jefferson later said, that "the will of the majority is in all cases to prevail." These reasonable and perhaps inevitable deductions from the Spirit of '76 were widely prevalent in America during the Articles of Confederation period. Many of the solid citizens deplored such "mad democracy" and longed to curb it, but they could not evade the fact that the will-of-the-people concept was now firmly planted in American minds as one of the premises of political thinking.

Yet plainly that concept conflicted with the doctrine of fundamental law which was also, and concurrently, treasured by Americans. Popular sovereignty suggests *will;* fundamental law suggests *limit.* The one idea conjures up the vision of an active, positive state; the other idea emphasizes the negative, restrictive side of the political problem. It may be possible to harmonize these seeming opposites by logical sleight of hand, by arguing that the doctrines of popular sovereignty and fundamental law were fused in the Constitution, which was a popularly willed limitation. But it seems unlikely that Americans in general achieved such a synthesis and far more probable, considering our later political history, that most of them retained the two ideas side by side. This propensity to hold contradictory ideas simultaneously is one of the most significant qualities of the American political mind at all stages of national history, and it helps substantially in explaining the rise to power of the United States Supreme Court.

For with their political hearts thus divided between the will of the people and the rule of law, Americans were naturally receptive to the development of institutions that reflected each of these values separately.

The legislature with its power to initiate programs and policies, to respond to the expressed interest of the public, embodied the doctrine of popular sovereignty. The courts, generally supposed to be without will as Hamilton said, generally revered as impartial and independent, fell heir almost by default to the guardianship of the fundamental law. It did not avail for Jeffersonian enemies of the judicial power to insist that a single department could exercise *both* the willing and the limiting functions. The bifurcation of the two values in the American mind impellingly suggested that the functions should be similarly separated. And the devotion of Americans to both popular sovereignty and fundamental law insured public support for the institution that represented each of them.

CONSEQUENCES FOR AMERICAN CONSTITUTIONALISM

This dualism of the American mind, symbolized on the one hand by "political" institutions like the Congress and the Presidency and on the other hand by the Court and the Constitution, helps account for a good deal that seems baffling in later history. In logical terms it might appear strange that the nation should resoundingly approve the New Deal in 1936 and a few months later stoutly defend against attack the Supreme Court that had cut the heart from the New Deal program. But the paradox is related as branch to root to the historic dualism between popular sovereignty and the doctrine of fundamental law that developed with the birth throes of the American political system. The separation of the two ideas in the American mind had been emphasized by intervening events: strongminded judges had added new arguments for the Court's constitutional prerogative; congressmen and presidents, busy with more pressing concerns, had been content except for fitful rebellious impulses to let those arguments go unchallenged; and the cake of custom had hardened over the original disjunction. But it was made possible at the outset by our native tendency to harbor conflicting ideas without trying, or caring, to resolve them.

The United States began its history, then, with a Constitution that posed more questions than it answered and with a Supreme Court whose birthright was most uncertain. The temper of the times and the deepseated inclinations of the American political character favored the future of both these institutions and at the same time prescribed their limits and helped determine their nature. American devotion to the principle of fundamental law gave the Constitution its odor of sanctity, and the American bent for evading contradictions by assigning values to separate compartments allowed the Supreme Court to assume the priestly mantle. But like most successes, in politics and elsewhere, this one had a price. The failure to resolve the conflict between popular sovereignty and fundamental law perhaps saved the latter principle, but by the same token it left the former intact. And this meant that the fundamental law could be enforced only within delicately defined boundaries, that constitutional law though not simply the creature of the popular will nevertheless had always to reckon with it, that the mandates of the Supreme Court must be shaped with an eye not only to legal right and wrong, but with an eye to what popular opinion would tolerate.

We have seen, then, that the Constitution makers postponed some of the most vital questions confronting them, that the Constitution and the Supreme Court inherited the quasi-religious symbolic quality attached to the doctrine of "higher law," but that the dogmas of popular sovereignty also continued to survive and flourish and therefore influence constitutionalism. The consequences of all this were several. For one thing the Constitution itself could not become the certain and immutable code of governmental conduct that some of its latter-day idolaters imagined it to be. Conceived in ambiguity as well as liberty, it could never escape that legacy. The framers had said in effect: with respect to certain questions, some of them very momentous, the Constitution means whatever the circumstances of the future will allow it to mean. But since those circumstances were almost sure to vary, the result was that alterability became the law of the Constitution's being: it might mean one thing in 1855, something else in 1905, and something still different in 1955, depending upon what circumstances, including popular expectations, warranted.

To be sure, as the years went on there was a certain accumulation of fairly well-fixed interpretations, and the picture of a constitutional system in eternal flux should not be overdrawn. Some constitutional clauses are explicit enough (and frequently unimportant enough) so that argument about their meaning is improbable. It is unlikely that the states will ever be permitted to grant titles of nobility (Art. I, sec. 10); federal judges, once hired, can feel secure against direct wage cuts (Art. III, sec. 1). Other phrases often rather technical in nature, like the "ex post facto" clause (Art. I, sec. 10), seem to resist the winds of innovation more efficiently than others. Moreover, because the illusion of continuity must be respected, great constitutional changes are likely to come slowly. Nevertheless only a very bold constitutional scholar would declare that he *knows* how the commerce clause or the due process clauses will be understood by the next generation. And when we count up the clauses whose past is variable and whose future is uncertain they far exceed in significance if not in number their more stable fellows.

THE COURT'S CONSTITUTIONAL POWERS AND DUTIES

As for the Supreme Court, its nature has also been heavily and permanently influenced by the factors just described. As might be expected, any description of the judicial function in America is shot through with paradoxes. To begin with, the observer confronts the fact that the Court does inherit a responsibility for helping to guide the nation, especially with respect to those long-term "value questions" that are so vital to the maintenance of a just political order. A good many gallons of ink have been spilled over the issue of whether such a heavy assignment should have devolved on the judiciary. John Marshall, "the great Chief Justice," has been accused of seizing the bitter cup all too gladly and thus setting a pattern of usurpation for future judges to follow. Insofar as this indictment rests on the supposed "intent of the framers," it suffers from the weakness already remarked: that so few of the framers had any clear views one way or another about the subject.

On the other hand, insofar as the charge is that the nation was unwise to delegate this duty to the judges (or allow them to assume it), it may be right, but is also perilously near to irrelevance. For this amounts to saying that America was unwise to be the nation that it was. The American mind conceived a dichotomy between the willed law of legislative enactment and the discovered or pronounced law of the Constitution, and "judicial review" was, as we have seen, one result. The fallacy of making such a distinction may be palpable enough from our modern perspective, but the fact remains that it was not palpable to Marshall's generation, and nothing very helpful is accomplished by arguing that it should have been.

Nor is it much more profitable to urge that the Court should now put off the responsibility it once so eagerly took up, even if it be conceded that the original arrogation was unwise. Historical accident and bad logic may explain the inception of judicial review, but by now the American nation has lived with the consequences for more than 150 years. Our courts and, even more important, our legislatures have been shaped by the understanding that the judiciary will help in charting the path of governmental policy. A rough division of labor has developed from that understanding, for it is assumed that the legislature can focus largely on the task of "interest representation," while passing on to the courts a substantial share of the responsibility for considering the long-term constitutional questions that continually arise. Appearances may be deceptive. Congressmen may self-righteously insist that they serve both the Constitutional Tradition and their Constituents, but the needs of these two masters seem to coincide with remarkable invariability; and it is fair to infer that interests and pressures play the larger part in the legislative process.

Surely this is no indictment of that process, for the American tradition respects, as has been said, the will of today's popular majority, and interests must therefore be paid due heed. But the American tradition also sets great store, as we have also seen, by the set of values associated with the "rule of law," which history has rightly or wrongly consigned in heavy part to the judiciary. In a world of abstractions, one might argue that this historic division, since it defies good sense, ought to be obliterated. But in the world that history has given us, the almost certain result would be that pure calculation of interest-group pressures defined the course of government in the United States. It is too much to ask that a legislative process as interest-dominated as ours abjure its traditions at this late date and take on the functions of a high court as well. Yet until it does, the judiciary must accept its own traditional responsibility, lest the very idea of limited government be lost. Critics may legitimately debate whether the Court should play a greater or lesser part in directing the ship of state. That it must play some part is the penalty of its heritage.

THE CONDITIONS OF JUDICIAL CONTROL

Yet once this is said, it must immediately be added—or reiterated—that the tradition which transmits this power to the Court likewise prescribes the conditions of its exercise. The nation expects the judges to aid in deciding policy questions, but the nation is prone, with sublime inconsistency, to grow fiercely resentful if the aid becomes repression, if the judges bypass certain ill-marked but nevertheless quite real boundaries, two of which merit special consideration.

In the first place, there are the limitations implied by the fact that the Supreme Court is expected to be both a "court" in the orthodox sense of the word and something very much more as well. A full account of the confusions fostered by this seeming contradiction would almost involve a recapitulation of Supreme Court history. Legions of judges and their devotees have believed, or professed to believe, that constitutional law was a technical mystery revealing itself in terms of unmistakable precision to those who had the key, that the Constitution was the record and the judges merely the impartial phonograph that played it, a group of men who somehow managed to stop being men when they put on their robes and would not dream of letting their subjective value judgments affect their understanding of the Constitution. No court was ever like this, no system of law was ever so sure a guide to its interpreters. And the myth of a perfect judiciary perfectly administering a perfect Constitution was therefore deeply impaired in the twentieth century by writers who pointed out what some perceptive observers had always known—that judges are mortal. Like senators and presidents, it was said, judges may have prejudices, and those prejudices may affect their understanding of the Constitution. In fact, the critics went on, the American Supreme Court, so far from merely and imperturbably reflecting eternal constitutional verities, is a willing, policy-making, *political* body.

All this was perfectly true as far as it went, and it provided a useful antidote to previous oversimplifications. But the trouble was that it tended to foster an oversimplification of its own: "legal realists," impressed by the discovery that the Supreme Court was more than a court, were sometimes prone to treat it as if it were not a court at all, as if its "courthood" were a pure façade for political functions indistinguishable from those performed by the legislature. Such a view bypasses everything that is really interesting about the institution and obscures, as much as the discredited old mythology ever did, its true nature.

For the fascinating thing about the Supreme Court has been that it blends orthodox judicial functions with policy-making functions in a complex mixture. And the Court's power is accounted for by the fact that the mixture is maintained in nice balance; but the fact that it *must* be maintained in such a balance accounts for the limitations of that power. The Court's claim on the American mind derives from the myth of an impartial, judicious tribunal whose duty it is to preserve our sense of continuity with the fundamental law. Because that law was initially stated in ambiguous terms, it has been the duty of the Court to make "policy decisions" about it, that is, to decide what it means in the circumstances existing when the question is presented. But though the judges do enter this realm of policy-making, they enter with their robes on, and they can never (or at any rate seldom) take them off; they are both empowered and restricted by their "courtly" attributes.

They cannot, for example, even decide a question unless it is presented in the form of a "case" between two or more interested parties; and the Supreme Court early, and wisely, held that to render "advisory opinions" even to the President would be incongruous with the judicial function. Sometimes the Court is criticized for leaning over backward to find technical and, to a layman, unduly "legalistic" reasons for leaving important constitutional questions unsettled. Often the drag of precedent inhibits the judges from revising constitutional principles as quickly as might be desirable. And finally there are whole large areas of constitutional determination which the Court deliberately and rather consistently leaves alone (for example, the issue of whether a state has "a republican form of government," Art. IV, sec. 4) on the grounds that the questions therein raised are not appropriate for judicial determination.

Any individual decision along any of these lines may well be subject to criticism, for the judges of the Supreme Court, being men, can err. But it is the greatest of nonsense to generalize the criticism into impatience with the Court's "legalistic" demeanor as such, since the logical conclusion of such a criticism is to align the judicial power squarely with the legislative power and to erase the differentiation of function that is the Court's basis for being. And it is also wrong to suppose that the Court's insistence on such attributes of judiciality is a mere pose, designed to hoodwink the public without hampering the judges. In certain spectacular cases in our history the Court has seemed to take leave of courtly procedures in order to remedy an injustice, real or fancied. Such a landmark of judicial temerity was the decision of 1895 which outlawed a national income tax, and no sophisticated student of the Court would deny that it can sometimes forget its "legalistic" trappings and can at other times refashion them to serve the judicial purpose of the moment. But in most cases such technical legal limitations do play a part that is not sham but perfectly real. The judges have usually known what students have sometimes not known—that their tribunal must be a court, as well as seem one, if it is to retain its power. The idea of fundamental law as a force in its own right, distinguishable from today's popular will, can only be maintained by a pattern of Court behavior that emphasizes the separation. If departures from that pattern are too frequent and too extreme, the emphasis will be lost and the idea itself will be imperiled.

One consequence, then, of the Supreme Court's peculiar origins is this necessity that it perform legislative (or quasi-legislative) tasks with judicial tools, which is roughly akin to the assignment of playing baseball with a billiard cue. But its problems do not end there. A second result, as has already been intimated, is the need for the judges to reckon, in making rules and guiding policy, with the imperatives of public opinion no matter how impeccably "judicial" is the method by which the rules are arrived at. This is not to say that the Court should consult the latest bulletins on the popular climate and shape its judgments accordingly. But it is to say that public concurrence sets an outer boundary for judicial policy-making; that judicial ideas of the good society can never be too far removed from the popular ideas. The Republic might have been dedicated at the outset to the principle of pure popular sovereignty, and in that event the Supreme Court would have inherited only the important but secondary responsibility of statutory interpretation. On the other hand, it is imaginatively, though not perhaps practically, conceivable to establish a governmental system in which the fundamental law absolutely controls the public will, and in such a system the Court might enjoy utter independence. But America, as we have seen, chose neither of these worlds, but tried to have the best of them both: the upshot is that the Court, while sometimes checking or at any rate modifying the popular will, is itself in turn checked or modified.

America has thus had two sovereigns, but this somewhat outlandish arrangement has been maintained only because each of the partners has known the meaning of self-restraint. In the critical literature of the past generation or two, one has read much about judicial tyranny, and the vision of a populace bent on social reform but shackled by an unfeeling Court's despotism seems to have beguiled more than one observer. In truth the Supreme Court has seldom, if ever, flatly and for very long resisted a really unmistakable wave of public sentiment. It has worked with the premise that constitutional law, like politics itself, is a science of the possible.

The Contours of Court History

There is a final point, which is at the same time very much like a summary of the discussion so far. We have seen the both the meaning of the Constitution and the nature of the Supreme Court's authority were left in doubt by the framers, that circumstances nonetheless conspired to favor the early growth of both constitutionalism and judicial power, but that those same circumstances also helped to set the terms within which these institutions would develop. The Constitution became a symbol of American patriotic devotion, but a symbol whose continued force depended on its continued flexibility in the face of shifting national needs. The Supreme Court became a venerated institution, half judicial tribunal and half political preceptor, sensitive but not subservient to popular expectations, obliged by its tradition to share the duties of statesmanship, but equally obliged to be alert that its share did not exceed its capacities.

The history of the Court and its treatment of the Constitution can be broadly understood as an endless search for a position in American government that is appropriate to these conditions imposed by its genesis. The quest is laden with difficulties because the paradoxes of the Court's existence can only be reconciled, even temporarily, by the most delicate balancing of judgments. It is unending because every such tentative reconciliation is sure to be disturbed ultimately by the relentless course of history, and every such major disturbance sends the judges forth on another chapter in their odyssey.

In each chapter certain dominant judicial interests take form, certain dominant values emerge, and the Court can be observed struggling to formulate a judicial role that will reinforce those interests and values within the subtle limits of judicial capability. We need not pause just now over the issue of whether these preoccupations and postures are consciously chosen, nor need we trouble ourselves that individual judges may vary in the degree of their conformity to the pattern, except insofar as this may affect the pattern itself. The refinements of the judicial motivation process are intriguing to be sure, but too much concern with them may cause an observer to miss the broad trends that give meaning to an epoch in constitutional history. Conceding that there are variations within the framework, we can nevertheless identify three great periods in American constitutional development: 1789 to the close of the Civil War; 1865 to the "Court revolution" of 1937; and 1937 to the present. The judicial interests and values that characterize each period are sufficiently articulated to be significant; and the Court's struggle to define its role as great new historical movements alter the backdrop, supplies a further element of dramatic change and uncertainty. If the framers had tried to settle all "constitutional" questions that confronted them; if they had even assumed the more modest task of specifically circumscribing the judicial power; if the doctrine of legislative supremacy had been a little more firmly intrenched in 1789; if judges like Marshall had been a little more inclined toward abnegation and a little less inclined toward politics, the uncertainties would be very different, the tale would be of another order. But then the country it was told about would not be the historical United States.

Two

The Establishment of the Right to Decide: 1789–1810

AMERICANS HAVE ALWAYS experienced a peculiar difficulty in accommodating themselves to one of the least contestable observations made in the preceding chapter—that the Supreme Court is a willful, policy-making agency of American government. In the long and crowded history of antijudicial polemics the most persistent angry charge has been that the Court, in this situation or that, has been guided by its prepossessions rather than by the unambiguous mandates of the fundamental law. On the other hand, the defenders of the Court in such debates (that is, those who approve the policy decisions in question) have ordinarily and with indignation rejected this impeachment, insisting that the judges were the helpless instruments of constitutional logic. Since the combatants have a bewildering way of shifting sides from year to year or at any rate from decade to decade, a watcher of the constitutional skies might draw a somewhat puzzling conclusion—that for many Americans the Court is the echo of the Constitution when it agrees with them and the voice of subjective prejudice when it does not.

The effect of this musical chairs game is unfortunately to obscure any coherent view of what the Court is really up to at any given time. Those who like the Court's record in that time are indisposed to admit that it is up to anything except its mythic business of consulting the oracle; and those who disapprove its record are too wrathful over the current usurpation to offer reliable judgments.

Nevertheless it is perfectly apparent to the detached observer that the Court's decisions do tend to fall into patterns that reflect current judicial views of what ought to be done; and that these views, though heavily influenced by the nature of the forum that issues them, are nonetheless policy determinations. The very question of what subjects should claim judicial attention, involves an avowed or implicit decision about what is most important in the American polity at any given time, for the Court has always enjoyed some leeway in controlling its own jurisdiction (though less in the past than it does now). The Court's "interests" are likely indeed to be affected by the historical context, but historical imperatives can be strengthened or weakened by the Court's eagerness or reluctance to accede to them. And since the constitutional questions that do successfully claim the attention of the Court are often those least answerable by rules of thumb, the predilections, the "values" of the judges, must play a part in supplying answers to them.

From 1789 until the Civil War, the dominant interest of the Supreme Court was in that greatest of all the questions left unsolved by the founders—the nation-state relationship. And the dominant judicial value, underlying the drift of decision in widely different areas, was the value of preserving the American Union. To be sure, the judges of the Supreme Court were not entirely single-minded and so of course other interests, other values, intruded upon the judicial mind and clamored for attention. Marshall and, indeed, the American bench and bar in general, were deeply concerned over the question of property rights, and it is possible to interpret the decisions of the Marshall court in terms that emphasize this preoccupation. Early in Taney's era Jacksonian distrust of finance capitalism found expression in judicial decisions; later the issue of slavery ran its dark course through constitutional law. Such matters as these profoundly engaged the judges' interests, and there is no disposition here to minimize the part they played in shaping legal doctrine or to deny that in isolated cases that part might be the crucial one.

But the question of nation-state relationships was in this era so closely entwined with such issues as property rights and slavery that to touch one was to touch the other, and we can be sure that it was never far from the judges' minds even when they seemed for the moment to be focusing on something else. And the motive of preserving the Union is persistently suggested by decision after decision, the one factor that makes sense out of apparent doctrinal inconsistencies, the often-inarticulate major premise that binds even such disparate spirits as Marshall and Taney together in a common cause.

It is hardly surprising that this should be so considering the drift of American history during the period, the evasiveness of the Constitution on these points, and the extremely tentative nature of the Court's own status. The states' rights and nationalist fetishes were the great herrings across the trail of American politics. Where reason and prudence were arrayed against him, a partisan could always invoke the dogma of states' rights or national sovereignty and feel fairly confident that tempers would rise and good sense depart. The nation lived in a nearly constant alternation of fears that it would cease being a nation altogether or become too much of one. And the Constitution alone could not serve to quiet these misgivings, for, as the warring camps soon discovered, it could be cited on either side, depending on whether a "strict construction" or a "loose construction" were adopted.

These ubiquitous questions thus inhered in almost every constitutional case the Supreme Court faced. At the same time, the Court's very title to decide them depended upon the Union's preservation, and this made it almost sure that the judges would put that value first. Hamilton hoped to strengthen the nation by giving capitalism a stake in its survival. Whatever the failures of that particular program, just such a marriage of interest and principle was accomplished by the establishment of the federal judiciary.

Within this broad category of interests then and with this dominant value of unionism for guidance, the Supreme Court of the pre–Civil War years sought to define its role. The relevant query for the judges—as for a student of the period—was not whether the Union ought to be maintained and made "more perfect"; there was all but unanimous agreement about that. The problem was how the Court could most usefully serve the cause it had espoused, or, to put it in another way, what view of the Constitution was best calculated to preserve the Union—and thereby the Supreme Court.

With the advantage of hindsight we can see that the judges had three major "role problems" before them. In the first place they must establish, not merely in theory but in practice as well, the doctrine of *judicial independence.* It is true that this doctrine was well rooted in colonial tradition and that the framers had tried to implement it by providing life tenure during "good behavior" for federal judges and by prohibiting reduction of their salaries. But it is also true that Congress was given powers, such as impeachment and control of the appellate jurisdiction, which were quite adequate to obliterate judicial independence if Congress were determined to do so.

Second, the Court must gain acceptance for the idea that among the powers thus independently exercised was that of *judicial review,* that is, the power to refuse to enforce an unconstitutional act of either the state or national government. And finally that power itself must be nourished and cultivated so that it will grow into the doctrine of *judicial sovereignty,* or the idea that a law may be held unconstitutional if the Court thinks it is, even though the case is not plain, and that the Court's opinion to this effect is binding on other branches of government. These problems need not be met in just this order; they need not be resolved with absolute finality. But they must be dealt with and partially answered if the Supreme Court is to play a significant part in the long struggle to preserve the Union.

YOUTHFUL UNCERTAINTIES

It is hard for a student of judicial review to avoid feeling that American constitutional history from 1789 to 1801 was marking time. The great shadow of John Marshall, who became Chief Justice in the latter year, falls across our understanding of that first decade; and it has therefore the quality of a play's opening moments with minor characters exchanging trivialities while they and the audience await the appearance of the star.

Such an impression is not altogether unjustified. The Supreme Court was, as we have seen, uncertain of its standing in those early years. When John Jay refused to resume the chief justiceship in 1801, he told President Adams that he had no faith the Court could acquire enough "energy, weight and dignity" to play a salient part in the nation's affairs. Each justice was burdened with the ridiculous chore of riding circuit, turning up twice a year to attend circuit court in each of four or five federal districts, which meant that judicial energies were dissipated in endless travel under the semiprimitive conditions of the day. Several statesmen of distinction like Edmund Pendleton of Virginia and Charles Cotesworth Pinckney of South Carolina refused appointment to the Court, and several more resigned in favor of greener pastures, including two Chief Justices, John Jay and Oliver Ellsworth. Few cases came to the Court compared with the torrents of later years, and even fewer were very important. Not one decision holding a state or federal law unconstitutional was handed down. And in most of the cases that were decided the practice of delivering opinions *seriatim* (a separate opinion by each judge) diffused the impact of the judgments and made it all the less likely that the Court would be regarded as an equal partner in the federal triumvirate.

Of course constitutional questions were arising. It would have been strange if they had not in these years when the Constitution itself was being tried on for size. But for the time being most of them were fought out in the legislative branches, in cabinet meetings, or in the forum of public opinion. The first Congress, acting in accord with the conditions

attached to ratification by several of the states, proposed twelve amendments, ten of which were ultimately ratified and became the "Bill of
Rights." The bill to incorporate a national bank raised the grave question
of whether the national government's authority should be broadly or
strictly construed, for no such incorporation power was specifically
granted in the Constitution. Madison in Congress and Jefferson in the
cabinet sharply opposed the proposal, arguing for strict construction,
while Hamilton's astute defense of the broader viewpoint not only won
the day but became one of the great state papers of American history. The
issue was not to reach the Supreme Court for almost thirty years.

Even when the rod of power was explicitly offered, the judiciary displayed some reluctance about grasping it. Certain ticklish questions of
international law were arising in connection with the Neutrality Proclamation of 1793, and, although President Washington wanted the Court's
advice in solving them, the Court declined to give him any, arguing that
"advisory opinions" were inconsistent with the judicial function. And
somewhat earlier, when Congress had tried to invest the judiciary with
authority to settle claims of invalid war veterans, two Supreme Court justices sitting on the circuit court joined a district judge in modestly rejecting the assignment. The law, they declared, is unconstitutional, because "the business directed by this act is not of a judicial nature" (first
Hayburn case). All this suggests a Court bypassed in the major power
struggles of the day and by no means eager to have greatness thrust
upon it.

But this does not mean that the Court of the 1790's was unmindful
of its potential as a factor in American government. In fact, as the *Hayburn* case suggests, the judges were quietly laying the groundwork of
power even while power itself was allowed to slip away, were preparing
for a time when great matters, such as the issue of the Bank, would come
within the judicial purview. The refusal to perform "non-judicial" functions reflected a shrewd insight—that the Court's position would ultimately depend on preserving its difference from the other branches of
government. The Congress and the presidency would always have roots
in the power structure of American society, while the Court must find its
support in the popular belief that the judiciary stands apart and defends
the fundamental law. And the decision in *Hayburn,* with all its appearance of self-denial, was bold enough in other respects: it rested on the
cardinal premise that the judiciary could disregard a legislative act which
it believed was unconstitutional.

That premise, the very essence of the Court's future greatness, was taking vague but perceptible shape throughout these years. Hamilton had supplied an invaluable cue in the *Federalist Papers* by flatly claiming such a power for the judiciary; and those papers were already become a venerated source of constitutional guidance. State court judges were following his lead from time to time, asserting their right to determine the validity of state laws in the light of the state constitutions. The members of the Supreme Court themselves, not only in *Hayburn* but in other cases, were giving voice to the idea of judicial review in ways that allowed them to avoid being called to account for all the idea's implications. Justice Paterson indulged in 1795 in some high-sounding language about the judicial duty to declare unwarranted legislative acts void; but the occasion was a jury charge in the course of circuit court proceedings, and it was not at all clear that the doctrine he enunciated had any practical effect on the outcome of the case. In several other cases, decided by the Supreme Court, the justices quite evidently assumed in their opinions that they *could* set unconstitutional state or federal laws aside, but they elected in these circumstances not to do so. This approach had the double advantage of disarming critics concerned with the outcome of the immediate cause and at the same time adding a brick or two to the edifice of precedent on which the judicial future would depend.

Nor was the Court of this era as neglectful of the nation-state relationship problem as its failure to hold a state act unconstitutional might suggest. In fact, its first real foray into hotly disputed constitutional realms indicated zeal and audacity somewhat in advance of the times. In the course of the ratification controversy, more than one apprehensive Antifederalist had noticed the phrase in Article III which extended the judicial power to controversies "between a State and citizens of another State," and had darkly suspected that it might be invoked to subvert state sovereignty. Did the clause mean that an individual could sue a state in the federal courts? So it might seem from the language alone, but the Constitution's defenders, including Madison, Hamilton, and Marshall, rejected the inference and soothed this fear of its detractors: no state, they said, would be haled into federal courts under the authority of this clause, for the sovereign is not subject to suit. Now however, in 1793, the Supreme Court chose to think otherwise. When two citizens of South Carolina brought an action against Georgia for the recovery of debt and Georgia refused to appear in her own defense, the Court declared that states were suable and rendered judgment for the plaintiff.

The practical consequences of this doctrine were grave enough, for the states had been playing fast and loose in fiscal matters for years; and the doctrine, if enforced, might expose them to harassment by a swarm of creditors. But, even worse, the theoretical premise of the decision was an outright challenge to state sovereignty. The judges had forthrightly recognized that they were being asked to make their first great decision about the nature of the Union and had held, in the words of Justice Wilson, that "*as to the purposes of the Union, therefore, Georgia is not a sovereign state.*" The point seems sensible and indeed almost inevitable if the Union was to have meaning, but 1793 was too soon to state it so baldly. A gale of opposition at once arose from all sides, and a constitutional amendment denying that states were suable in federal courts by citizens of other states, was proposed and later ratified (Amendment XI). The larger question of the nature of the Union was postponed for the more devious talents of Marshall to cope with. The pre-Marshall justices had made two mistakes their great successor usually managed to avoid: in their ardor to establish an ultra-Federalist doctrine they had spoken overplainly; and they had spoken thus in support of a doctrine that immediately imperiled the concrete interests of most of the states. The resulting united protest was too strong for the Court's nascent independence to withstand, and the judges' fingers were badly (though not fatally) singed.

As *Chisholm* v. *Georgia* suggests, then, the pre-Marshall Court was fully conscious that its greatest problem was the nation-state relationship, and it was heavily disposed to create, or to encourage the creation of, a consolidated national union. And as tentative gropings toward a doctrine of judicial review suggest, the Court was also perfectly aware that it could carry out this imposing assignment only if it possessed final authority to decide questions of constitutionality. Why then did it not proceed at once to undermine state sovereignty and to assert the full range of the judicial prerogative? Why, for example, did the Court allow more than a decade to pass without directly invalidating a state law on constitutional grounds? Why are the statements of the doctrine of judicial review artfully concealed in innocuous decisions or pronounced so equivocally as to leave the whole matter in doubt?

In part the answer is that the judges understood, whether consciously or instinctively, their limitations as well as their opportunities. They realized that the Constitution did not explicitly accord them the power they coveted and that public opinion had not yet filled in this gap in the organic law. They realized that the characteristically unqualified logic of Hamilton, however convincing and tempting it might seem, was not quite apt for their purposes. The essayist Hamilton could sweep premises, argument, and conclusions together in a single brave statement at a single moment in time. The constitutional judge—or the would-be constitutional judge—needed time as an ally and could not afford to treat it so cavalierly. The judicial empire, if there was to be one, had to be conquered slowly, piece by piece. An idea could be implied today, obliquely stated tomorrow, and flatly asserted the next day. But months and years had to pass before the judiciary was ready to give that idea fully effective life as a principle of decision. Meanwhile the forthright logic of Hamilton was being transmuted into the less tidy but more potent logic of public consent, as the original idea worked its way into the consciousness of educated Americans. And then, when the moment for real action came, the ground might be ready.

The Menace of Jefferson and the Caution of Marshall

The ground might indeed have been ready in 1800 if the nicely ordered political world of the Federalists' dreams had behaved itself as they thought they had a right to expect. The Court, as we have seen, had laid the basis for judicial review in its pronouncements of the past ten years. The idea was now familiar to most of those who thought about such matters, and there is no reason to believe that many of them staunchly opposed it. Neither, to be sure, is there evidence that they fully understood its implications as a doctrine of judicial *supremacy*, or expected that the Court would use its veto in any but a clear case; but some of those implications could wait a bit longer for the future to unfold them. Judicial nationalism had been set back on its heels by the reaction to the *Chisholm* case, but in 1796 the Court had dealt state sovereignty an almost equally grievous blow when it held that the peace treaty with Great Britain overrode state laws affecting the rights of British creditors, and the reaction had not been disastrous, however ill-tempered. The judiciary's time for greatness might have seemed at hand.

But the world of politics chose this moment to display a mind of its own. The Federalists, in a fine frenzy engendered partly by fear of France and partly by well-founded doubts about their own ability to hold the American electorate's support, had passed the Alien and Sedition Acts in 1798. The judges of the federal bench were almost to a man ardent Federalist partisans, and they had enthusiastically shouldered the task of enforcing the Sedition Act, which was designed, among other things, to visit savage punishment on those who criticized the national administration. Supreme Court justices like Paterson, Iredell, and above all Samuel Chase earned the hatred of Jefferson's fast-growing Republican party, not only by presiding over the convictions of men who had called John Adams names ("hoary headed incendiary") and otherwise maligned Federalism, but by revealing on the bench a vengeful partisanship that rekindled pre-Revolutionary memories of the king's courts. Insult was added to injury when federal judges undertook, even without benefit of a statute, to punish under the English common law those who violated Washington's Neutrality Proclamation or the Treaty of Peace with Great Britain. Justice Chase, not content with giving partisan speeches from the bench, openly and eagerly participated in political campaigns against the monstrous threat of Jeffersonianism.

This would have been a bad sort of game for the judiciary to play under any circumstances, but in light of the political realities of the time it was almost suicidal. The Alien and Sedition Acts called forth the Kentucky and Virginia resolutions which challenged, in language composed by Jefferson and Madison, respectively, the whole doctrine of national supremacy and unity upon which the very existence of the Supreme Court hinged. The party of Jefferson won the election of 1800, and the victors came to office with an understandably bitter distrust of the national judiciary which had so eagerly joined in the persecution of Republicans. The outgoing Federalists did their part to make a bad situation worse by passing the Judiciary Act of 1801, creating a number of new federal judgeships which were hastily filled by Adams, and reducing the number of Supreme Court justices from six to five. This law was not without merits, but those merits were forgotten in the justifiable Republican anger at its obvious partisanship. The Federalists, having lost the other two branches of government, hoped to maintain their control nonetheless by intrenching a pro-Federalist judiciary protected by life tenure.

It is little wonder that the noble rage of Jefferson's party, once focused on the task of winning a national election, was now directed at the federal judiciary and its head and symbol, the Supreme Court. When Adams, as one of the last acts of his administration, appointed the Federalist John Marshall to the Chief Justiceship, the Republicans felt they had endured enough such Parthian salvos and began to map out a counter-campaign of their own. The Judiciary Act of 1801 was repealed only a little more than a year after its passage, notwithstanding Federalist cries that the repealing act was itself unconstitutional. John Adams' "midnight appointments" of new federal judges were thus for the most part wiped away. As for the remaining members of the federal (and Federalist) bench, the awful power of impeachment was to be invoked: the judiciary must bow to the will of the people—which was, of course, in Jeffersonian theory the will of the Republicans—or be turned out. The principle of judicial independence was faced with its first great challenge.

This threat to judicial independence loomed over the Marshall Court during the first few years of his incumbency and inevitably conditioned what might be called the strategy of judicial behavior. Marshall desired, as much as Wilson or Jay had, to establish the power of the judiciary on solid ground and to use the power to defend the cause of national union. Their Court had in its first few years prepared the way for this and was proceeding gradually but surely along the way when the Jeffersonian tempest, generated in part by the judiciary's own folly, burst forth. As a result of it, Marshall's opportunity was perilously difficult for him to grasp, and in fact the great day when the Court would declare a state law unconstitutional was postponed for almost another full decade. Not until then, or nearly then, was it clear that localist sentiment in the American body politic was less robust than he had feared it was. Not until then did he know that judicial prestige was durable enough to warrant some risks, that judicial independence was at least relatively secure. Not until then did the Court begin to be a major factor in American government.

Important as Marshall is in the history of American jurisprudence, it is not his appointment that marks the Court's coming of age, for the Court, like an individual, grew up slowly. Marshall did establish almost at once the custom of letting one justice's opinion, usually his own, stand for the decision of the whole Court, and this custom gave the judicial pronouncements a forceful unity they had formerly lacked. But in spite of this the Court after 1801 was for some time no more formidable than it had been before; judicial independence had not yet been firmly established; the real bite of the doctrine of judicial review had not yet made itself felt; the problem of the Union was still comparatively untouched. Marshall was holding back, awaiting a more propitious future. His preeminence among builders of the American constitutional tradition rests not only on his well-known boldness, his "tiger instinct for the jugular vein" as an enthusiastic metaphorist once called it, but also on his less-noticed sense of self-restraint.

The famous case *Marbury* v. *Madison* in 1803 appears to contradict this proposition but in fact confirms it. The decision is a masterwork of indirection, a brilliant example of Marshall's capacity to sidestep danger while seeming to court it, to advance in one direction while his opponents are looking in another.

In its closing hours the Adams administration had done its competent best, as we have seen, to fill up federal offices with loyal anti-

Jeffersonians. But events were moving rapidly, some details were apt to be neglected, and when Jefferson took over, the commission of one William Marbury to be Justice of the Peace in the District of Columbia had not been delivered to him, though it had been signed and sealed. The new President was indisposed to mend this oversight of his predecessors, so Marbury asked the Supreme Court for a writ which would compel Jefferson's Secretary of State, Madison, to hand over the commission. This created what seemed a painful and unpromising dilemma for Marshall and his Court. If they upheld Marbury and ordered delivery of the commission, the order would surely be ignored by Madison, the Court would be exposed as impotent to enforce its mandates, the shakiness of judicial prestige would be dramatically emphasized. If on the other hand they did not uphold Marbury, they would give aid and comfort to Jefferson and might seem to support his denunciation of the "midnight appointments." The latter course was impossibly distasteful to an ardently Federalist bench; the former was humiliating and might well be risky.

But Marshall was equal to the occasion. Marbury's commission, he said, is being illegally withheld from him by the Jeffersonian administration and a writ can appropriately be directed to a cabinet official when he fails his duty. However, the Supreme Court is not the proper tribunal to supply Marbury with a remedy in this case, for the Court does not possess the power to issue writs in cases of this kind. It is true that Section 13 of the Judiciary Act of 1789 seems to grant the Court such power, but that provision is itself invalid. For the Court's original jurisdiction is defined in the Constitution, and a congressional act like this one, which adds to the original jurisdiction, is therefore unconstitutional. And an unconstitutional law is void and must be so treated by the Supreme Court. Mr. Marbury then must look elsewhere for redress of his just grievance— with the Court's best wishes.

A more adroit series of parries and ripostes would be difficult to imagine. The danger of a head-on clash with the Jeffersonians was averted by the denial of jurisdiction; but, at the same time, the declaration that the commission was illegally withheld scotched any impression that the Court condoned the administration's behavior. These negative maneuvers were artful achievements in their own right. But the touch of genius is evident when Marshall, not content with having rescued a bad situation, seizes the occasion to set forth the doctrine of judicial review. It is easy for us to see in retrospect that the occasion was golden. The attention of the Republicans was focused on the question of Marbury's commission, and they cared very little how the Court went about justifying a hands-off policy so long as that policy was followed. Moreover, the Court was in the delightful position, so common in its history but so confusing to its critics, of rejecting and assuming power in a single breath, for the Congress had tried here to give the judges an authority they could not constitutionally accept and the judges were high-mindedly refusing. The moment for immortal statement was at hand all right, but only a judge of Marshall's discernment could have recognized it.

As for the statement itself, it exemplifies the gift for argumentative effectiveness, the masterful sense of strategy, that is illustrated in Marshall's whole approach to the case and was perhaps his supreme talent. He was able to endow his arguments with the flavor of the irresistible through a combination of lucidity and self-confidence:

> The question of whether an Act repugnant to the Constitution can become the law of the land, is a question deeply interesting to the United States; but, happily, not of an intricacy proportioned to its interest. It seems only necessary to recognize certain principles, supposed to have been long and well-established, to decide it.

Marshall then proceeds to an examination of those principles for the benefit of the few who might not realize how "long and well-established" they were. These hypothetical adversaries are chosen with great care— they are evidently those who would deny the power of judicial review *altogether*. Imagine a law that clearly violates the Constitution, says Marshall, for example, a duty on state exports explicitly violating Article I, section 9. Surely the judges are not bound to enforce such an act, to treat it as valid. Now many, though not all, of Marshall's listeners would probably concede this point as far as it goes; the real questions for them would arise when the statute was not a *clear* violation of the Constitution, or when judges purported to speak on constitutional questions not only for themselves but for the other branches as well, to presume that the judicial finding of invalidity was final. These queries are not met at all in the argument of the *Marbury* case, and by ignoring them Marshall succeeds in beclouding them. Attacks on the discretionary scope and the finality of judicial review are henceforth confused with attacks on the minimal power Marshall here contends for, and the attackers thus find that though they aim for the weakest point in the judicial armor they almost invariably hit the strongest. The *Marbury* argument is justly celebrated, but not the least of its virtues is the fact that it is somewhat beside the point.

The *Marbury* opinion then is far from suggesting that Marshall was rash or even very bold in exercising judicial supervision at this stage of his career as Chief Justice. The decision was criticized for its dictum that the executive *could* be called to account by judicial process, but since the requested writ was in fact denied, no really great heat was generated even on this point. And as for the argument for judicial review, at the time only the Federalists paid much attention to it, and they of course were warmly approving; the Jeffersonians shed few tears over the voiding of a law that had been passed by Federalists in the first place.

The decision does suggest, however, that Marshall, though choosing the path of discretion in the immediate occasion, did not for a moment forget the long-term objectives—enhancement of judicial power in general and diminution of state autonomy in particular. The relevance of the *Marbury* case to the struggle against state autonomy is easy to miss, because the Chief Justice's specific target is a national statute. But the argument for holding an unconstitutional law void is phrased in very broad terms, and it applies equally whether the enacting body is Congress or a state legislature. In fact two of Marshall's three argumentative illustrations of obviously invalid laws would be just as apposite if state, rather than national, power were being called into question. The important point is that the Court may refuse to enforce an unconstitutional law, whatever its source may be. *Marbury* is thus not, as it might appear at first glance, a digression from the long-run struggle against excessive localism; on the contrary, it is a crucial skirmish in that campaign, for when state laws are later judicially challenged, the precedent of *Marbury* stands ready to back up the challenge.

THE ORDEAL OF JOHN MARSHALL:
THE IMPEACHMENT THREAT SUBSIDES

Meanwhile, however, the antijudicial brew of the Republicans was simmering and Marshall was constrained to adhere to the course of measured caution that *Marbury* represents. No one knew better than he that the ambitious assertions of that case would be quite meaningless in the face of concerted political resistance from the other branches, and he had no wish to provoke more united opposition than he already faced. In 1803, the very year of the *Marbury* decision, the Congress proceeded to the impeachment of John Pickering, Judge of the United States Court for the District of New Hampshire. This unfortunate man was hopelessly insane and a drunkard; his behavior on the bench for three years had been picturesquely irrational. There was no doubt that he now lacked the capacity to discharge the duties of office, but the Constitution provides no method for removal except "Impeachment for, and Conviction of, Treason, Bribery, or other high Crimes and Misdemeanors" (Art. II, sec. 4). Could a man who was clearly out of his mind and therefore not responsible be convicted of "high Crimes and Misdemeanors"? If not, could he be impeached?

The answer of the Republicans was to offer a theory of the impeachment power that would transcend such technical limits. As Senator Giles of Virginia was to put it: "Impeachment is nothing more than the enquiry, by the two Houses of Congress, whether the office of any public man might not be better filled by another. . . . A trial and removal of a judge need not imply any criminality or corruption in him." Pickering was convicted of high crimes and misdemeanors in spite of the legal anomaly this involved, the broad theory of the impeachment power being clearly implicit in the finding. But the principal interest of the theory's framers was not of course its first demented victim. Having given the idea a trial run, they now proposed to apply it to Samuel Chase of the Supreme Court, their particular bête noire among Federalist judges, and then to any other judicial menace to Republican aims, including John Marshall.

If the program had succeeded, the doctrine of an independent judiciary would have foundered and the whole future history of the Court might have been profoundly altered. Marshall's alarm can hardly be exaggerated. Apparently despairing of the chances for full independence, he privately suggested that Congress might be given appellate jurisdiction over Supreme Court decisions, as an alternative to impeachment. As a biographer remarks, we could not credit that Marshall ever subscribed to such an extraordinary notion if it had not been set forth in his own hand and the letter preserved. But the suggestion is a measure of his fear for his precious tribunal, of his conviction that a formal surrender of final authority might be the price that had to be paid in order to preserve any authority at all.

But the program did not succeed; it turned out that a lesser price would serve the purpose. The House, under the whip of the malignant John Randolph, duly brought impeachment articles against Chase, charging him with misconduct in the sedition trials of Fries and Callender in 1800, in his treatment of a grand jury at Newcastle in the same year, and in his political harangue of another grand jury in Baltimore in 1803. However, in conducting the impeachment proceedings before the Senate, Randolph and his cohorts seemed unable to decide whether to rest their case on charges of criminality or on the radical Republican theory that Congress could impeach merely for conduct it disapproved. The former charges were hard to prove, especially in the face of the formidable legal counsel that had assembled on Chase's behalf; yet the latter theory might well not receive the support of the necessary two-thirds of the Senate, and the whole cause might thus be lost. Instead of resolving this dilemma, the impeachers mingled criminality and mere objectionable conduct in a hopeless tangle. Those who might have supported one kind of charge were repelled by the other, and the Senate ended by finding Chase not guilty.

Mismanagement by the impeachment leaders undoubtedly contributed to this result. But the essential explanation is that many members of the Senate, including some Republicans, were not yet incensed enough with the judiciary to vote to destroy its independence. And their wrath was moderate or non-existent because the Court under Marshall had really done so little to incite it. The charge that the judiciary was tyrannically imposing a Federalist will on a Republican-minded nation did not square with the immediate facts of judicial behavior, whatever suspicions might be entertained about Marshall's long-term aspirations. And this impression of a non-aggressive bench had been further confirmed when, only a few days after *Marbury*, the Supreme Court sustained the validity of the law repealing the Judiciary Act of 1801. A Court that would pass up an opportunity to strike at this law, which all good Federalists regarded as the acme of Republican wickedness, could hardly be thought of as a despotic monster.

The failure of the Chase impeachment is one of the signal events in the history of the federal judiciary, because it set a precedent against loose construction of the impeachment power and thus supported the doctrine of judicial independence. And the price paid for this benign result was not the great one Marshall had feared—the vesting of an appellate authority in Congress—but simply a measure of present judicial self-restraint. Throughout the nation's future history this lesson can be read again and again: paradoxical though it may seem, the Supreme Court often gains rather than loses power by adopting a policy of forbearance.

THE LION STIRS AT LAST: *FLETCHER V. PECK*

Marshall at any rate continued to take this lesson to heart for some years after Chase was saved from martyrdom. Of course it was by no means as clear to Marshall and his contemporaries as it is to us that impeachment was no longer an omnipresent danger. After his only real clash with Jefferson's administration, the trial of Aaron Burr for treason in 1807, demands for impeachment were heard once more. In this case Marshall seems to have been provoked by the partisan heat of the moment and by his hatred of Jefferson to depart from the pathway of caution. His interpretation of the treason clause of the Constitution made it quite impossible for Jefferson's administration to convict Burr, and his vulnerability to the consequent Republican attacks might appear all the greater when we reflect that the interpretation was of very doubtful validity.

But this time the antijudicial crusade, though extremely noisy, got nowhere at all. No doubt its progress was to a degree thwarted by the administration's involvement in other concerns, for the War of 1812 was already impending. But surely it can also be inferred that the doctrine of judicial independence had itself become a formidable shield against partisan assaults. The fact that the doctrine was now established and recognized did not mean that the judiciary was henceforth free of any threats from the congressional side. Under sufficient provocation the weapon of impeachment might yet be called into use, and in any event the less drastic but formidable power to restrict appellate jurisdiction was still untried. Henceforward Marshall and his cohorts could feel sure that such antijudicial action would not be undertaken lightly, that the Supreme Court's prestige was a factor to be reckoned with. In those first few stormy years of the Republic's history, the members of Congress and of the executive department had demonstrated over and over that the Constitution was less important to them than were political results. The records of both parties were strewn with evidence of this, but the Federalists' Sedition Act and the Jeffersonians' Louisiana Purchase are enough to illustrate the point. The judiciary had thus been left free to claim the Constitution for its own, to identify its own prestige with the prestige of fundamental law, and Marshall, with his happy combination of audacity and discretion, had made the most of the advantage.

Now at last then, after the reverberations of the Burr incident had subsided, Marshall was ready to follow the course which the judicial maneuvers of the past had made possible. He was ready to declare state law unconstitutional, to show how the judiciary's carefully nurtured power and prestige could be employed to help preserve the Union.

The case, *Fletcher* v. *Peck* in 1810, involved the notorious Yazoo land-grant scandal. The details of this outrageous but fascinating affair are too intricate to be traced here; a good, long story must be shortened unmercifully. In 1795, Georgia had sold at a bargain price a huge tract of land comprising most of the modern states of Alabama and Mississippi. It quickly became known that all but one of the members of the legislature who voted for the sale had been bribed to do so, and a newly elected legislature, inflamed with righteous indignation, hastened to rescind the grant. However, before this virtuous step could be taken, the original purchasers had resold millions of acres of the land to supposedly innocent third parties, and the question of their titles' validity now came before the Supreme Court. The argument was that the rescinding act was a violation of the Constitution and that the third-party titles were therefore still sound.

John Marshall and a unanimous Court agreed. The rescinding act was invalid and must be held so by the Supreme Court; this much was clear. But the exact basis for the holding was far from clear, for Marshall seemed reluctant to rest his judgment on one ground alone, probably because of the lingering difficulties each argument separately presented.

At one point he seemed to declare explicitly that the rescinding act impaired the obligation of contracts in violation of Article I, section 10, of the Constitution. But this declaration encountered two serious objections: that the contract clause was probably meant to apply to contracts between private individuals and not between the state and individuals; and that in any event a grant is not a contract carrying an obligation. Marshall met both of these hazards and purported to dispose of them, but we may doubt that he was fully confident he had done so.

At another point he intimated that the Georgia act was a violation of the ex post facto clause, but the trouble here was that the clause had been held applicable only to criminal legislation some twelve years before, and the law now in question of course concerned purely civil matters. At still another point he suggested that the rescinding act might be invalid merely because it offended against "the nature of society and of government," in other words natural law; as Justice Johnson, concurring, put it: "the reason and nature of things: a principle which will impose laws even on the Deity." And in the end Marshall said: "The state of Georgia was restrained, *either* by general principles, which are common to our free institutions, or by the particular provisions of the Constitution of the United States" from passing the rescinding law and applying it to innocent purchasers. (Italics added.) This statement scrambled the various possible arguments in a single indiscriminate mixture.

Yet the importance of the results accomplished by this seemingly turgid rhetoric was considerable. To begin with, it laid the basis for the momentous rule that the state is bound by its own contractual obligations. Marshall may have been toying with the idea of claiming for the Court the power to overthrow laws which violated such agreements on the basis of natural law or "right reason" without reference to any specific constitutional clause. This idea was abroad in the land at the time, and hints of it keep turning up in Supreme Court opinions for many years to come. At first glance it might seem that this carte blanche for judicial governance would be very appealing to Marshall, for it would supply him with a roving commission to invalidate any law he disapproved, subject only to the proviso that the incantations of the natural-law tradition must be recited. But he surely realized that the Court's future lay with the tangible Constitution itself rather than its invisible and most disputable higher-law background, that a Court which claimed the power to go beyond the Constitution would be dispensing with its most valuable support and might end by possessing no power at all. In the long run, therefore, he preferred to moor his arguments in the language of the Constitution. For the moment, however, since the contract clause alone was not yet strong enough to support the great principle that the state must abide by its agreements, he was willing to use the natural law as a supplementary prop. Later, when the contract clause had reached a higher stage of legal maturity, the talk of natural law and right reason was dispensed with and the principle rested squarely and explicitly on the contract clause.

But in the second place and in some ways more important, *Fletcher v. Peck* is the first clear precedent for the general proposition that the Supreme Court is empowered to hold state laws unconstitutional. That this power exists is the unstated premise of the whole decision, unstated because Marshall simply assumed that there was no room for argument on the point. He declared what no one would dispute:

> But Georgia cannot be viewed as a single, unconnected sovereign power, on whose legislature no other restrictions are imposed than may be found in its own constitution. She is a part of a large empire; she is a member of the American Union; and that Union has a constitution the supremacy of which all acknowledge, and which imposes limits to the legislatures of the several states, which none claim a right to pass.

Then he blandly took a long leap from this resounding truism to the holding that the Georgia law was invalid. We have seen with what circumspection the Court had been edging toward this climactic declaration in the preceding two decades; now at length its careful efforts were rewarded. The justification for Marshall's assumption of power is to be found by looking to the past, back to the judicial arguments in such cases as *Hayburn* and *Marbury*, back to the acceptance of jurisdiction in *Chisholm*, back to the whole elaborate process by which Marshall and his predecessors built support for the doctrines of judicial independence and judicial review. The argument need not be stated now because that process has imbedded it in the ideology of the nation.

Fletcher v. *Peck,* then, marks the end of the beginning of the Court's long struggle to find its place in the American governmental system. It is a milestone at which we can pause to assess the accomplishments and lessons of the past, and the problems of the future. Some of the initial uncertainties that confronted the four judges in Philadelphia in 1790 have been at least tentatively resolved. The idea of judicial independence has become an operative doctrine. The power of judicial review over national and state legislation has been not only claimed in theory but applied to concrete cases. The judges have begun to learn the arts of judicial governance: the necessity to avoid, if possible, head-on collisions with the dominant political forces of the moment; the undesirability of claiming too much too soon; the great advantage of taking the long view, especially when others take the short; the usefulness of diverting criticism from weakness to strength; the importance of identifying judicial claims to authority with the claims of the Constitution. These doctrines, these arts, are now available to the judiciary as it turns its attention to the cause of national union, and they are potentially of great service to that cause. But we must not mistake half a loaf for the whole; though the preliminaries are over, much remains undone. Judicial independence is a formidable reality, but it remains to be seen whether it can be sustained in the face of real adversity. Judicial review in Marshall's carefully phrased formulation is fairly well accepted, but judicial sovereignty is not; and until the Court's opinion on constitutionality even in debatable cases is regarded as final, the influence of the judiciary on national affairs can only be peripheral. These remaining problems dominate the agenda of the Court's next twenty-five years; and their resolution depends partly on the roll of the historical dice and partly on the wisdom of the judges in directing the institution that has fallen to their charge.

THREE

THE MARSHALL COURT AND THE
SHAPING OF THE NATION:
1810–1835

S O FAR THE STORY of the Supreme Court has been largely prelude.
The judges have been deviled by uncertainties about their own status
in the young American polity and about the power and malevolence
of the forces that might imperil that status. Since the constitutional
agreement of 1789 was inexplicit about the nature and scope of judicial
authority, the Court has inherited the responsibility for drawing up its
own commission, one line at a time, and the task has been delicate. Only
gradually has it become apparent that the Court is being accepted as a
symbol of constitutionalism and can therefore count on a solid measure
of public support. Only with experience has it become clear to Marshall
and his judicial brethren that the Republicans are not after all savage rev-
olutionaries, that their bark is worse than their bite, and that the rule of
law can therefore survive even though the Federalist party may not. In
such a prelude, amid such uncertainties, the Court has been able to lay the
argumentative bases for future accomplishments; it has fashioned some of
the tools which may later be used to help govern America. But it has not
yet been in a position to exert much real influence on the course of affairs.
It has built its own fences with some cunning, but has not so far done
much to build the nation.

However, with the War of 1812 and its immediate aftermath a new
stage in the Court's history was inaugurated. We have seen that the slow
accretion of precedents and confidence culminated in 1810, when the
judges at last felt secure enough to hold a state law unconstitutional. Logically, the Court was then ready to begin to make its weight felt in the
political order, to defend and foster in a concrete way the principle of
national union. Now this logical development was stimulated and

strengthened by the war's impact on American attitudes and political alignments.

Many of the old Federalists, especially in New England, had fiercely opposed "Mr. Madison's war," had talked darkly of seceding from the Union, and had espoused a states' rights position strangely reminiscent of the extreme Republicanism of the Virginia and Kentucky resolutions. The politically dominant Republicans, on the other hand, were forced, in defending their war, to embrace the idea of nationalism, and to abjure in part their own localist tradition. Since they were in the ascendancy, this meant that the creed of nationalism enjoyed an unprecedented, if temporary, popularity and—the other side of the coin—that localism was for the moment bereft of really powerful defenders. To be sure localist sentiment soon revived and its exponents were as vocal as ever. But the nationalist spirit, once awakened, could not be dismissed at will. These events had intruded a cross-current in the Republican ideology; leaders like Madison and Monroe though by no means unqualified nationalists were not consistent localists either; the tradition they spoke for was now ambivalent on the great question of the nature of the Union.

This ambivalence persisted for some years and gave John Marshall his opportunity to use the judicial instruments he had been preparing. But his way, though now passable, was still far from easy. The Court after all was in the process of attaining a position more exalted than any attained by a judicial tribunal in modern world history; great tasks were impending. For one thing it was necessary both to confirm and to extend the Court's claim to authority, to transmute "judicial review" into "judicial sovereignty." Granted that it was proper for the Court to adjudge questions of constitutionality, did this imply that the Court's judgment was final? Did it imply that the judges could call the other branches to account even when the question of constitutionality was doubtful? Did it imply that the Court would exercise a general supervision over some governmental affairs that fell outside the traditional judicial orbit?

To Marshall it implied all this, for he was firmly convinced that the more America was guided by judges the happier and more just its system would be. But others, in politics and out, were not ready to bear the Chief Justice's mild yoke, and there was always a threat that overweening judicial power would encounter resistance or counterattack more formidable than its recently established independence could withstand. Though moving onward and upward, then, the Court must still tread carefully.

Secondly and simultaneously, the Court of Marshall's remaining years was engaged in using its still nascent authority to establish the substantive constitutional principles on which the American polity should rest. It was interpreting the document of 1789 so as to provide maximum protection to property rights and maximum support for the idea of nationalism. Usually these two objectives were conjoined, so that a pronationalist constitutional doctrine best served the cause of property rights and vice versa. The national government was not at this time much inclined to interfere in commercial affairs, whereas the states, one or the other, presented a constant threat to the stability of currency, the sanctity of debts, or the freedom of business enterprise. Thus Marshall, happily for his peace of mind, was able to assure himself that he made property rights more secure when he deprived the states of power by enhancing the power of the nation. If these two primary values of his had conflicted, his soul-search would have been agonizing. But they seldom did conflict, and his historic achievements in the cause of union were therefore not clouded by confusion of motives.

He had troubles enough without adding internal uncertainty to them. The antinationalist front of the Republicans (soon to be called Democrats) had indeed been impaired, but specific and bitter centers of opposition still developed when specific provocations aroused them, and almost every major decision was met by a storm of intemperate denunciation from some politically potent quarter. Even worse, as the 1820's neared their end, it became increasingly apparent that the tide of states' rights sentiment was rising if not in volume at any rate in intensity. From time to time he was compellingly reminded of a fact that all Supreme Court justices must learn to live with: that the Court's decrees are backed only by its own prestige and ultimately by the willingness of the President to help enforce them. Over and over he was reminded that Congress could destroy in a day the judicial independence that had been building for decades.

In this context Marshall faced his great task of augmenting the judicial power and shaping the Constitution into a charter for nationalism. These two interwoven themes run through nearly all his decisions; each case raises the question of the Court's authority together with that of nation-state relationship, and the Court must always decide one question in the light of the other, taking care that its nationalist zeal does not compromise its own status or that claims for judicial power are never so extreme as to vitiate the crusade for nationalism. And little by little, in spite of the delicacy of this balancing feat, in spite of the deep antagonism of affected litigants, in spite of the rising wave of states' rights sentiment, the job is done. The Court's empire of decision is extended and stabilized as firmly as it ever can be in a governmental arrangement that rests on inference and acquiescence rather than on final definition. The great operative phrases of the Constitution—the supremacy clause, the contract clause, the necessary and proper clause, the commerce clause—are impregnated with the nationalist meanings so dear to Marshall's heart. And most important of all, these judicially contrived mutations in the character of American constitutionalism are generally accepted by the nation they are designed to guide.

How were these remarkable results achieved? How was the Court able, in the face of these adversities, to have its way? Partly the answer goes back to factors mentioned in previous chapters—the American attachment to the idea of fundamental law and the gradual identification of the Supreme Court with that idea. Partly the answer is to be found in the judges themselves and most of all of course in Marshall—the judicial sense of strategy and timing, the rhetorical virtuosity which should never be undervalued, the capacity to engender respect even among those who disagreed. Partly, as has been said, the difficulties were eased by the temporary ambivalence of Republican opinion on the nature of the Union.

But the Court's progress was also aided by a basic disability of the localist movement—its very lack of unity. The states were so individualistic that they defeated themselves, for it was (and is) a peculiarity of the states' rights doctrine that its partisans were devoted to it only when their own oxen were being gored, when nationalism presented a specific threat to a concrete interest. If states' rights could be associated with a common and long-term economic issue like slavery or the tariff, then the affected states would stand long and firm against their mutual adversary. But if Virginia had a problem today that Maryland did not share, Virginia's outraged protest in the name of states' rights would attract little support from Maryland any more than Maryland's similar protest tomorrow would bring Virginia rushing to her standard. Both states were being true to the fractional principle that lay at the heart of the states' rights doctrine. But, because of their adherence to that principle, the Supreme Court, with its eye steadily on a single target, was spared the calamity of confronting a united opposition. The Court left such potentially unifying issues as the tariff and slavery pretty much alone, and it was not even necessary, then, to divide to conquer, for the opposition had thoughtfully divided itself.

THE COURT OVER THE STATES

One of the Court's great problems was presented either by direct or by implied challenge in nearly every significant case of the era: the problem of its right to review decisions of state courts involving the validity of acts undertaken by the state governments. Such a right was granted to the Court under Section 25 of the Judiciary Act of 1789; state court decisions that denied a claim made in the name of the federal Constitution, laws, or treaties could be reviewed by the Supreme Court by a "writ of error." And of course if the state court was thought to have erred, its judgment could be reversed and any state law it rested on invalidated.

That was the Supreme Court's nominal statutory authority, but it was one thing for Congress to pass such an empowering act and another thing to persuade the states to yield to it. From the first, localists had contended that Section 25 involved an unconstitutional encroachment on state sovereignty, and although the Court had several times exercised this supposedly unwarranted power with comparative impunity, the rumbles of protest had never quite been stilled. The case of *Martin* v. *Hunter's Lessee* in 1816 compelled the Court, which had so far tried to ignore the arguments against Section 25, finally to meet them head on.

The case involved the title to some 300,000 acres of Virginia land which had once belonged to Lord Fairfax but which had been confiscated by the state in Revolutionary times partly on the ground that Fairfax and his heirs were enemy aliens. Virginia had proceeded to grant a section of the land, which it now claimed as its own, to David Hunter, who later sought in the courts of Virginia to eject the Fairfax heirs. But in the meantime of course the Revolution had ended, the Treaty of Peace with Great Britain had been signed, the national Constitution had come into being, and the new national government had been endowed with the power to make treaties. It was argued that both the Treaty of Peace and Jay's Treaty of 1795 confirmed the titles of British subjects to land in America and that the Fairfax title was therefore still valid.

In spite of this, the Virginia Court of Appeals held against the Fairfax heirs, and the Supreme Court of the United States, having granted review of this holding on a writ of error, ordered it reversed. The Virginia court, which was headed by Spencer Roane, an ardent states' righter and bitter foe of Marshall, pondered this order for a while and then decided to ignore it, arguing that Section 25 was itself unconstitutional. The Virginia judges conceded of course that they were bound to observe the federal

Constitution, but they insisted that the meaning of the Constitution was for them to decide and that the Supreme Court had no power to impose its own interpretation upon them. It was this contention, so fatal to the prospects for both judicial supervision and centralism, that faced the Court in *Martin* v. *Hunter's Lessee*. If the Constitution was to mean whatever the various states wanted it to mean, the cause of national union was lost at the outset.

Justice Story spoke for the Court, Marshall having disqualified himself because he had been financially involved with the Fairfax interests. Story had been appointed by Madison in 1811 as a New England Republican, but now, after five years on the Court, he was as nationalistic in his views as Marshall himself. Indeed the supreme bench consisted of two Federalists and five nominal Republicans, and yet Marshall was seldom to have much difficulty enlisting his fellows in the nationalist crusade. His success in doing so has often been attributed to the witchcraft of his strong and charming personality; Jefferson had once predicted that "it will be difficult to find a character with firmness enough to preserve his independence on the same bench with Marshall." There can be no doubt that Marshall was an immensely attractive and convincing colleague, but it seems reasonable to suppose that the judges who came to share his nationalist views were beguiled not only by him but by a growing awareness that the Court's status and their own depended on the strength of the Union. It is hardly surprising that the Supreme Court, an intrinsically national institution, should be drawn to the doctrine of nationalism.

Story's powerful opinion in this case followed a pattern which can be traced through most of the great nationalistic decisions of the era. In the first place, he felt called upon to argue, or rather to assert, that the Constitution was the creation of "the people of the United States" as the Preamble says, and not of the several states. This contention, which may seem merely abstract, was essential to his purpose. Since at least 1776, most Americans had conceded that the people were the ultimate source of sovereignty and that the people could therefore, as Story says, "invest the general government with all powers which they might deem proper and necessary." If the Constitution was the work of the people, the powers it granted the national government *could* be as extensive as sovereignty itself. But if, on the other hand, the states had created the Constitution, it was arguable that the powers of the national government must stop at the point where they encroached on state sovereignty, and this very argument had been insisted upon by the embattled Virginians. The assertion that the Constitution represented the higher sovereignty of the people enabled Story to controvert the argument that state sovereignty is inviolable; if the people, in enacting the Constitution, wanted to modify state sovereignty, they had an incontestable right to do so.

The second great step in the opinion was to contend that the people *did* want to modify state sovereignty and had given evidence of that desire in the language of the Constitution. Article III extends the judicial power to all *cases* arising under the Constitution, laws, or treaties. There is no suggestion that the judicial power must stop short if a case originates in a state court rather than a federal. Since the language is general and is not restricted by the context or by necessary implication, it must be assumed that any case presenting a federal question is within reach of the judicial power, whatever may be the tribunal in which it arises.

This opinion contains, in more or less explicit statement, practically all the major items in the bag of tricks the Marshall Court was to use in future years against the minions of disunion. It invokes the doctrine of popular sovereignty to accomplish traditionally Federalist ends, a gambit that was particularly frustrating to the Court's Republican opponents, who were accustomed to think of themselves as the champions of that doctrine. The doctrine is then used by Story to deprecate the idea that state sovereignty was left intact at the time the Union was formed. Next he sets forth the proposition that national powers should be construed generously, a notion disastrous to states' rights when its implications are developed. From these principles "in respect to which no difference of opinion ought to be indulged," as Story says, he is able to infer a supervisory power for the Supreme Court so broad that it embraces all state tribunals. And finally this panoply of authority is used to defend property rights against spoliation by a capricious public. Each of these themes will be echoed over and over in the decisions of the future; each of them serves a vital purpose in the judges' struggle to make America the nation they believed it ought to be.

The specific problem of the *Martin* case—whether the Court's power under Section 25 could be maintained—was not of course entirely settled by Story's argumentative dexterities. In the years that followed, whenever a state felt aggrieved by a Court decision, the familiar cry against Section 25 was again heard. In 1821, in *Cohens* v. *Virginia,* Marshall not only reiterated Story's basic points but interpreted the Eleventh Amendment, that supposed warranty of states' rights, so as to permit individuals to appeal to the Supreme Court even though a state was the other party in the litigation. The Amendment, said Marshall, prevents individual suits against states only if the action is "commenced" by the individual; if the state has initiated the action (for instance, by arresting a person), the person can still bring the state into the Supreme Court to defend itself against an appeal.

At this point, the Virginian defenders of states' rights felt that judicial sophistry had surpassed itself, since not even a constitutional amendment had arrested its course. They urged that the Court's authority be curbed by statute or by more carefully drawn amendment, and hereafter throughout the 1820's hardly a session of Congress went by without a proposal to modify, in one way or another, the doctrine of judicial control. These threats were serious enough to alarm the Court and its friends, but in truth none of them ever came very close to succeeding. As John Taylor of Caroline complained, the apathy of the "sister states," when one of their number was assailed, for a long time made a united front of states' rights sentiment impossible to assemble. Meanwhile, decision after decision accustomed the nation to accept the Court's view of its own function; each year that passed, each holding that was submitted to, made it a little harder to question that view. When South Carolina radically assailed the whole principle of nationalism in the Nullification Ordinance of 1832, its formidable adversaries included not only Andrew Jackson but a federal judiciary which had become a focus of public respect and a symbol of Union.

THE ENHANCEMENT OF NATIONAL POWER

One handicap of the Supreme Court during these early years and indeed throughout its history was its divorce from the sources of political power. Seven men in Washington, armed with nothing save their robes and their intellects, seem pitiful rivals to state legislatures, congresses, and presidents who command the machinery of government and are backed by the mighty force of the electoral process. But the Court's apparent weakness was also, as we have seen, a kind of opportunity. Because it was an independent, small, cohesive body, it could maintain a long-term view that gave it a decided advantage over opponents divided between a variety of special, temporary concerns and often confused in the basic premises of their opposition.

This advantage is further illustrated by the great Marshallian decisions involving the question of national legislative authority. Story's argument in the *Martin* case that national powers should be liberally construed enabled him to contend that Congress had a right to pass Section 25 and thus to make the Court the dominant tribunal of the nation. But his interest and Marshall's in the doctrine of liberal construction went far beyond its use to bolster judicial status. They wanted to enhance national power in all respects, partly because this would simultaneously restrict the power of the states, but partly too because they anticipated awesome tasks for the nation and wanted to insure that it was constitutionally equipped to deal with them. And the Court's success in accomplishing this aim must be attributed in no small degree to self-contradiction among the forces that opposed it.

McCulloch v. Maryland in 1819 is by almost any reckoning the greatest decision John Marshall ever handed down—the one most important to the future of America, most influential in the Court's own doctrinal history, and most revealing of Marshall's unique talent for stately argument. It involved a state tax on note issues of the Bank of the United States, which had been incorporated by act of Congress in 1816. The government argued that such a tax on a federal instrumentality was invalid and need not be paid. The state replied that the incorporation of the Bank exceeded Congress' constitutional powers and that in any event the states could tax as they willed within their own borders. These contentions raised vast and difficult questions both for the present and the future. The Bank was viewed with special loathing by the states' rights advocates; any decision upholding its claim to exist and denying the state's claim to tax could be counted on to infuriate them. And not the least of their heated objections would be the familiar one that the Court had no power in spite of Section 25 to entertain the cause. On the other hand, it was clear to Marshall, as it has been to posterity, that a national government restricted in its powers by Maryland's narrow interpretation would be incapable of the great tasks that might lie before it.

Speaking for a unanimous Court, Marshall therefore upheld the constitutionality of the Bank's incorporation, and in doing so set down the classic statement of the doctrine of national authority. The argument he advanced was not new; its main outlines had been endlessly debated since the first Congress and Hamilton's famous paper urging the Bank's establishment; and much of it had been given judicial expression by Story in 1816. But Marshall deserves the credit for stamping it with the die of his memorable rhetoric and converting it from a political theory into the master doctrine of American constitutional law.

Because the argument is logical it lends itself to summary, falling into three major phases. The first is concerned with the problem of the nature of the Constitution itself. Two crucial premises are laid down: First, the Constitution emanates from the hand of the sovereign people and speaks in broad language so that it can "be adapted to the various crises of human affairs." We must never forget that "it is a *constitution* we are expounding." These premises infuse the second phase, which concerns the nature of the national government the Constitution created. The people made that government supreme over all rivals within the sphere of its powers (Art. VI), and those powers must be construed generously if they are to be sufficient for the "various crises" of the ages to come.

The third phase is simply the application of these weighty principles. The power to incorporate the Bank is upheld under the clause endowing Congress with the power to make all laws "necessary and proper" for carrying into execution the other powers (Art. I, sec. 8); the words "necessary and proper" are interpreted generously, in accord with the principles advanced, to mean "appropriate" and "plainly adapted." The Maryland tax is invalidated, because since "the power to tax involves the power to destroy," to uphold the tax would grant the state the power to defeat the national government's supremacy; an inferior (in these matters) would be empowered to destroy a superior. But no summary can convey the air of high seriousness that pervades the opinion, the magisterial dignity with which it marches to its conclusions, the sense of righteous certitude with which it announces them. It was such qualities as these that made it persuasive to contemporaries and to the generations to come; and to appreciate these qualities the reader must go to the opinion itself.

The reaction was what might have been expected. In the North and the East the decision was praised; in the South and West, where the Bank was especially unpopular, the Court was roundly condemned. But even in Virginia, the fastness of such philosophers of Republicanism as Jefferson, Roane, and Taylor, the assailants curiously compromised their own position by putting the immediate issue of the Bank ahead of the broader issue of principle. Most of them denounced the Court for *not* holding the incorporation statute unconstitutional, thus of course tacitly conceding that the Court had the power to do so. Yet surely if the Court had the exalted power of overthrowing an act of Congress, it was not unreasonable to suppose that it also had the right to disapprove state laws. And if it did have these high prerogatives the Court must have some discretion in exercising them, that is, it could not be condemned merely because Spencer Roane, wielding the same power, would have decided the case differently.

In short most of the critics conceded too much for the good of their own criticisms. Their proper course would have been to deny that the Court had any business judging the validity of either national or state laws. But as usual they were more concerned about the immediate, concrete issue than they were about such a general doctrine as judicial sovereignty or even states' rights; and once again the Court profited from the fact that it alone seemed to understand the value of consistency and generality.

Much the same lesson can be drawn from the "Steamboat Monopoly Case," *Gibbons* v. *Ogden* in 1824, in which the Court was confronted for the first time by the problem of interpreting the commerce clause. A quarter-century before, the New York legislature had granted Robert R. Livingston and Robert Fulton the exclusive right to steamboat navigation in the waters of New York, and in the course of time the monopoly had extracted a similar privilege from Louisiana. The value of this controlling position in the two great port states of the nation was of course enormous, and rival states were deeply resentful of the arrangement. The *Gibbons* case involved an action for encroachment on the monopoly, and the defendant contended that the state had no right to grant it in the first place, because navigation is "commerce among the several states," which is the business of Congress.

This contention raised a series of questions that were destined for long and checkered careers in the development of constitutional law. First, what *is* interstate commerce? Does the term cover only buying and selling, or does it apply to such activities as navigation? Second, once we have determined what interstate commerce is, what is the extent of the power to regulate it? Third, what is the effect on the states of this grant of power to Congress? Must they stay out of the field altogether, or do they have a concurrent right to control it? It is not too much to say that the future of America as a nation depended on the answers that were given to these questions.

And Marshall, with his usual foresight, was well aware that he stood at another major constitutional crossroad. The opinion, like so many of his great ones, is a deft blend of boldness and restraint. In answer to the first two questions, he advanced the kind of broad, nationalistic definitions that the Hamiltonian tradition approved. Commerce, he said, is not merely buying and selling; it includes "every species of commercial intercourse," and this is true whether we are talking of either interstate or foreign commerce. Nor does interstate commerce stop at state boundaries; a journey that begins in Boston and ends in Philadelphia is subject to congressional power from start to finish. Of course, so inclusive a definition amply covers navigation. As for the extent of Congress' power to regulate a subject, once it is found to be in interstate commerce, that power is "complete in itself, may be exercised to its utmost extent, and acknowledges no limitations other than are prescribed in the Constitution." It is no less than the power "to prescribe the rule by which commerce is to be governed."

Perhaps only in the perspective of the future can it be understood how much these words meant; a twentieth-century observer looking back on them is impressed because he knows that the definitions have proved elastic enough to justify all the extensive commercial enterprises in which the national government has since engaged. But to contemporaries the most urgent question was yet to come: are the states precluded from acting in the commercial area thus defined? And at this point Marshall grew curiously evasive. He stated sympathetically the argument that the commerce power is exclusive, remarked that it had "great force" and said: ". . . the court is not satisfied that it has been refuted." He came as close to formally approving the doctrine as he could without quite doing so. But, he went on, it is not now necessary to decide this issue, because the New York monopoly law conflicts with a federal coasting license statute. Whether or not the commerce clause alone would invalidate the state law, surely it must be admitted that the federal coasting license law does, for the Constitution makes congressional enactments "the supreme law of the land." The lucrative but controversial monopoly was thus at last brought to an end.

Once again, as so often in the past, Marshall had managed to achieve imperishable results while sidestepping the area of greatest controversy. In other commerce clause cases he refined the notion of interstate (and foreign) commerce somewhat further by holding that goods were still subject to national control so long as they remained in their original shipping packages (the "original package doctrine"); and confused the question of state regulatory power still more by allowing a state to maintain a dam that blocked a navigable stream. No watchful guardian of states' rights could contend that Marshall had erected constitutional barriers to all state commercial regulation. Surely he had implied that some such regulation might be prohibited by the commerce clause alone, and surely his dicta about the extent of the commerce power had opened up the possibility of prodigious congressional regulation in this field. But it was present actualities, not implications and possibilities, that most concerned his contemporaries, and they found it hard to condemn a judicial stroke that slew the hated monopoly, whatever the flourishes that accompanied it. Jefferson and a few like him were horrified by *Gibbons,* but in general the decision was welcomed; the fact that it did after all overthrow a state law and hammer a few more nails in the coffin of state sovereignty was easy to minimize in the face of its immediately popular conclusion.

JUDICIAL ALLIES AND PRIVATE RIGHTS

One of the Supreme Court's peculiar characteristics is that it attempts to decide questions of policy without the advantage of conventional political resources. The judges have no organized party machine to call on for guidance and encouragement; they are spared both the penalties and the benefits of direct electoral support. But this does not mean of course that the Court has no constituency, if we can use that word in a somewhat looser and more informal sense than is usual. No institution in a democratic society could become and remain potent unless it could count on a solid block of public opinion that would rally to its side in a pinch. And the Supreme Court has historically been blessed with two kinds of supporters—those who venerate it and are prepared to defend it as the symbol of continuity and fairness, who are attached to the idea of the rule of law; and those who happen to be gratified by the course of policy the judges are pursuing at the moment. In practice the latter invariably claim also to be the former, and perhaps the problem of separately identifying the two groups is futile and somewhat academic. It is enough for our purposes to say that the Marshall Court had such a constituency to draw on and that the growth of constitutional doctrine on the subject of private rights is illuminated if we realize that this is so.

An essential element in that constituency, though by no means the whole of it, was the American legal fraternity, or as it has been called in a fine phrase, "the inner republic of bench and bar." In these early days lawyers were already occupying the pivotal position in American political affairs that they have occupied ever since. And they tended to reinforce the Supreme Court, partly no doubt because they represented the affluent "haves" who would profit from the stable, nationalized structure Marshall was building, but partly too because their training had taught them to esteem the rule of law which Marshall and his associates stood for. It was not only that men like William Pinckney and Daniel Webster vindicated Marshallian doctrine with the magic of their oratory in formal argument before the supreme bench; they and their lesser colleagues also helped, in letters, in conversations, in appearances before lower courts, in state legislatures, and in Congress, to generate the atmosphere of consent that made Marshall's achievements possible.

These stout allies played a significant part during Marshall's era in the development and acceptance of doctrines protecting the property owner, most particularly by way of the contract clause of the Constitution. In fact if their activities were not part of the historical record, they would have to be postulated in order to account for a process of legal growth that would otherwise seem autonomous. It will be remembered that Marshall had stepped very tentatively in *Fletcher* v. *Peck,* the first contract clause decision. The principle that the state must abide by its own contractual commitments rested on flimsy historical grounds and presented certain grave logical difficulties; therefore the vague mandates of natural law were invoked to augment the force of the contract clause argument. Two years later, in 1812, he offered an interpretation of *Fletcher* that made it sound less ambiguous than it was: in that case, he said, it was decided "on solemn argument and much deliberation" that the contract clause "extends to contracts to which a State is a party." The statement of the point is clear enough at this stage, but it is after all only a statement; nothing apparent had happened to quiet the misgivings he seemed to have in *Fletcher* about the doctrine's acceptability.

Seven years later the famous case *Dartmouth College* v. *Woodward* came to the Supreme Court. The question was whether the state legislature could validly alter the charter which had been granted to Dartmouth College in 1769 by the British crown. A complex imbroglio of theology and politics had resulted in a law changing the name of the college to Dartmouth University and vesting control over it in trustees and overseers largely appointed by the governor; in effect, Dartmouth was to be converted into a public institution. The old trustees fought back by pointing out that the charter had granted them the sole right to fill vacancies in their number "forever" and contending among other things that the state law violated the federal contract clause. This was a bold assertion and seemingly not a very promising one, since it involved, in addition to the heretofore somewhat doubtful idea that the state is bound by its own contracts, two even more novel propositions: that a charter is such a contract and that it is inviolable even though its holders have no "beneficial interest" at stake.

It might be thought that the burden of all these meanings would be more than the contract clause could bear, especially when we consider that Marshall himself appeared to have so little confidence in it only nine years earlier. But Marshall not only affirmed all three interpretations but did so with an economy of argument unusual for him. On the first he offered no argument at all, simply taking it for granted that the state must stick to its agreements; the trimmings drawn from the natural law tradition were now dispensed with, and the contract clause alone was the basis for decision. The idea that a corporate charter is a contract within the meaning of the clause was also assumed rather than argued. Finally he came to the only point that really troubled him—that the contract clause was primarily designed to protect the private property rights of individuals and that the trustees have no such beneficial interest in Dartmouth College; they would not personally lose anything if the charter were overthrown. But, said Marshall, although the framers of the contract clause may have been chiefly concerned with protecting private property, they did not use language that excludes a charitable institution like Dartmouth, and we must therefore assume it is included. "The case, being within the words of the rule, must be within its operation likewise" unless the result would be "obviously absurd, or mischievous, or repugnant to the general spirit" of the Constitution.

The startling thing about the *Dartmouth College* case is not this last point, which follows reasonably enough if we accept the two that precede it, nor yet those two points themselves; but the fact that they were announced so confidently and seem to have provoked so little dissent. Indeed the Superior Court of New Hampshire, though holding against the trustees, had conceded that the contract clause extended to contracts between states and individuals and had assumed that a charter granting privileges to individuals for their own benefit would be protected by the contract clause. Yet by these concessions the contract clause, once apparently innocuous, became a mighty instrument for the judicial protection of property rights against state abridgment. How did it happen that Marshall could forge such an instrument so off-handedly? How did the tentative suggestion of *Fletcher* in 1810 become the confident assertion of *Dartmouth* in 1819?

The explanation is that the Court's "constituency" had been at work on its behalf in the meantime. The idea that the contract clause might serve to protect private property from the states and the corollary idea that corporate charters could be included in such protection—these embryonic ideas had caught hold in the minds of lawyers and judges, had been fostered and developed by them, and had thereby been raised to the status of mature constitutional doctrines. By 1819, they were so well intrenched that the Supreme Court needed to do little more than stamp them with its formal sanctions. The *Dartmouth* decision is important then, not for its own accomplishments but for its acknowledgment of results already achieved. Businessmen, secure in the possession of inviolable state-granted charters, could thank their stars for "the inner republic of bench and bar" as well as for John Marshall.

Marshall wanted in fact to improve the property holders' lot even further. In the same year he invalidated a New York bankruptcy law on the ground that it infringed the contract clause. The special vice of this law was that it released debtors from obligations contracted before its passage. A creditor might legitimately feel aggrieved if he loaned money under one set of rules and was forced to try to collect it under another. But, it was argued, if the law already exists, the lender knowingly takes the risk that his debtor will be released by bankruptcy and therefore cannot complain of unfairness if it so turns out. However, Marshall, in holding that the Constitution barred retrospective interference with contracts, used language intimating that *prospective* interferences were also prohibited. His ambitious objective was to forbid any state law that impaired contracts in any way, and the acceptance of such a principle would have greatly enhanced the value of the contract clause as an instrument for the protection of private rights. But at this point even his usually acquiescent brethren called a halt, and in 1827 the Court voted, four to three, to uphold a state bankruptcy law as applied to debts contracted after its passage. Marshall dissented, and it is plain that the decision bitterly disappointed him; but he had much reason for self-congratulation all the same. With the help of the contemporary bench and bar, he had transmuted a clause of modest pretensions into a broad inhibition on the commercial laws of the states. He had maneuvered America a few steps closer to his own idea of the good society.

THE ACHIEVEMENT OF JOHN MARSHALL

Few intellectual feats are more difficult than the assessment of history while we are living it, and perhaps the problem is all the greater for those who are themselves playing the leading roles. In his last years, Marshall was beset with misgivings about America's future, full of gloomy convictions that he had failed in his campaign to establish judicial sovereignty and to cement the bonds of national union. The states' rights movement was waxing ever stronger and more vocal under the ministrations of John C. Calhoun; the Court had recently been defied in two spectacular cases by Georgia, and President Jackson's unwillingness to back the judges had underlined the Court's ultimate dependency on external support. The old Federalist dream of rule by "the wise, the rich, and the good" seemed more chimerical than ever, as the spirit of Jacksonian democracy swept the nation.

But, ominous though these developments appeared, Marshall was wrong to think that they spelled the failure of his programs. Not even he, the architect-in-chief, realized how securely the cornerstones of American constitutionalism had been laid. His error probably was that he hoped for absolute certitude in a system that had been dedicated by its framers to the principle of relativism. We cannot say that the doctrine of judicial sovereignty was established beyond the shadow of doubt by *Cohens* v. *Virginia* in 1821, or that the broad construction of national powers was settled once and for all by *McCulloch* v. *Maryland* and *Gibbons* v. *Ogden,* or that the *Dartmouth* case stilled all uncertainties about the contract clause. We cannot say that at one moment the constitutional basis for union was an aspiration and at the next a firm reality, for constitutional history does not move in this way. The vagueness of the Constitution on these issues gave the Court its chance to be creative, but by the same token it was decreed that the creations would never be final and perfect. The Court's title to power, being inferred rather than explicitly stated, must always be somewhat tentative; interpretations of the Constitution, being fashioned by the historical context rather than by the fiat of 1789, must submit to the verdict of later history, as well as the past. With all his subtlety and shrewdness, Marshall's mind was attracted by absolutes, and the contingency of the constitutional universe never ceased to trouble him.

But if we can tolerate, as Marshall could not, a world of half-certainty (and if we enjoy, as he did not, the perspective of the future), we can see that his forebodings were excessive, and his accomplishments greater than he knew. The doctrine of judicial sovereignty was still subject to occasional challenge in moments of stress; men like Jackson and Calhoun were unwilling to admit that the Supreme Court was the *only* authority on the Constitution's meaning. But surely the judicial monopoly, though imperfect, was very impressive. The nation in general thought of the Court as the principal authority and conceded its right to supervise the states in most matters. When the Court impinged on the great primary interests of a state or region, a line might be drawn; but in the considerable distance before that line was reached judicial sovereignty held its sway. The Supreme Court was now far more serene and formidable than the precariously balanced institution Marshall had taken over in 1801. America's devotion to the idea of fundamental law and the Court's ability to capitalize on opponents' errors had made sure of that.

This establishment of judicial hegemony was itself a highly important victory in the struggle to promote the principle of national union, for it meant (with the qualifications already mentioned) that the Constitution spoke with one voice throughout America. But the other substantive principles Marshall had laid down also served that purpose and were also more solidly fixed than Marshall, in his somber old age, imagined. The national-power doctrines of *McCulloch* and *Gibbons* were to have their great day in a more remote future when the national government felt inclined to use the constitutional sinews Marshall's court had provided; until then their significance was more moral than practical. But the corollary doctrine—that the states may not encroach on these federally reserved realms—was well accepted and immediately relevant. These limitations on state power based on the doctrine of national supremacy, plus such specific limitations as those derived from the contract clause, helped open the way to the development of commercial enterprise on a national scale in the next half-century.

Marshall was right in thinking that he had failed to resolve for America the great problem of nation-state relationships. No court could finally settle an issue of such dimensions, an issue that had already brought the nation near the brink of civil war. But he might justifiably have felt that he and his Court had made a priceless contribution to its settlement, had fashioned out of judicial materials an ideology of seasoned strength to which those who cared for the Union could repair, had established a pattern of control that would help to shore up the Union even though nothing but bloodshed could ultimately save it. He could have comforted himself with the thought that no court in world history had ever done so much to affect the destiny of a great nation.

FOUR

THE COURT UNDER TANEY: THE NATURAL HISTORY OF JUDICIAL PRESTIGE

W HEN JOHN MARSHALL DIED in 1835, the anguish of his admirers was compounded partly of grief for a beloved national
figure and partly of apprehension that Jackson would appoint
Roger B. Taney to succeed him. It is one of the commonplaces of American history that those who have learned to live with the governmental
order of their own day nurse an often excessive dread of its passing. They
forget how many times their forebodings of the past have turned out to
be bugbears; they forget that the bonds of continuity in America are remarkably strong. And so it was in 1835. Taney had been a staunch oppo-
nent of the Bank of the United States and had, as Secretary of the Treasury, deprived the Bank of the federal deposits that were its lifeblood.
This made him, in the eyes of anti-Jacksonians, a "political hack" and "a
supple, cringing tool of power," for the Bank was their darling. The prospect of a Court appointed by Democratic presidents and headed by Taney
seemed dark indeed; Marshall's carefully wrought jurisprudence would
be demolished and the nation would be exposed to the unchecked ravages
of agrarian, states' rights radicalism.

Their depression deepened when the event they had feared actually
occurred. Taney was appointed, and confirmed by the Senate after a bitter
wrangle in March of 1836; five members of the Court were now Jackson
appointees, only Story and Thompson surviving from the Marshallian
golden age. Webster, the "godlike Daniel" whose name and heart were
so intimately associated with the old Court, wrote: "Judge Story thinks
the Supreme Court is *gone,* and I think so too." Then three decisions
handed down in Taney's first term seemed to confirm their misgivings.
Each of the cases had been heard by Marshall, but decision had been
postponed; the holdings of the new Taney Court were in each case at

variance with the position Marshall would have taken, according to his close friend Justice Story. The dismay of the Whigs was acute. "Under the progressive genius of the new judicial administration," said one journal, "we can see the whole fair system of the Constitution beginning to dissolve like the baseless fabric of a vision."

For a long time historians accepted these despairing outbursts as if they actually, or at any rate nearly, described the constitutional policies of the Taney Court. The legend of Taney and his brethren as radical democrats, hostile to property rights, nationalism, and Marshall's memory, was stronger than the facts that would have emerged from a reading of the decisions themselves. But as the decisions finally were read and compared with those of Marshall's time, as the whole doctrinal course of the Taney Court was traced, it became apparent that the legend was badly misleading. The old jurisprudence had not been broken down after all, or even very greatly altered: the claims of property were still well protected, the nation was not constitutionally fragmented, judicial power was not surrendered. In fact, the position of the Supreme Court as the final arbiter of constitutional questions had become, within a few years of Taney's accession, more secure than ever before. The concept of judicial sovereignty, which Marshall had nurtured so lovingly and defended against so many challenges, was by 1840 an almost unquestioned premise of American government.

This congenial result, unexpected by the Webster-Story fraternity and long unnoticed by history, was achieved in perfectly unsurprising ways. The living Marshall himself of course deserves much of the credit. Numerous though his enemies were, even they had found it hard to resist being impressed by his dignity, his self-righteousness, and his intellectual power; and his constitutional edifice had been well made.

But the death of the great Chief Justice was almost as decisive as his life in bringing about the triumph of judicial sovereignty. For one thing it made him a saint. Within a surprisingly short time the justices of the Supreme Court, regardless of who appointed them, were paying almost unanimous lip service to his memory; those who had chided him so willingly while he was alive now cited him, like scripture, in their own behalf and flinched at the charge that he would have disagreed with them. For another thing, Marshall's death diverted judicial partisanship, or rather turned it upside down. Though many Americans came to venerate Marshall, many others could never forget that he was a Federalist and a very opinionated one at that, and thus a residue of animosity always handicapped the Marshall Court.

Now the Chief and a majority of his associates were Jackson-approved, and this meant that the anti-judicial tradition of the Democrats lost much of its edge. On the other hand, the Whigs (the successors to the now-dead Federalist party), though they might bemoan the loss of their idol and deplore the advent of Taney, were committed to a prejudicial philosophy they could not lightly forswear. Their natural propensity to support the Court could be depended upon to reassert itself when and if they realized that the Taney regime was not likely to attempt a real constitutional revolution. Unless the Court erred on the side of either extreme—unless it enraged the Democrats by an excess of Marshallian nationalism or antagonized the Whigs by an outright reversion to localism—the chances for a kind of judicial "era of good feelings" were very good.

Whether the chance should become a reality depended of course on the wisdom of the judges who confronted this opportunity. The old idea that they seriously undermined Marshall's constitutional structure has already been mentioned; there is very little to it. But in recent years there has been some disposition to reverse the idea, and to treat the Court of the Taney era as if its doctrines were a consistent extension in all important respects of tendencies Marshall set going, as if no concessions at all to shifting political winds had been made.

The trouble is that neither of these comparatively neat analyses will quite square with the untidy, pragmatic welter of doctrines that has actually been bequeathed to us by the Taney Court. It is true that the jurisdiction of the federal courts was in some ways extended beyond the limits Marshall had recognized—in admiralty cases, for example, and in cases involving the right of corporations to bring federal suits. It is true that the basic dogmas of Marshall's contract-clause interpretation were not challenged and that in some cases the Taney Court was as dogmatic about the sanctity of contracts as even Marshall had been. It is true that the national government's supremacy over the states was repeatedly upheld. But it is also true that the Court elsewhere restricted the range of jurisdiction that is asserted or implied in some of Marshall's great opinions, qualified the constitutional privileges enjoyed by corporations, and granted the states a degree of autonomy in commercial matters that Marshall would undoubtedly have denied them.

The fact is that the Court from 1836 until 1857 was pursuing a non-doctrinaire course to which only the loosest kind of descriptive generalizations can apply. The Court was adjusting itself to the contours of a changing America, relaxing the rigidities of Marshallian dogma when that seemed desirable, retaining or strengthening others, and fashioning some new dogmas of its own, producing a constitutional jurisprudence that had been pragmatically fitted to the nation of the day. If we see the process either in terms of pure judicial imperialism or pure judicial abnegation, we are missing the important point—that the Taney Court by giving ground at some salients was able to advance upon others, thus maintaining a quantum of jurisdiction at least equal to that exercised by Marshall but composed of elements somewhat different from those the great Chief Justice himself might have chosen. And we might miss the even more significant point that the result of this adjustment process was to fortify the judicial power by creating an atmosphere of public acceptance more complete than the Court had ever before enjoyed. Marshall's historic task had been to establish the frontiers of judicial supervision; the function of the Court under Taney was to consolidate the most essential of these gains by a deft combination of tenacity and flexibility. The function was so well performed that not even the monumental indiscretion of the *Dred Scott* decision could quite destroy the judicial imperium.

THE NATION-STATE PROBLEM AND
THE COURT'S POLICY OF MODERATION

The theme of the adjustment process by which this result was achieved was compromise. To be sure, this theme was far from new in the Court's history; even Marshall had been well aware that half a loaf is sometimes better than none, and no wise Court has ever forgotten this platitude. But the need to compromise is a matter of degree depending in part on the historic context. Marshall in the most creative period of his tenure faced a situation that permitted the Court to pursue a comparatively bold and unambiguous policy with impunity. In the years from 1836 to 1857, the American political world was torn by conflicts so bitter that a frankly doctrinaire Court would have wounded both itself and the cause of union. As always, the Court was dedicated to keeping the Union secure, if only because its own existence depended on that security. But there is a season for everything, and in the climate of the Taney era the Court could best sustain the Union by preserving its own status as a national tribunal. And that meant that constitutional doctrines must be framed in a spirit of moderation.

One of the 1837 decisions that so alarmed the Whigs was *Mayor of New York* v. *Miln,* in which the Court had upheld a state regulation applying to ships entering the port of New York. The law impinged on foreign commerce, and Marshall's disciple Story argued that it should be overturned under the doctrine, which he derived from the Steamboat Monopoly Case, that Congress' power over foreign and interstate commerce is exclusive. This was of course the extreme nationalist position applied with a rigor that Marshall himself had not insisted upon. The other extreme was Justice Thompson's view that the states could regulate interstate and foreign commerce as much as they chose unless the state law conflicted with an actual federal statute.

But the Court majority steered between, sustaining the law on the ground that the state had merely been exercising its "police power" for the welfare of its citizens, not regulating commerce; thus the question of whether the national commerce power was exclusive did not arise. A flat answer to that question, either yes or no, would have infuriated an important segment of American opinion. The Court's resort to what has been called the "convenient apologetics" of the police power enabled it to avoid both the frying pan and the fire; and the additional advantage was that the doctrine was arguably rooted in one of Marshall's own decisions which had permitted a state, on similar grounds, to block a navigable stream. Even the Whigs, if they had really thought the matter over, could not reasonably contend that a prolocalist revolution had taken place.

Although the police-power doctrine was therefore in some ways very convenient, the distinction it made was always slippery, for it depended, as Taney was to say, on the idea that a state regulation which affected commerce had been passed with the motive of protecting health and welfare, rather than regulating commercial affairs. Motive is always an elusive entity. Moreover, since Revolutionary times, the states had woven a complex network of regulations which were frankly commercial and which often touched foreign and interstate transactions: here the police-power "apologetics" were not even relevant. So the Court found it increasingly difficult to evade the direct question of whether the states could regulate commerce as such. In 1851, they resolved the question, again by compromise. The states, said the Court, are precluded from regulating commerce as such when the particular subjects regulated are "in their nature national, or admit only of one uniform system . . . of regulation." On the other hand, if the subject is one that is local in character, appropriate for diverse plans of regulation, depending on local peculiarities, the states may regulate that commerce until Congress itself chooses to take over the subject (*Cooley v. Board of Wardens*).

This ingenious disengagement from the horns of the dilemma was not entirely satisfying to those, like Taney himself, who had argued for full concurrent state power in the commercial field; nor to those all-out nationalists, like Justice McLean, who had insisted that the states must leave commerce strictly alone. But neither localist nor nationalist could claim that the Court had wholly yielded to the other; each could justifiably feel that the announced doctrine in some part embodied his views.

In other fields a comparably moderate realignment of doctrine can be traced. The other two 1837 decisions that had alarmed the disciples of Marshall like a fire bell in the night were *Charles River Bridge* v. *Warren Bridge Co.* and *Briscoe* v. *Bank of Kentucky.* The first involved an application of the contract clause, that sacred cow of Marshall's jurisprudence, and because the Court refused to find in the clause new restrictions on state power, the cry of heresy was raised.

The proprietors of a toll bridge in Massachusetts argued that their state-granted charter implied a promise that the legislature would not authorize a competing bridge; in short that, without explicitly saying so, the state had endowed them with a constitutionally guaranteed monopoly. The Court simply held that no such inferences would be drawn; public grants should be strictly construed. There is no challenge to the basic principles of Marshall's contract-clause doctrine—that a charter is a contract that binds the states—nor is there evidence in later contract-clause cases that the Taney Court was reckless of property rights, as the Whigs had feared. The states were held to the letter of the doctrines Marshall had enunciated, and the most that can be said is that the new Court usually declined to expand those doctrines so as further to inhibit state powers. By thus conceding the states some leeway in commercial affairs and at the same time insisting that they abide by the promises they had actually made, the Court had once more found a middle—and generally popular—ground.

As for the *Briscoe* case, it undoubtedly represents a concession to localism. One of the evils that had most perturbed men of substance during the Articles of Confederation period was state issuance of currency, and the Founding Fathers had hoped to debar a return to that sorry state of affairs by providing, in Article I, section 10, that no states might "emit bills of credit." Marshall had enforced the clause rigorously when Missouri issued interest-bearing certificates receivable for debts due the state. Since they circulated as money, they were bills of credit. But now Justice McLean, in a Court opinion that is a triumph of incoherency, approved the issuance of currency by a bank owned and controlled by Kentucky. An uninitiated observer might protest that such a bank was the equivalent of the state itself and equally bound by the constitutional prohibition. Justice Story, who dissented, had no doubts about it. But the new Court thought otherwise, and state autonomy in money matters was given increased vitality.

But against the centrifugal thrust of such a decision and a few others of a similar tenor, we can balance a series of judgments which reasserted the principle of national supremacy: for example, a ruling that the incomes of federal employees are exempt from state taxation under the doctrine of *McCulloch* v. *Maryland;* a second that the extradition of fugitives from justice to foreign countries is an exclusive prerogative of the national government; and a third permitting a corporation chartered in one state to do business in another unless specifically barred by the second state's laws. In this last case partisans had argued on the one side that Alabama *could* not, under the "privileges and immunities" clause (Art. IV, sec. 2), exclude a Georgia-chartered corporation, and on the other side that the corporation was *automatically* excluded, without a specific Alabama law, because the Georgia charter was useless anywhere else. Characteristically the Taney Court faced by these extreme contentions chose to compromise.

And compromise was appropriate to the Court's historic circumstances in a double sense. After the burst of creative enterprise under Marshall, the judiciary had need to slow the pace of its constitution-making process so that America could grow used to the house John Marshall had built, so that the doctrines could be adjusted a little to fit the facts of the changing economic order, so that the judicial power could be consolidated. Great advances in history, if they endure, are often followed by such a period of retardation and adaptation. But beyond this, a propitiating temper was called for by the conditions of the day, especially when the great question of nation-state relationships was even indirectly raised. For America was moving toward Armageddon with frightening inexorability, and passions were stirring as never before. If the task of the Marshall Court had been to champion nationalism against the states' rights movement, the task of the Court in Taney's era was to champion temperance and reason against the extremism that threatened to dissever the Republic. For a long time it performed that task remarkably well.

THE PRIDE OF POWER AND THE SLAVERY QUESTION

But throughout these years, as the judges charted point by point their path of moderation, a specter stood near their elbows, and as time passed this presence became harder and harder to ignore. Its name, of course, was slavery. In an attempt to exorcise it, the Court mortally endangered the judicial temple which they and their predecessors had so painfully erected. For a time it seemed that the labor of nearly seventy years would be blown away by the holocaust following one dramatic lapse from judicial self-restraint.

It is easy for a modern observer to see, looking back, that the slavery question was too big and too explosive to be decided by a court. We know, whatever mythologists may say, that there are practical as well as technical limits on the Court's jurisdiction. The great fundamental decisions that determine the course of society must ultimately be made by society itself. If they are also, as they are apt to be, decisions that profoundly engage the emotions of the whole people, this is all the more reason for the judiciary to leave them alone; the Court's place is not on the battlefield or in the center of the political arena. And we know that, as it turned out, only bloodshed could settle the slavery issue.

The judges of the 1850's knew some of these things but unfortunately not all, and others were perhaps too easily forgotten in the heat of the moment. They should have realized that their power was built on a lively sense of its own limitations; this was the lesson of the Court's past successes—and failures. They should have known that slavery was a judicial untouchable, for it had already, in 1850, brought the nation to the brink of civil war. But they were children of their time as well as judges. By the 1850's the slavery issue was clouding the gaze of seemingly wise men all over America; it is perhaps too much to expect that the vision of the Supreme Court would remain unimpaired.

For a while the Court majority resisted the temptation to plunge into the flames. To be sure, as early as 1842 Justice Story had struck back-handedly at slavery when, speaking for the Court, he overturned a Pennsylvania law. It conflicted, he said, with the federal Fugitive Slave Law, and he went on gratuitously to hold that *any* state legislation touching fugitive slaves was invalid because the national power over that subject was exclusive. Since the national law was almost unworkable without state co-operation, the effect of this decision was to hamper the apprehension of fugitive slaves under the guise of defending the power to apprehend them. The decision was angrily criticized. But the tumult such as it was soon died down, and the Court thereafter left the slavery question pretty much to the mercies of the political branches of government.

In 1851, it was confronted with the contention that slaves had become free when they entered free states or territories. Behind this argument lurked the perilous question of whether Congress could prohibit slavery in the territories of the United States, as it had done in the Missouri Compromise. With nice discretion, the judges skirted the volcano's edge, holding in *Strader* v. *Graham* that the status of the Negroes in question depended on the laws of the state where they now lived—Kentucky. Since Kentucky regarded them as slaves, the Supreme Court was bound by that fact; and the question of their status during former sojourns in free areas did not arise.

By this kind of circumspection the carefully nurtured judicial prestige was temporarily kept intact in these hazardous hours. But the Court's high repute was in some ways its danger. The political order was abundantly demonstrating its inability to cope with the slavery issue without dissevering the nation. The line defining the practical boundaries of the Court's power, though implicitly recognized in decisions of the past, had seldom been acknowledged, and prevailing mythology tended to obscure its existence. Perhaps, then, this highly esteemed group of nine men could succeed where the political parties were so grievously failing. Perhaps a pronouncement from them would settle the questions evoking the slavery controversy, or at any rate help in settling the thorniest of them all—the question of slavery in the territories. The nation was in deadly jeopardy. It would be tragic for the Court to withhold its hand, if that hand might save the Union.

Such exalted ideas of the Court's power were advanced repeatedly during these years by supposedly responsible statesmen and publicists. The judges were sure to listen, and they were tempted to heed. Perhaps, however, they had also been impressed by the ominous words of Northerners like Seward and Chase, who had accused the Court of partiality to slavery and denied that the country need accept a proslavey decision. The old familiar challenge to judicial sovereignty had not been heard much lately, and its reappearance now may have given the judges pause. At all events a majority of them were still apparently unconvinced that they could bell the cat when *Dred Scott* v. *Sandford* came before them in 1856. Scott had been taken as a slave into Illinois and into the northern part of the Louisiana Purchase. Illinois law forbade slavery, and the Louisiana Purchase territory north of the southern boundary of Missouri had been declared free by the Missouri Compromise in 1820–21. Scott, now in Missouri, sued his present owner in federal court, arguing that these journeys to free areas had made him a free man. This raised the fiery question of whether Congress could bar slavery from the territories, but did not require the Court to answer the question. The judges might have replied, under the analogy of the *Strader* case, that they were bound by Missouri law, regardless of Scott's status when he had lived elsewhere. Since Missouri regarded him as a slave that would settle the matter, and the problem of Congress' power need not be answered, pro or con. A majority of the Supreme Court agreed to take this course; an opinion was actually written by Justice Nelson.

But at least one judge, McLean, was dissatisfied with this prudent arrangement. It became known that he, an ambitious politician and a firm abolitionist, intended to dissent, arguing that Scott became free when he entered the free territory of the Louisiana Purchase. This necessarily involved the contention that Congress had the power to enact the Missouri Compromise which had made that area free. A majority of his fellow judges believed in fact that the Compromise was invalid, and they were unwilling to let McLean go unanswered, if the question was to be posed at all. Besides there was always the beguiling idea that a forthright statement from the Court might settle the whole, terrible issue and retrieve simultaneously the cause of both the Union and the South. Cheered on by his fellows and by the newly elected President James Buchanan, Taney therefore produced the most disastrous opinion the Supreme Court has ever issued. Dred Scott, he said, cannot bring suit in federal courts, first, because Negroes are not and cannot be citizens in the meaning of the federal Constitution; second, because, since the Missouri Compromise exceeded Congress' powers and is unconstitutional, he is still a slave in spite of his sojourn in free territory; and, third, because Missouri law regards him as a slave and the Supreme Court is here bound by Missouri's determination.

Eight separate opinions, including the Chief's, were filed by the judges in this case, and the task of unraveling them is more formidable than it is rewarding. What mattered to the nation was that a six-judge majority had denied the right of Negroes to be citizens and the right of Congress to control slavery in the territories.

The tempest of malediction that burst over the judges seems to have stunned them; far from extinguishing the slavery controversy, they had fanned its flames and had, moreover, deeply endangered the security of the judicial arm of government. No such vilification as this had been heard even in the wrathful days following the Alien and Sedition Acts. Taney's opinion was assailed by the Northern press as a wicked "stump speech" and was shamefully misquoted and distorted. "If the people obey this decision," said one newspaper, "they disobey God." Senator Seward fostered a dramatic but improbable story that Buchanan and Taney had villainously plotted this stroke on behalf of the slavery interests in a whispered tête-à-tête during the President's inauguration ceremonies, and the idea of a corrupt bargain between President, Congress, and Court became a theme of party politics in the next few years.

Of course no such explicit conspiracy existed. But Taney had connived in an exchange of information between Justices Catron and Grier and the incoming President, apparently out of sincere conviction that the leader of the nation in such parlous times should be informed about so grave an issue. It was not the least of his mistakes. The first and greatest had been to imagine that a flaming political issue could be quenched by calling it a "legal" issue and deciding it judicially.

But the notion that the Court could legitimately co-operate with the "political" branches in dealing with such an issue was almost equally self-destructive, for the Court's claim to public regard rested heavily on the belief that its work was distinguishable from "politics." In 1850 the Court enjoyed popular support as nearly unanimous as can ever be expected in a diverse democratic society. It was playing a modest but significant part in the affairs of the nation. Eight years later, it had forfeited that position, and its role in the American polity was nearly negligible. Taney and his fellows had been almost irresistibly provoked to do what they did in the *Dred Scott* case; the Chief's errors were well intended and understandable; he does not deserve the infamy that was so long associated with his name, for he was during most of his tenure a wise and good leader of the Court. But the fact that he had these virtues does not make his errors in this case any the less woeful; the fact that the Court under him had reached the pinnacle of its historic prestige merely heightens the tragedy of its decline.

The extent of that tragedy is revealed by the peculiar transvaluation of values that took place in connection with the case of *Ableman v. Booth* in 1859. Ableman, a Milwaukee editor, had assisted a fugitive slave to escape from federal custody, and was therefore arrested for violation of the national Fugitive Slave Law. The Wisconsin Supreme Court ordered him released on a writ of habeas corpus, and the order was obeyed. However, the national government then appealed to the Supreme Court of the United States, which held that the state courts had no business to interfere with the conduct of federal law and that the Fugitive Slave Law was constitutional.

Now the first point was of course the very keystone of the Supreme Court's jurisdictional arch; this was the principle for which Marshall had fought so shrewdly and effectively. If the national government and its judicial arm can operate only by the leave of the several states, the nation is not a nation and the Supreme Court is not a supreme court. Yet the decision was violently attacked, the state was urged to resist, the cry that the Court had no power thus to overrule a state was heard, not only in Wisconsin, but throughout the North.

This was the doctrine of nullification, familiar since the Virginia and Kentucky resolutions of 1798–99, re-energized by the mordant genius of Calhoun in 1832, and now becoming an article of faith below the Mason-Dixon line. That it should be invoked by a northern state as a challenge to the Court is a measure of the witless inconsistency of some Northern opinion but is also a measure of judicial bankruptcy. The Court's effective existence depended on acceptance of the principle of national authority, and there was no hope that this principle would be entertained in the South one minute after an anti-slavery opinion was rendered. The judicial constituency had always been drawn from those who had a stake in nationalism, and in 1859 that meant the North. But the monumental indiscretion of *Dred Scott* had forfeited Northern allegiance. For the first time in its history, the Court seemed almost friendless (for the fair-weather friendship of the South provided very cold comfort).

DECLINE WITHOUT FALL

The gloomy view of the judiciary's estate that is suggested by these events seems confirmed when we glance briefly at the Court's vicissitudes during the war years that followed. War is never a favorable environment for judicial power. It is characterized by emotion and quick, drastic action; and courts are not well equipped to cope with either. But natural handicaps are not enough to account for the impotency of the Supreme Court during the Civil War. It was of course, necessarily, the court of the Union, for the Confederacy was going its own way. But a substantial proportion of Union opinion associated the Court with the Confederate cause, unfairly but nonetheless stubbornly. It was hardly to be expected that its mandates would be eagerly sought or greatly heeded.

Taney, the luckless scapegoat of this judicial ice age, added another item to the Unionist score against him when less than three months after Lincoln's inauguration, he challenged the President's power to suspend the writ of habeas corpus for wartime purposes. He ordered that John Merryman, a Maryland secessionist being held in military prison, be brought before him on the writ, and when the commanding general refused to comply, Taney ordered that the general himself be haled into court in order to be fined and imprisoned for his disobedience. The marshal seeking to carry out this assignment was denied admission to the fort by the general, and Taney addressed himself to the President, calling on Lincoln to "perform his constitutional duty." The President did not reply. The only immediate reward for Taney's zeal was another shower of venom from the Northern press against this "hoary apologist for treason."

The Chief's point was in fact pretty well taken. Lincoln had wielded executive power somewhat recklessly during those early months of hostilities. It is at least doubtful that the President alone had the power to suspend the writ of habeas corpus, and it was not unreasonable to ask that he get congressional approval before he did so. But any chance that the Court might play the role of a moderating force, holding the government within sensible boundaries as it waged the bloody war, had been squandered in 1857.

And the Court majority knew it. Taney's willingness in the *Merryman* case to add to the judicial sea of troubles was not characteristic of the Court as a whole while the shooting continued. The judges found reason to refuse jurisdiction on cases involving such ticklish questions as the trial of civilians by military commission and the Legal Tender Acts. A decision adverse to the Union government in either might well have brought the temple crashing about their ears. The Court also upheld the power of the President to make war in the legal sense without waiting for a congressional declaration. Surely, it might be said, the day of the Supreme Court as a powerful factor in America was done. The Civil War was not only testing whether the nation could long endure; it was also demonstrating that the experiment of an independent and influential national judiciary had failed. The aged Chief Justice was not alone in believing that the Court would never "be restored to the authority and rank which the Constitution intended to confer on it," that is, the status it had attained under Marshall and himself.

But like Marshall, who died with similar forebodings weighing on his spirit, Taney and his colleagues had built better than he knew. On the foundation Marshall had bequeathed, the Taney Court had fashioned a system of jurisprudence and a judicial image; and the nation had learned to accept one and to admire the other. The judges had maintained a clear line of connection between Marshall's doctrines and their own. This was wise because it preserved the essential idea of the fundamental law as a steady river of continuity in otherwise capricious political seas. They had used the judicial veto, and this was important because it not only kept the notion of constitutional limit alive but reminded those who might forget that judicial sovereignty had not atrophied. But their discipleship to Marshall was discriminating; the veto had been handled discreetly; the Taney judges were aware that both the economic and the political world had changed since Marshall's time. They had managed to strike a middle ground that reconciled the American will for change with the desire for order and stability, the American's wish to have his way with his respect for the rule of law. Their reward had been the homage of the nation.

This achievement had been endangered by the audacious assumption in *Dred Scott* that the judiciary could solve the major problem facing America. But the public habit of reverence was strongly ingrained by those years of painstaking cultivation, and not even this calamity could stamp it out altogether. How many such adversities the judiciary could sustain is another question. The fact is that this wound, though grievous, was not fatal. The qualities of the American mind that had made the Court of the past possible had not disappeared. Americans, so to speak, had needed the Supreme Court to help express their own peculiar medley of governmental aspirations. When the war was over that need would reawaken.

FIVE

CONSTITUTIONAL EVOLUTION IN
THE GILDED AGE: 1865–1900

I N THE OPENING CHAPTERS of this volume it was suggested that the
Civil War marks the close of one great epoch in the history of judicial
review, and the beginning of another. For the Court, as for many individuals, the war wrought profound changes both internal and external,
changes so basic that it might well take decades to realize their dimensions. No person or institution or nation that had endured that experience could ever be the same as before; men like Henry Adams, who had
lived abroad during the conflagration, were astonished—and somewhat
appalled—when they returned to see the altered America that had
emerged from the flames. And the judges of the Supreme Court, though
lacking, perhaps, Adams' peculiar gifts of detachment and insight, had
equal reason to rub their eyes. Their constitutional universe had been similarly transfigured.

For one thing, the nation-state problem had changed its nature dramatically. The Marshall and Taney Courts had been perennially haunted
by the danger that centrifugal forces would tear the nation apart, and
their jurisprudence had been shaped with that terrible threat always in
mind. The Northern victory scotched this bugbear; when Chief Justice
Chase declared in 1869 that ours was "an indestructible Union, composed of indestructible States," he spoke with a just confidence unknown
to his predecessors.

The second great difference between the old constitutional environment and the new was slower to reveal itself fully but in the long run even
more important to the future of judicial review. It was, of course, that
capitalism, developing at a rapid but relatively moderate tempo in prewar
years, had been given an enormous accelerating thrust by the war and was
now proceeding at a pace of headlong expansion that was unexampled in

the nation's history. The agrarian nation Jefferson and Marshall had known was now the industrial-mercantile nation that Hamilton had envisioned. The change had not really occurred overnight; in the 1850's this metamorphosis had been clearly enough foreshadowed. But in the 1850's the problems of slavery and the Union had claimed a very heavy share of attention from those who had thought about constitutional questions, and the constitutional implications of the rise of capitalism were correspondingly obscured. Now those implications were evident and were soon to be unavoidable. In 1866 the judges faced what was in effect a new judicial environment; and it was getting newer all the time.

For as capitalism expanded, it impinged on the lives of individuals as never before; as it became the most important fact in American life, it became the most troublesome fact as well. Men began to say, first from scattered quarters, then in a steadily augmenting chorus, that the power of government should be used to control this giant, to mitigate the harm to individual and collective welfare that it might do if left unchecked. And, conversely, others began to say, with a vehemence and volume far greater than in the past, that the giant would serve the community best if it were allowed to go its own way, that governmental tinkering with the economy was both futile and mischievous, that laissez faire should be the watchword of the day. The question of whether government should control capitalism, and how much it should control it, moved to the center of the American political arena and was never very far from that center for the next seventy years.

The results of all this for judicial review in the postwar era were several, but the most significant was that the Court's focus of interest was radically modified. The dominant interest of the Court in the past had been the nation-state relationship, and the dominant judicial value, as I have said earlier, was the preservation of the Union. The war did not of course obliterate the nation-state issue, for that issue is interminable in a federal republic. But its importance in the judicial order of things became much less, both absolutely because the very existence of the Union no longer hung in the balance and relatively because the greater issue of economic control had arisen to dominate the political scene. The postwar Court was no more disposed to leave the question of economic control alone than Marshall was disposed to leave the question of federalism alone. He had taught his successors to view themselves as vital factors in the governmental process, he had tried within the limits of judicial capacity to guide and coerce America along paths of his choosing. Whether or not he had succeeded in all his aims, he had at any rate succeeded in planting a judicial tradition of mentorship. The judges who now began coming to the Court—men like Chase and Bradley and Field—felt authorized to help America decide what kind of nation it should be. And since the gravest problem facing America was government regulation of business, that problem gradually became the major interest of America's constitutional court.

But if the Court's tradition helps explain why it was likely to focus now on the economic control issue, the tradition is also useful in predicting where the judges' preferences would lie in the evolving conflict between the proponents of control and of laissez faire. Marshall's darlings had been the nation and the property-owner, and most Supreme Court judges between 1789 and 1860 had shared these twin affections to a greater or lesser degree. Now that the national government had vindicated its existence in trial by battle, its health seemed reasonably assured, and it no longer required the solicitous protection of the Court. But the property-owner (that is, the businessman) began in the 1870's to be harried by government; "legislation by clamor," in William Graham Sumner's phrase, threatened to penalize him and hamper his freedom of action— to prevent him, as his admirers saw it, from helping the community by helping himself. A Court committed by its tradition to the cause of property rights, composed of judges who were inevitably drawn largely from the ranks of the "haves" and who were of course by definition lawyers and thus imbued with the conservative bias that has always characterized the American legal fraternity—such a Court was almost certain to throw its weight against the regulatory movement and on the side of the business community.

In this second great period of constitutional history, then, running roughly from the end of the Civil War to 1937, the major interest of the Supreme Court as a molder of governmental policy became the relationship between government and business; and the major value of the Court (to carry on the terminology used in earlier chapters) was the protection of the business community against government. The nation-state relationship, once salient, was now subordinate; the fear that the states would wound or destroy the nation was replaced by the fear that government, state or national, would unduly hinder business in its mission to make America wealthy and wise.

But to say this is the beginning of analysis, not the end. Historians like Charles Beard and J. Allen Smith and Brooks Adams were telling us, as early as the first decade of the twentieth century, that the Supreme Court was remarkably friendly to the pleas of "vested wealth." Those who at first recoiled in horror from such a suggestion have now generally subsided, and the fact has been incorporated among the standard assumptions of students of the era. The challenging question is not whether the Court of 1865–1937 favored the business community but what was the nature and degree of that favoritism, how was it implemented, to what extent was it qualified and self-restrained? In short, what role did the Court work out for itself in the light of its new interests and values? As suggested earlier in this volume, the Court's whole history can be viewed as a constant, or at least repeated, readjustment of role to suit the circumstances of each succeeding judicial era. What were the readjustment problems faced by the Court in this new age of burgeoning capitalism and regulatory government? How did the Court meet them?

The historical record that supplies the answers to these questions can be divided into two subperiods, the first extending roughly from the Civil War to 1900, the second ending with a bang and a good many whimpers in the fateful spring of 1937. And it is of course the first of these subperiods that concerns us for the remainder of this chapter.

Valor and Discretion: The Problem of Military Trials

An unwary reader, examining the behavior of the Court in the early postwar years, might easily get the impression that the foregoing paragraphs exaggerate the predominance of the government-business relationship in this judicial era. For some time after the shooting ended, the Court was heavily concerned with after-echoes of the war and with the knotty problem of Reconstruction for the conquered South. These issues were imposing enough in their own right to preoccupy the minds of the judges, and it would not be surprising if the Court had concentrated on them exclusively. But the significant fact is that even in the thick of these postwar difficulties the problem of economic control persists in peeping through; even while the guns are still reverberating or the "bloody shirt of the Rebellion" being most violently waved, the judicial opinions hint strongly of a quite different world which the judges themselves are perhaps as yet only dimly aware of.

True, there are few such hints in the decisions involving the war-endangered problem of military trials. In 1862, President Lincoln had authorized military commanders to seize and try by military tribunal civilians who engaged in "disloyal practices," even in areas remote from the actual conflict where the civil courts were duly functioning. Although in fact this authority was used quite sparingly, in principle it represented a startling transgression on individual rights, and the executive order was bitterly criticized in some quarters.

However, in 1863 it was applied in Ohio by General Burnside to the notorious "Copperhead" Clement L. Vallandigham who had, in a public meeting, denounced the "wicked, cruel, and unnecessary" war and had urged resistance to such extraordinary powers as those granted by the presidential order. Burnside promptly arrested him, presumably under that very order, and a military commission, finding him guilty of aiding and comforting the enemy, sentenced him to detention for the balance of the war.

Then Lincoln, apparently somewhat embarrassed by Burnside's zeal and always alert to the opportunity for a jest, commuted the sentence and ordered Vallandigham sent into Southern territory, where he could be free to comfort rebels to his heart's content. Meanwhile the prisoner had applied for a writ of habeas corpus to the United States circuit court in Cincinnati, and the writ had been denied. He and his supporters wished of course to pursue the issue to the Supreme Court in the hope that the Lincoln administration might be declared to have acted illegally. But the approach they chose, seemingly on the assumption that it was the only way now available, was to petition that the Supreme Court call up the record of the military commission for review by a writ of certiorari. This writ was, and is, a standard form by which the Court exercises control over inferior tribunals, but the use of the writ is confined by law to certain types of cases. The Court held, quite rightly, that its powers of review consisted only of those granted by the Constitution and Congress, and that it had not been authorized by either of those agents to call up the proceedings of a military commission in this way. Vallandigham was left to seek his satisfaction elsewhere, and he did, running for governor of Ohio in 1864 and polling nearly 40 per cent of the total vote.

The members of the Court may well have thanked providence for the jurisdictional technicalities that removed Vallandigham's cause from their ken, for the scars of the *Dred Scott* decision were as yet by no means healed, and a "pro-Copperhead" decision would not have been received kindly by Unionist opinion. However, in 1866, when *Ex Parte Milligan* came before them, the fighting was over, and the judges felt that a backward slap at the wartime military trials was now in order. In 1864, Lambdin P. Milligan, a citizen of Indiana, had played a leading part in a plot by the Order of the Sons of Liberty to set free prisoners of war and take over by armed force the state governments in Indiana, Ohio, and Illinois. He had been tried by a military tribunal and sentenced to hang. Milligan, like Vallandigham, then asked the circuit court in Indianapolis for a writ of habeas corpus.

So far the cases of Vallandigham and Milligan would appear to be kindred in all important respects. But from the viewpoint of the Supreme Court when it received Milligan's appeal, there were two significant differences. For one thing, a law of March 3, 1863, though suspending the privilege of the writ of habeas corpus, had provided that if a grand jury had met after a man was taken into custody and had failed to indict him, the prisoner could require the court concerned to order his release. This seemed to give the circuit court undoubted authority to hear Milligan's case, and moreover it strongly suggested that Congress had tacitly forbidden military trial if the civil courts were open and grand juries were duly being assembled. The circuit court to which Milligan applied professed doubts on these and other points and passed the issues up to the Supreme Court by the process known as "certification." This mode of appellate jurisdiction is provided in the Judiciary Act, and thus the jurisdictional difficulties that barred the way in the case of Vallandigham did not arise. The question of the validity of the military trials was clearly and regularly before the Court.

The second difference between the two cases was of course that the war had ended by the time Milligan's case reached the Supreme Court. Some commentators have made more of this point than is warranted, suggesting that the Court gratuitously seized upon a technicality to escape jurisdiction in the first case because the atmosphere was supercharged with danger for a Court that presumed to interfere with the conduct of the war. As we have seen, there was nothing gratuitous about it; in order to reach Vallandigham's case, the judges would have had to invent jurisdiction that was not provided by law. But this is not to say that they were unaware of the difference between the military trial question in 1863 and in 1866. Their awareness shows in a contrast of the spirits of the two decisions, the cautious opinion of Justice Wayne in the first case, restricting himself to the jurisdictional issue, eschewing any implications about the propriety of such trials, and the boldly venturesome majority opinion in *Milligan,* suggesting with oratorical flourishes that the Court was now ready to resume its place as a leading participant in the councils of the nation.

A majority of five now felt prepared to say that no one, not even Congress, could authorize military trial of civilians when the civil courts were still open. The remaining four judges were not willing to go so far, but they concurred that Congress though possessing the power to authorize military trials in war, had not exerted it here, and that Milligan must go free. Justice Davis' majority opinion is the more remarkable in that he not only deals with an issue unnecessary to the decision (for he agrees that Congress had not authorized the trial, and the question of whether it could have done so is thus hypothetical) but intrepidly asserts, in effect, that the Supreme Court is the final judge of what constitutes military necessity.

This is not the Court of the wartime years, smarting under the lash of criticism that had immediately followed *Dred Scott,* modestly forbearing from interference in the great affairs of state. It has shown itself willing to wait until the national temperature has dropped somewhat below the boiling point, but there is no mistaking the intimation, made as soon as that stage of excessive peril is past, that the Court is moving back to its accustomed seat of power as fast as circumstances will allow. There is no danger that America will be deprived of judicial guidance in coping with the problems that the postwar era has in store.

Unfortunately one of those problems, though temporary, was calculated to generate almost as much heat as the war itself. This was the problem of Reconstruction in the South, for the Republican party, now riding high, was determined upon a policy of revenge and self-perpetuation. To those ends Congress had divided the South into military districts under military commanders and had provided for military trials in the areas at the commanders' discretion. Under the rule of the *Milligan* case such trials were plainly invalid, but in that case the Court had been looking back at a situation in the past, and now it was looking squarely at a present danger.

The enemies of Reconstruction hastened to bring up a case that would force the Court to stand on the *Milligan* logic and declare the Reconstruction Acts unconstitutional, but they encountered a series of jurisdictional checks. A request for an injunction to prevent Johnson from enforcing the laws was turned down on the ground that an injunction could not lie against the President. Similar suits against the Secretary of War and military officials encountered from the Court the declaration that they presented "political questions" (that is, abstract questions of sovereignty rather than the immediate question of whether John Doe was being deprived of particular rights) and were not justiciable. The would-be litigants seemed on the point of success in *Ex Parte McCardle,* involving a Mississippi editor arrested by a military commander, for his right to appeal in a habeas corpus proceeding seemed clearly guaranteed by federal law. But the Court delayed action until Congress itself provided a checkmate by passing a bill that deprived the Court of the jurisdiction under which McCardle's cause had been brought. The Court unanimously—and, we may guess, thankfully—held that this act was valid, that Congress' power over appellate jurisdiction was plenary. And the upshot was that the Reconstruction Acts, though palpably unconstitutional under the *Milligan* doctrine, were never tested in the Supreme Court.

THE COURT'S NEW SPIRIT AND THE LEGAL TENDER ISSUE

The generalizations that can be drawn from the military trial cases are two. The first is that the postwar Court is wary of involving itself in issues so emotionally charged that a decision might precipitate ruthless counterattack from the dominant political forces of the nation. But the second is that, with this caveat duly in mind, the judges still feel it their right and duty to help America decide the fundamental issues that confront it. An understanding of the delicate distinction that is here implied is crucial to an understanding of the Court's historic place in American life. The Court tacitly acknowledges an informal but very real limit on its jurisdiction: the most explosive issues are "non-justiciable." Sometimes (as in war) the most explosive issues will also be the most "important," and then the Court is likely to play a rather modest role in national affairs. But this modesty is brought on by knowledge of the explosiveness of the question rather than by awe at its importance. Neither Marshall nor his predecessors nor his successors have, until lately at any rate, displayed much diffidence about substituting their judgment for that of others when the moment for doing so seemed auspicious. But they have displayed a fairly consistent awareness that for everything on earth there is a season.

The willingness of the postwar Court to remount the heights of power, foreshadowed in the *Milligan* case, is further illustrated in a series of other cases involving problems of war and Reconstruction. And now the King Charles's head of economic control does begin to break through the more immediate judicial preoccupations.

Perhaps the most ambitious, though abortive, of these early postwar ventures into judicial supervision was the attempt to adjudicate the weighty issue of legal tender. During the war the Union government, being in some fiscal difficulties, had issued $450,000,000 in "greenbacks" (that is, paper money which was not redeemable in coin and thus owed its value, if any, to the government's declaration that it was legal tender for "payment of all debts, public and private"). The question of whether Congress had power to issue such fiat money and compel creditors to accept it was an old one, and a case (*Roosevelt* v. *Meyer*) challenging the law's validity reached the Supreme Court in 1863. But the Court escaped jurisdiction by the simple, if inexcusable expedient of misreading the Judiciary Act in such a way as to prohibit a Supreme Court hearing. We must assume either that the judges were unfamiliar with the law that furnishes their very basis for being, or that they deliberately chose a Pickwickian interpretation in order to avoid deciding, in wartime, a question so central to the conduct of the war. It is hard to think of a third reasonable explanation.

At any rate this decision postponed the constitutional issue of legal tender, as *Vallandigham* had postponed the war trials issue, until the war was over. Even then the Court approached the matter cautiously, avoiding constitutional problems by strict construction of the statutes, agreeing that Congress had power to issue greenbacks, but not grappling with the ultimate question, which was whether creditors must accept them. However, in 1869 this question was squarely presented by a creditor who refused to take payment in paper for a debt contracted in 1860, before the passage of the Legal Tender Acts. And in 1870 a Court majority held in *Hepburn* v. *Griswold* that the refusal was justified because the law, at least as applied to debts contracted before its passage, was unconstitutional.

Chief Justice Chase's opinion for the majority has been roundly criticized by generations of observers, not only on the ground that it undertook to argue and decide a question inappropriate for judicial treatment, but also on the ground that the Chief Justice failed to make a good case for the point of view he did adopt. His argument was that the legal tender requirement was not a "necessary and proper" means of carrying out the war powers, and this involved him in an essentially economic treatise on the evils of soft money, hardly a matter that falls within the range of judicial expertness. He further sought to prop up this slender reed of logic by contending that the law violated the "spirit" of the Constitution because it was unjust; and the letter as well because, by decreasing the value of the creditor's accounts receivable, it took money without "due process of law."

The noteworthy things about the decision from the viewpoint of this chapter are that it illustrates, as *Milligan* did, the postwar Court's eagerness to impose its wisdom on the government in connection with momentous issues, and more particularly a growing compulsion to defend property rights against all who might assail them. The question at stake was the power of the national government to control its own currency, a power which, as Justice Bradley was to say, may be "absolutely essential to independent national existence." The audacity of the Court's decision to restrict this authority by its own fiat is breathtaking when we consider that the *Dred Scott* case lay only thirteen years in the past. And the invocation of the due process clause, though it seems a kind of afterthought here, is prophetic. For it was by way of this clause that the Court was ultimately to claim the overloadship of economic policy that is asserted so daringly, though lamely, in the *Hepburn* case.

But the *Hepburn* doctrine itself, including its novel gloss of due process, enjoyed the shortest life of any important doctrine ever promulgated by the Court. Justice Grier, who helped to make up the five-man majority, had retired before the decision was announced, and on the very day of announcement President Grant nominated two new justices, Strong and Bradley, to bring the Court to its full complement of nine. The *Hepburn* vote had been on strict party lines—five Democrats against the law (counting Chase who was busily becoming a Democrat at this time) and three Republicans for. The two new appointees were of course Republicans and could presumably be counted on to uphold the Legal Tender Acts, if they got a chance to do so. They helped to provide that chance by voting to accept jurisdiction in two cases which raised an issue similar to *Hepburn* and agreeing to reconsider the constitutional issue. And in 1871, only fifteen months after *Hepburn*, a new majority held that the Acts were constitutional in all respects (the *Legal Tender Cases*). Thus Chief Justice Chase's tortured logic and his doubtful interpretations of constitutional doctrine died in infancy. But the spirit of his opinion—the implied superiority of judicial wisdom, the insistence that no issue is too big or too intricate for judicial governance, the solicitude for the aggrieved possessing class—these lived on in decisions of the future, as we shall see.

The Fourteenth Amendment and the Slaughter-House Cases

The *Legal Tender Cases* then blended the motifs of war and Reconstruction with the more purely economic themes that were to dominate the Court's value system in the near future. Somewhat the same qualities were apparent in the *Slaughter-House Cases* of 1873, one of the great landmarks in American constitutional history. But here the harmonies were even more complicated, for the eternal issue of federalism could also be detected, running through the opinions and influencing their result.

The cases involved the Fourteenth Amendment, the second and, as it turned out, most pregnant of the three major constitutional changes that had been imposed by the triumphant Republicans on the nation in general and the defeated South in particular. In its first section the Amendment declared that:

> No State shall make or enforce any law which shall abridge the privileges or immunities of citizens of the United States; nor shall any State deprive any person of life, liberty, or property, without due process of law; nor deny to any person within its jurisdiction the equal protection of the laws.

This sentence, especially in its last two clauses, was to become perhaps the most adjudicated and discussed sentence in the federal Constitution, but in 1873 its meaning was uncertain and its significance highly conjectural. In order to understand both its future importance and its contemporary ambiguity, we must glance backward again at pre–Civil War constitutional history.

For one thing it must be realized that the Bill of Rights (Amendments I–VIII) had been held to limit the federal government alone, not the states. This was Marshall's doctrine in *Barron* v. *Baltimore* (1833); it had never been seriously controverted; the states could therefore infringe on individual liberties as they willed, except for relatively mild restrictions like the contract clause or the ex post facto clause. The second point worth special note is that the due process clause, which appears in both the Fifth Amendment as a limit on the nation and in the Fourteenth as a limit on the states, had usually been interpreted as having only a procedural meaning. That is, it did not prevent government from depriving a person of life, liberty, or property, but simply guaranteed that certain standard procedures would be observed before a person was so deprived. In this sense the concept of due process did not import a very strict curb on government power, for it meant that only the *manner,* not the *object,* of legislation was subject to judicial scrutiny. And yet having said this, we must also admit that the difference between manner and object, between procedure and substance, is not always so clear-cut in practice as it may appear in conception, and that there had existed for some time an undercurrent of feeling that the due process requirement could be, and perhaps should be, enlarged into a general prohibition against "unjust" or "arbitrary" legislation. Such a prohibition, if recognized, could now apply to both the national government and the states through the Fifth and Fourteenth Amendments, respectively.

These two points lead to a question or rather a series of them: what was the quoted sentence of the Fourteenth Amendment designed to accomplish? Was it intended to reverse *Barron* v. *Baltimore* and make the Bill of Rights applicable to the states, that is, were the "privileges or immunities" it speaks of those that have heretofore been protected against national action alone by the Bill of Rights (free speech, jury trial, etc.)? Was the due process clause merely meant to outlaw unfair legal procedures in the states or to forbid all governmental action infringing on property which a court might regard as unjust? Was the "equal protection" clause to be taken literally? Did it mean that the states' laws could enforce no discriminations at all between persons? If the sentence meant all of these things, or even a substantial part of them, then the federal system had been drastically revised, for the whole domain of civil rights now fell under the protection of the national judiciary.

Unfortunately these questions are easier to state than to answer. The best evidence is that the Congress that passed, and the state legislators who ratified, the Amendment had extremely mixed or extremely vague ideas about the meaning of these terms. Only the query about due process can be answered with anything resembling confidence; it is most unlikely that those who participated in establishing the Amendment expected it to protect property in a broad way from all forms of state-imposed injustice, for the phrase had usually been construed much more narrowly. Yet even here there is a modicum of doubt, and with respect to the other clauses the doubt becomes full-fledged confusion.

However, as has been remarked earlier in this volume, ambiguity of constitutional language and uncertainty about constitution-makers' intent is the very *sine qua non* of judicial review as it has operated in the United States. The Court itself could not have been the institution it was if the framers in 1789 had spoken more plainly about the judicial power. Great clauses like the commerce clause and the contract clause could not have been shaped to the judicial purpose if they had been drawn more precisely. It is arguable that the Fourteenth Amendment was a kind of license for the Court to proceed at will within broad limits, to make of these phrases what it felt was right and feasible. That is, after all, what the Court had done with other imprecise mandates. If the framers of the Fourteenth wanted their brainchild to be treated otherwise, nothing would have been easier than for them to say so. They did not, and their failure to clarify their intentions provided the Court with a golden opportunity to inaugurate a new era in the history of judicial review.

Now to return to the *Slaughter-House Cases*. In 1869, a "carpetbag" legislature in Louisiana had passed a law granting a monopoly in the slaughtering of livestock to a single New Orleans corporation. Other

New Orleans butchers were understandably outraged by this invasion of their occupational freedom, but under traditional interpretations of the Constitution it seemed that they would be forced to grin and bear it unless the legislature could be persuaded to change its mind. The pre-war Constitution would have offered the Supreme Court no way to redress their grievance, even if it had the will to do so, for the states' control of such economic matters had been recognized as plenary so long as the contract clause was not violated.

But now the butchers had two new cards to play. The first was the Fourteenth Amendment ratified in 1868 and hence applicable to the legislation. And the second was the Honorable John A. Campbell, one-time Supreme Court justice and now one of the greatly successful lawyers of the day. There was a saying, "Leave it to God and Mr. Campbell," and the butchers gladly put their case in the hands of those high authorities. Mr. Campbell rose to the occasion with a lengthy, scholarly, and powerful argument that the Fourteenth Amendment had revolutionized the American system by bringing the rights of man, including of course the right to occupational freedom, under national judicial protection. Already, in 1873, he was showing the Court the way to provide business with relief from governmental meddling: the Fourteenth Amendment had enacted the principle of laissez faire into the American Constitution.

The Court was visibly shaken by this brilliant improvisation, but a majority was not quite convinced. Five to four, through Justice Miller, it rejected the butchers' claims. The "privileges or immunities" clause, said Miller, does not secure against state action the great basic rights that are protected against national action by the Bill of Rights. It refers only to certain special rights of national citizenship, such as the right to travel freely about the country, the "right to use the navigable waters of the United States," etc. The freedoms guaranteed against national action by the Bill of Rights are at the mercy of the states, just as they have been since *Barron* v. *Baltimore.* As for the argument that the due process clause accomplished Mr. Campbell's aims, it is not sustained by any "construction of that phrase that we have ever seen, or any that we deem admissible." And as for the equal protection clause, it is clearly a provision to protect the Negroes in their newly won freedom and has no applications to the case in hand.

One interesting thing about this decision is the contrast between what it seemed to do and what it actually did. It seemed to slam the door on the question of whether the Amendment had radically altered the federal relationship, and on the subquestion of whether property rights were to be granted broad national protection. The answers, one might think, were both emphatically "no." But, in the event, the decision turned out to mean only that these two great developments were postponed until the magical process of "judicial inclusion and exclusion" could bring them about more subtly and gradually. Outright acceptance of Campbell's argument would have imposed upon the Court the vast and perhaps unmanageable problem of protecting all civil rights against state abridgment; moreover, it would have left the Court small room to maneuver, to feel its way toward self-chosen goals within the limits of the politically possible. While seeming to dash all hopes for a constitutional check of this sort, Miller had actually made it possible for the American constitutional system to evolve, as it always has, by slow "Burkean" accretions rather than by a single great mutation; and he had left the Court free to define, as it had in the past, its own role in the national polity.

Moreover, this process of closing the door but leaving it unbolted served another purpose, probably unsuspected by Justice Miller, but nonetheless important in the Court's dawning future. It helped to consign the redoubtable problem of Negro rights to a rather trivial place in the judicial agenda and thus removed an incumbrance that might have been most troublesome. With nicely mingled idealism and opportunism, the victorious Republicans had forced through not only the "War Amendments" (XIII, XIV, XV) but a series of "civil rights acts" designed to secure the Negroes in their newly won privileges of citizenship. Miller's narrow definition of "privileges or immunities" disposed of any likelihood that that constitutional clause would help the freedmen. And a few years later the national civil rights acts were emasculated by the holding that the "enforcement clause" of the Fourteenth Amendment did not authorize Congress to legislate against transgression by private persons on the rights of individuals, Negro or white. This left only the due process and equal protection clauses which Miller had brushed aside so disrespectfully and which for a good many years were to play little part in insuring such meager privileges as the Negro enjoyed. Outright and flagrant state discriminations based on race might be struck down by the judicial arm, but indirect and informal distinctions were tolerated, and legally enforced segregation of races were permitted so long as the facilities provided were "substantially equal" (the adverb was generously construed). And of course, except in very special circumstances, the discriminatory behavior of private persons was beyond the reach of the courts and Congress alike. The judges thus avoided the distractions and the diffusion of energy that might have hampered them, if they had chosen to defend both the businessman and the Negro at the same time.

The Drift toward Constitutional Laissez Faire

Now, and to an increasing degree as war and Reconstruction recede into the past, the Court's history becomes a history of response to the advance of what was later to be called "the general-welfare state." The development of this preoccupation is foreshadowed, as I have suggested, in such immediately post-war decisions as *Hepburn* and in the opinions of *Slaughter-House* dissenters like Field and Bradley. Whether they were more prescient than their majority associates or simply more passionately devoted to the defense of property, the fact is that these judges were ready in 1873 to interpret the Fourteenth Amendment as a general restriction on economic legislation.

But the Court majority was more hesitant, and for good reasons. For one thing, some, like Justice Miller, were undoubtedly disturbed by the enormity of the assignment Mr. Campbell had urged upon them. Miller may have been, as his biographer says, more "reconciled to the exercise of power by the political branches of government" than most of his colleagues, but others probably shared some of his misgivings and had to be won over gradually to the radical construction espoused by Bradley and Field. For another thing, it is probably true that the judges in 1873 had not yet become fully alert to the nature and extent of the welfare state "menace." The Granger Movement, an attack on corporate autonomy and especially the railroads, was already under way in the Midwest; but it was still possible in 1873 to view such developments as atypical, temporary, and therefore only mildly alarming. The specter of full-fledged paternal government, of state socialism, had already begun to haunt the dreams of Field, but others still slept fairly soundly.

And finally, as I have intimated, traditional legal doctrine hindered the program of judicial empire-building that Mr. Campbell proposed. The states had always been allowed a pretty free hand to regulate economic affairs under their reserved "police power." The Marshall-Taney view of national power under the "necessary and proper" clause had been uniformly permissive. The term "privileges and immunities" had reposed innocuously in Article IV of the Constitution since 1789, and no court had forced it to bear the weight of implications that Campbell now suggested. Due process had been regarded chiefly as a procedural guarantee.

In these early postwar years, then, and partly for these reasons, the majority seemed willing, if not entirely content, to leave economic affairs to the "political branches of government." The self-denial of the majority in *Slaughter-House* was matched in 1869 by *Paul* v. *Virginia,* sustaining state regulation of the insurance business and as late as 1879 by *Stone* v. *Mississippi,* which held that the state could prohibit lotteries, even when conducted by a corporation that had formerly enjoyed a state-chartered right to do so. Corporate charters are protected by the contract clause but, said the Court, this protection is subject to the implied qualification that "the public health or public morals" cannot be bargained away; that is, in these fields the state can change its mind and retract privileges it has previously granted.

These decisions, and others that might be cited, do suggest a judicial temper that was temporarily tolerant toward some forms of state interference with property rights. But as the years passed this indulgent mood became harder and harder for the Court to sustain and the threat of economic control became more real and more perturbing. Little by little the urge to intrude in economic affairs waxed stronger and stronger, the desire of Field and Bradley, expressed in *Slaughter-House,* was converted into the desire of the Court as a whole. By 1880 the majority was coming fully alive to the danger of economic control and to the need for some judicial action that would check it.

However, at this point, as I have suggested, the Court was handicapped in assuming this weighty but attractive assignment by its own inherited legal traditions. The judges had the will but not the way to protect business against what Joseph Choate was to call, in 1895, the "onward march of communism." What they needed was the due process clause in its 1900 form; what they had was the vague and relatively feeble clause of the Anglo-American legal tradition.

Their willingness to take to the ramparts on behalf of laissez faire is made clear enough in the decisions involving the commerce clause. When the weapons were at hand the judges were ready to use them. In this field, it will be remembered, the Court had available the doctrine of federal preemption (see pp. 56–57), drawn from such old decisions as *Gibbons* v. *Ogden* and *Cooley* v. *Board of Wardens;* and it was relatively easy to find state economic regulations invalid because they encroached on interstate commerce. The Court proceeded to do so in a series of decisions running in a seldom broken line from the year of Chief Justice Waite's appointment (1874) to the turn of the century. The states' power to tax interstate business activity was seriously impaired in such decisions as the *Philadel-*

phia and Reading Rail Road case in 1873, which outlawed freight tonnage taxes on interstate shipments; and other state attempts to control business within their borders fell under a similar ban in the 1870's. Perhaps the most important of these early decisions was the *Pensacola Telegraph* case in 1877, which precluded the states from granting telegraph monopolies, but it is only one of several. The rise of the regulatory movement was bringing commerce cases to the Court in growing numbers, and the judges were giving notice that state laws in this field would be scrutinized with a sharp eye.

This promise was honored with increasing consistency as time went on. There were some fourteen cases between 1877 and 1886 in which state regulations of commerce were held invalid, most of them on the ground that the subject in question was national in character and required a uniform rule which only Congress could provide. Nor does this include the most far-reaching of all, the *Wabash* case in 1886 which effectively forbade the states to regulate interstate railroad rates. And after this date, the tempo of such decisions increased still further; the states' power to tax and regulate business was more and more constrained by the doctrine that national commerce must be nationally controlled, if it is to be controlled at all.

Charles Warren, in his admirable history of the Supreme Court, describes Waite's tenure (1874–88) in terms of the ebb and flow of "nationalism." The non-nationalist period runs through 1880; thereafter nationalist tendencies begin to display themselves. The fact that the pre-1880 Court struck down a healthy number of state laws under the *Cooley* rule is apparently viewed as an enigmatic exception to its general attitude of tolerance toward state regulations, and that tolerance is otherwise evidenced by the judiciary's willingness to leave to the states the problem of Negro rights and by its failure in these years to use the Fourteenth Amendment to invalidate state business regulations.

This analysis mistakes the secondary for the primary. Of course the judges had opinions on the subject of nationalism, and they were growing increasingly aware during this period that business was becoming national in character. Truly intrastate commercial activity was far less common than it had been; more and more businesses had ramifications beyond the borders of a single state and were thus inappropriate for local regulation. The judges knew this and it was reflected, among other things, in their opinions.

But along with this knowledge there developed a complementary and to some extent transcendent feeling that government regulation in general was dangerously increasing and that the judiciary had a holy obligation to help avert the peril if it could. In the early stage the feeling could not be implemented via the Fourteenth Amendment, because judicial conscience did not permit an interpretation of the Amendment that was unwarranted by precedent. But in the commerce field, as we have noted, the precedent did exist, and the Court was inclined from the first to use the *Cooley* rule and related ideas against the regulatory threat. The fact that the decisions invoked the new realities of commercial nationalism was important; these realities added a significant weight to the balance, supplying a powerful argument and sometimes no doubt helping to change a judge's mind. But to suggest that considerations of nationalism were predominant is to confuse the postwar Court with its predecessors, to forget that the old issue of federalism was now becoming subordinate to the "higher" issue of economic control.

That subordination was made abundantly clear in the 1890's, when the Court was finally confronted with national regulatory statutes of major dimensions. Two cases in point are enough to illuminate the matter. After the *Wabash* decision, Congress finally bestirred itself to pass the act which established the Interstate Commerce Commission for regulating the railroads. The Commission's efforts were impeded from the onset by corporate opposition and court-contrived incumbrances. But the great blow fell in 1896 when the Supreme Court announced that the act did not endow the Commission with the power to fix railroad rates (*Cincinnati, New Orleans, and Texas Pacific Railway Co. v. I.C.C.*). As Justice Harlan remarked a year later, the Commission was now left with power "to make reports, and to issue protests. But it has been shorn, by judicial interpretation, of authority to do anything of an effective character."

The second illustrative case is equally edifying. It involved the Sherman Act, which had been passed by Congress in 1890 to "protect trade and commerce against unlawful restraints and monopolies." In 1895, the Court held that the law did not, and indeed could not, forbid monopolies in manufacturing, because manufacturing is not a part of interstate commerce and affects interstate commerce only "indirectly." To allow the national government to regulate this subject would be to permit encroachment on the reserved powers of the states (*United States v. E. C. Knight Co.*).

In the face of these decisions handcuffing national authority and in the face of the line of decisions already discussed which correspondingly restricted state control of commerce, it is a little hard to think of "nationalist" or "localist" considerations as dominant in the Court's value scale.

The inescapable implication is, on the contrary, that the Court's chief concern was to defend the principle of laissez faire and that both nationalist and localist doctrine were being pressed to subserve that end. The minions of the "onward march of communism" would find no comfort in the commerce clause, if the Supreme Court could prevent it. And to an impressive degree the Court could.

THE NEW FOURTEENTH AMENDMENT: THE TRIUMPH OF JUDICIAL CONSTITUTION-MAKING

However, if the battle of laissez faire was to be waged with effectiveness, some more potent weapon than the commerce clause was needed, for, versatile though that instrument was, it was not a universal answer to the individualist's prayers. Suppose a business falls clearly within the range of interstate or intrastate commerce; what is to save it then? Not the distinctions just discussed; they have been eliminated by definition. Yet unless some alternate doctrine can be discovered, the state and national governments will be left free to impose the most arbitrary restraints on business, and laissez faire will be, as far as constitutional limitations are concerned, a lost cause.

Precisely this point was made by counsel in *Munn* v. *Illinois,* the "Granger case" decided in 1877. Illinois and other western states had recently witnessed popular uprisings against the rate-fixing practices of the railroads and associated enterprises; the state law in question here set limits on the charges for grain storage in the Chicago area, but Illinois and her neighbors had also passed measures fixing maximum railroad rates, and conservative opinion had been deeply agitated by these assaults on free enterprise. Yet the lawyers who spoke for that element—specifically in this case for the grain elevators—were in rather the position of Mr. Campbell in *Slaughter-House:* their passionate conviction that the Constitution ought to prohibit these outrages was more impressive than their legal arguments that the Fourteenth Amendment had been designed to provide such a prohibition. Consequently, their arguments were heavily tinged with the idea that the Court had a moral duty to remake the Amendment into a bastion "behind which private rights and private property may shelter themselves and be safe" from "the will of the majority."

And this plea was meanwhile being echoed in the argument of other Granger cases before the Court, in speeches and legal periodicals, indeed almost everywhere the judges might turn, except of course in the "radical" press. The judiciary (and in fact America as a whole) were being deluged by a potpourri composed of Social Darwinist philosophy about the survival of the fittest and the virtues of economic freedom; scholarly appearing but largely irrelevant citations from the Anglo-American legal past; and admonitions that the judicial power alone had the means at its disposal to save the nation from suicide-by-regulation.

In the face of all this, it speaks well for the self-restraint of the Court that it rejected the immediate call to duty and upheld the Granger acts, including the grain elevator statute. Businesses like the present one, said Chief Justice Waite in the *Munn* case, are "affected with a public interest," because their owners have chosen to use their property "in a manner to make it of public consequence, and affect the community at large." When property is so used, its possessor must submit to public control, including rate regulation.

But the consternation of the proponents of laissez faire at this outcome demonstrates that they had not read the opinion carefully, or perhaps that, like so many critics of the Court in American history, they were more interested in an immediately favorable decision than in the long-term principle they had so fervently espoused. Had they read more attentively and thought more farsightedly, they must have seen that the majority's sales resistance was really weaker than a superficial reading might reveal, that their arguments had, after all, struck home. For Waite was careful to say that "under some circumstances" a regulatory statute might be so arbitrary as to be unconstitutional, and these mild words implied for the business community a concession whose value was beyond emeralds and rubies. It meant that the Court recognized, back-handedly to be sure but without question, that the due process clause of the Fourteenth Amendment imposed a substantive limit on economic legislation. Such an interpretation was too novel in 1877 to support an outright holding of unconstitutionality, but Waite had given the supplicants notice that their prayers were not unheeded, and also a kind of promissory note, redeemable when precedents had ripened a bit further and judicial backs had been stiffened a bit more.

The history of the Fourteenth Amendment for the remainder of the nineteenth century is one of gradual redemption of that promise made in 1877. But for some years the approach to the question was oblique, and the cumulative tendency of the decisions must have seemed equivocal to contemporaries. Instead of forthrightly invalidating a statute by applying a substantive view of due process, the judges chose to uphold the challenged laws, and concurrently to issue more or less explicit warnings that other laws in other circumstances might not be treated so tenderly. In 1886, for example, Waite allowed a Mississippi statute endowing a railroad commission with the power to fix rates, but he seized the occasion to remark that the Commission must beware of fixing charges so low that it might amount "to a taking of private property for public use without just compensation or without due process of law." If "due process" simply meant "due procedure," its historic connotation, the actual amount of the rates established was beyond judicial cognizance so long as the Commission observed procedural amenities like notice and hearing. Quite evidently Waite was assuming, though not for the moment employing, judicial power to restrain "injustice" if it should occur.

This assumption was a product, no doubt, of many converging factors: the multiplication of "welfare state" threats, the Macedonian cries of the business community and its legal and academic defenders, a growing awareness that an interpretation of due process which seemed impossibly novel and probably unnecessary a decade before could be made acceptable by slow accretion and might prove very useful in the cause of righteousness. As Waite wrote, the voices of two great contemporaries, Thomas M. Cooley and Stephen J. Field, must have been echoing in his mind. Cooley's classic treatise on *Constitutional Limitations,* first published in 1868, had become a canonical text for jurists, and his support of due process in its emerging form gave the stamp of scholarly approval to an interpretation that seemed ethically more and more imperative. Field had been from the start eager to embrace an interpretation that would protect freedom of contract; his dissents had been resounding in the supreme courtroom for years, and each term these organ tones must have seemed a little more compelling. Justice Harlan, perhaps the strongest-minded on the bench at the time except Field, was patently moved by the impact of all these gathering forces. In 1887, though upholding a Kansas prohibition law against due process attack, he remarked that the Court in evaluating such legislation is not bound by "mere forms," and continued:

> If, therefore, a statute purporting to have been enacted to protect the public health, the public morals, or the public safety, has no real or substantial relation to those objects . . . it is the duty of the courts so to adjudge and thereby give effect to the Constitution.

By the 1890's the development signalized by such pronouncements had run its course, and the concept of due process as a judicially enforced bar to arbitrary economic legislation was ready for action. Judicial minds had been gradually accommodated to an idea that had long since found its place in their hearts; dicta such as those just cited had accumulated in sufficient numbers so that "precedents" for the new doctrine could be readily invoked to satisfy a lawyer-like conscience. In 1890, the Court overturned a Minnesota railroad commission law on the ground that it "deprived the company of its right to a judicial investigation, by due process of law" of the reasonableness of rates. This seemed to mean that rates fixed by law or by commissions acting under law were subject to approval of courts, and ultimately the Supreme Court. There yet remained a margin of vagueness at this point, though the judges were obviously edging closer to their historic goal. But at all events doubts were swept away five years later in *Smyth* v. *Ames,* which flatly held that the judiciary has the last word on the reasonableness of rates, and even went on to propound what a later jurist called a "mischievous formula" for determining them. In 1897 the concept of "liberty of contract," so dear to Herbert Spencer and other defenders of laissez faire, was used as the basis for invalidating a state law; the Court as B. F. Wright says, "simply wrote the dissenting opinions of Justices Swayne and Bradley in the *Slaughter-House Cases* into the Fourteenth Amendment."

This holding completed the process of constitution-making that had begun with the dissents in that case. Ten years before, the Court had conceded, rather offhandedly, that corporations were "persons" within the meaning of the Amendment, and that concession was now seen to be of epic importance and of incalculable value to the business community. Combined with the now accepted idea of due process as a substantive limit on "arbitrary" laws, it meant that business, whether incorporated or not, was no longer wholly at the mercy of the popular will.

The development just chronicled is beyond much question the classic example of "government by judiciary" in the United States, and it is worthwhile to pause for a moment to underline some of its features. In the first place, it is noteworthy that the Court did not proceed by a single bound to this new doctrine and the new role that it made possible. This was the course urged by Field and other cheerleaders, but the majority preferred to grope more deliberately through the tangled thicket of modern government, to plant the judicial feet more warily. Strong men like Field, with a tinge of dogmatism, play an important part in American constitutional history, but less positive types like Waite are often more interesting because the problem of evaluating them is more subtle, and they tend to exemplify more faithfully the actual nature of American constitutional history.

For Field the problem was fairly simple: here is the businessman whom any just-minded judge should be honored to defend; and here is the due process clause; why not use it for that benign purpose? But the majority of his colleagues saw cross-threads in the tapestry: the proposed doctrine was strange and ill supported by precedent or public acceptance; impetuous and untimely decisions to assume the task of supervision might trap the judiciary in an impossible role of its own contriving. They held back, and this reluctance to make radical departures, to generalize adventurously, is characteristic of the historical Court. But it is also characteristic that their negative opinions provided an escape, that their "no" was qualified by a "perhaps."

That "perhaps" could swell to a certainty in the fullness of time by a process so subtle and complex that not even the craftsmen themselves would be fully aware of what was happening, and in the end both they and their observers could feel that the doctrine they applied was a familiar, indeed an immemorial, rule of law. Justice could be served, but the illusion of a changeless constitution need not be abandoned. And all this was achieved because the Court realized, whether instinctively or analytically does not matter, that the ambiguity of its mandate is both its limitation and its opportunity.

If due process had emerged as a dogmatic "rule" in 1873, it might have saved some corporate profits for a while, but the pressures of the welfare state would have forced the Court to scuttle it before long. The mature doctrine that became explicit in the 1890's was a far more effective tool of judicial governance, not only because it was now more securely backed by use and wont, but because it was flexible enough to mean anything the judiciary wanted it to mean. The Court could now help shape social policy toward capitalism, yet respect the boundaries imposed by economic necessity and political possibility.

The Tools of Judicial Supervision

With the maturation of substantive due process in the closing years of the nineteenth century, the Supreme Court was at length adequately equipped to play a part in resolving the major issue of the era—that of business-government relationships. The new Fourteenth Amendment and the commerce clause doctrines earlier described made almost every governmental intervention in economic affairs the business of the judiciary, to approve or disapprove, as discretion might dictate. The Court had finally adjusted itself and the Constitution to the altered conditions of the postwar order.

Old problems like slavery had been forgotten. The question of Negro rights, and with it the question of civil rights in general, had been relegated to a minor and almost negligible place among the Court's concerns. The once preponderant issue of federalism was now subordinated to the government-business preoccupation: the formerly ruling value of nationalism was replaced by a judicial ideal called economic freedom. The process of redefining the Court's role, a process impelled by the transfiguration of the nation itself, was not complete to be sure. But the enabling conditions had been met; the judges had surmounted traditional interpretations which would have left them impotent to play any significant role at all. They now had the tools, so to speak, to do the job to which they felt they were summoned by their legacy and their consciences. How they would use those tools, what role they would actually assume, what result they would work for arbitrating the business-government relationship—are questions for the next chapter.

Six

The Judiciary and the
Regulatory State: 1900–1937

I N 1900 THE SUPREME COURT'S POSITION is somewhat that of a
medieval knight-bachelor on the morning after his accolade. The long
novitiate as a squire has been served, the vigil has been kept, the rituals have been performed. The gilded spurs and the sword are ready, and
the world is waiting. Will the chevalier at once launch an intrepid campaign to slay all the dragons of "socialism" and rescue all the maidens of
"free enterprise"? Or will he exercise his hard-won rights and powers
moderately, bearing in mind that there are differences in vulnerability
even among dragons and that some maidens may be more virtuous than
others and more worthy of chivalry's attentions?

These were the two clear-cut alternatives open to the Court, and for
clarity's sake it would be gratifying to record that the judges elected one
or the other. But the fact of the matter is a little more intricate. Instead
of adopting either of these courses of action wholeheartedly, the Court
established a kind of dialectic involving both of them and managed to live
in this apparently uneasy state for the next thirty-odd years. Sometimes
the judges talked in this period as if they were determined to halt the
regulatory movement in its tracks and as if they had the will and power
to veto any political impulse they disapproved. Yet at other times, and
often even concurrently, they ratified many inroads on the free enterprise
ideal and sought only to moderate, not to stop, the growth of government intervention.

Such judicial dualism is easy enough to understand. The first notion—that the Court could and should use its new armaments to arrest
the drift toward regulation—had its origin partly in the deep sense of
horror that words like "socialism" generated in judicial breasts, and
partly in the rhetoric of judicial supremacy that had been accumulating

for over a century. Marshall's assertion in *Marbury* that "there is no middle ground" between the idea of judicial control and the idea of unlimited government; the statement of Davis in *Milligan* that the Constitution "covers with the shield of its protection all classes of men, at all times, and under all circumstances"; Field's repeated contentions that the Court had the authority and duty to defend "inalienable rights, rights which are the gift of the Creator" against all comers—such words had a certain impact on the minds of the judges themselves as well as of their auditors. The priesthood more than half believed the mythology it had helped to create; and the impulse to monarchize and kill with looks was therefore very strong.

But the same judges were at the same time more or less dimly aware of certain other factors and shared certain other attributes. Most of them had played some part in practical affairs, and their hostility to regulation in general was tempered by the realization that particular circumstances cannot always be governed by dogmatism. Moreover, the record of judicial history on which they drew was replete not only with mythic incantations like those of Marshall, Davis, and Field, but also with concrete examples of judicial forbearance. In a word, the Court of the past had often talked in absolutist terms, but had usually acted discreetly and flexibly. And the judges of the twentieth century were thus torn between the rhetorical and the historic forms of the judicial image. In general they used the veto power inherent in such doctrines as commerce and due process far more selectively and judiciously than the fierce champions of laissez faire would have preferred. The vision of judicial tyranny that emerges from some of the critical literature of the 1920's and 1930's, the picture of a great nation shackled helplessly by judge-made law, is pretty remote from the fact. Even in the heyday of judicial negativism, the affirmative note was also frequently sounding; many of the most notable negative decisions turned out upon close examination to be less absolutist than they at first appeared.

Yet neither can it be denied that the judges seemed recurrently tempted during these years to have done with temporizing, to attack with their bright new weapons, to rule by flat decree. This impulse emerged most often in dissenting opinions where language was least likely to be qualified by considerations of responsibility; it showed itself in an occasional majority decision during the first three decades, in cases which peculiarly outraged judicial sensibilities. Evidently there was a certain tension between the desire to influence and the desire to rule. In general, the chevalier conducted himself with reasonable modesty and decorum. But always in the background was the fond idea that a really intrepid assault might dispose of the dragons and that a world without them would be a pleasant place. Throughout the period there was a constant undercurrent of threat that the rhetorical could become the actual, if the provocation were great enough.

THE POWER TO TAX AND JUDICIAL SUBJECTIVISM

As the judges of the Supreme Court looked about them in the closing years of the nineteenth century and the early years of the twentieth, they could see threats to free enterprise rearing up on every side in numbers that seemed to increase year by year. They had rejected, as we have seen, the politically impossible plea of Mr. Campbell in the *Slaughter-House Cases* to establish a wall against all such invasions; and they were now faced with the nice task of distinguishing between interlopers that were tolerable and others that were not. Their moral instincts might be thought a sufficient guide by some, but what was needed was a legal rule, and it is hard to translate a moral instinct into a legal rule without losing something in the translation. The judges yearned for a formula, or set of them, which would objectively discriminate between permissible and impermissible economic statutes. If they acted merely in terms of a subjective ethic, they exposed themselves to the suggestion that perhaps the next man's ethic was as good as their own.

The power of taxation illustrates these problems with special force, for the power can be used, unless somehow checked, to accomplish prodigies of public control; yet it is peculiarly hard to formulate a rule that will limit it reasonably. And the Constitution provides little help; the clauses relating to taxation are few and hardly self-explanatory. It is not surprising, as the clamor for social justice grew, that the tax power was called upon to right wrongs, as well as to fill the public treasury.

From the point of view of the businessman, the most horrendous of these forays against capital was the federal income tax law, passed in 1894, which exempted incomes up to $4,000 and imposed a levy of 2 per cent above that amount. The law had been squeezed through Congress only after years of agitation; it was frankly an attempt to tax the well-to-do; and it seemed to many as it did to Justice Field "but the beginning" of "a war of poor against the rich" which would threaten the foundations of the Republic. Certainly it would at any rate deplete the pocketbooks of a good many solid citizens, and a constitutional challenge was rushed to the courts. It was argued among other things that the tax was invalid as applied to the income from real estate (that is, rents) and from personal property, because these were "direct taxes" and must be apportioned among the states in accordance with their population (Art. I, sec. 2). Apportionment by population would of course kill the principle of apportionment on the basis of ability to pay, which was the major concern of those who passed the law.

But the challengers faced the apparently grave difficulty that the Court had, in 1881, unanimously upheld the income tax that had been levied during the immediately after the Civil War; and their case was further undermined in advance by the ancient *Hylton* decision of 1796, in which it had been intimated that only "head taxes" and real estate taxes were "direct" within the meaning of the Constitution and thus subject to the apportionment requirement. Their glittering array of high-priced counsel, including such ornaments of the contemporary bar as George F. Edmunds and Joseph Choate, was therefore forced to argue that the Court should reverse "a century of error" in order to stop the "communistic march." Five members of the Court were ultimately persuaded, after elaborate argument and reargument, that this was indeed their duty, and the income tax law was scuttled by judicial fiat. The direct tax clause, so long neglected as a constitutional restraint, provided the judges with an objective formulation of their prejudice in favor of wealth. It is a kind of anticlimax that the enactment of the Sixteenth Amendment in 1913 deprived them of this self-created mooring post. It declared that Congress could, without apportionment, tax incomes "from whatever source derived" and most of the nice distinctions of the Income Tax decision came tumbling down; capital was again exposed to the communistic threat from which Choate and the Court had temporarily rescued it.

One of those distinctions, however, had long antedated 1895 and was destined to survive for many years thereafter. Among the vices of the income tax had been the fact that it applied to income from municipal bonds. It was thus, the Court had said, a tax upon the powers and instrumentalities of the state, and such intergovernmental taxation is forbidden by the principles of the federal system. This doctrine derived originally from Marshall's pronouncement in *McCulloch* v. *Maryland* (1819) that "the power to tax involves the power to destroy." It followed, thought Marshall's successors, that neither the state nor the national government could tax the other's instrumentalities, for the Constitution supposes the independent existence of both governments, and to allow such taxes would be to allow the taxing government to destroy the taxed government.

With the aid of such reasoning the Court had woven a complex web of reciprocal tax immunities, and it would be more wearisome than profitable to explore them in detail. It might be thought that the Sixteenth Amendment, empowering the federal government to tax incomes without apportionment "from whatever source derived," had relieved Congress of worries about taxing the income of state employees (whose offices had been held many years before to be state instrumentalities and thus exempt from federal taxation). But the Supreme Court ruled otherwise. From the point of view of this volume perhaps the chief significance of this whole doctrine is the light it sheds on the Court's prevailing habit of mind—the idea that government cannot be left judicially unsupervised in possession of a power that *might* be abused. It was suggested from time to time that it would be soon enough to worry when one government actually did seek to destroy or burden another by taxing its instrumentalities unreasonably, and that meanwhile the judiciary should leave the tax policy alone. But the Court of the twentieth century was not disposed to lift its hand from the reins even so conditionally.

Still another problem raised by taxation was presented when the taxing power was used to accomplish regulatory purposes. Such laws of course might endanger the sacrosanct principle of laissez faire, and some restraint on them was, therefore, evidently desirable, but how to frame such a restraint without frankly admitting that the Court was simply second-guessing the legislature on a question of social policy?

The difficulty is illustrated when we compare *McCray* v. *United States* in 1904, with the Child Labor Tax Case in 1922. In the former, the Court upheld a federal law imposing a heavy tax on oleomargarine colored to resemble butter, the obvious effect and purpose of the tax being to discourage manufacture of the product. The Court, said Justice White, cannot condemn an otherwise valid tax because it objects to the motives that prompted the law's passage, for those motives are not within the scope of proper judicial inquiry. This seemed to mean that regulatory results could be achieved by taxation without fear of court interference, a doctrine that would create vast opportunities for control. However, in later cases the Court began to hint that regulatory taxes might be subject to scrutiny if the provisions for collecting them were not clearly related to the gathering of revenue, and in the Child Labor Tax Case these hints were confirmed. Congress had laid a tax of 10 per cent on the profits of production industries that employed children, obviously banking on the assumption that the regulatory purpose of the tax would be beyond judicial cognizance. But, said the Court, "there comes a time in the extension of the penalizing features of the so-called tax when it loses it character as such and becomes a mere penalty with the characteristics of regulation and punishment. Such is the case in the law before us." The difference between this law and the law in the *McCray* case is that the purpose to control child labor is evident *on the law's face;* the purpose to inhibit manufacture and sale of colored margarine was not similarly evident.

But the trouble is that it *was.* Plainly the Court's ruling in the later case was prompted by the feeling that control over child labor was not and should not be vested in the national government, just as its ruling in *McCray* was explained by the feeling among the judiciary that it did no great harm to restrict the production of colored margarine. As judgments of social policy either of these pronouncements might be open to argument, but at least the argument would be relevant. The Court's difficulty was that it must try to cloak the social judgments in the form of constitutional rules, and the attempt was ultimately unavailing. A flat rule that the motivations of a tax could not be scrutinized would clarify the constitutional process, but it would allow governmental interference in fields which the judges thought best left free from interference. The alternative was the doctrine that the tax would be disallowed if its regulatory purpose was evident "on its face," and this reintroduced the subjective factor in judicial decision-making. For whether the judge finds an intent to penalize on the face of the law is likely to depend on whether he smiles or frowns on the purpose of the penalty. As so often in the cases of this era, the Court had been unable to develop an objective formula that would distinguish between acceptable and unacceptable departures from the free enterprise ideal. By their ultimate resort to subjectivism, the judges kept their hands on the reins and retained their freedom of discretion. But they made it harder to convince observers that judicial review was more than another step in the legislative process.

New Checkreins on the Commerce Power

This subjectivism of judicial control, evident enough in the tax field, becomes even plainer when we examine the Court's decisions involving interstate commerce. The judicial problem here was especially difficult to cope with though it is comparatively easy to state. The commerce clause is a grant of power to the national government, and the pre–Civil War courts had uniformly interpreted that power broadly. Unless such affirmative interpretations are qualified, they make it possible for national statutes to regulate the national economy unmercifully, and the battle for constitutional laissez faire is lost in advance. Negative formulas must, therefore, be devised, and in the *E. C. Knight* case of 1895, as we have seen, the Court answered this challenge by forbidding federal control of manufacturing on the ground that Congress may regulate only interstate commerce itself and that which affects interstate commerce "directly."

Another potent array of negativisms was assembled in *Hammer* v. *Dagenhart* in 1918. Spurred by the same reformers who were later to bring about the passage of the Child Labor Tax discussed in the preceding section, Congress had forbidden the passage through interstate commerce of products manufactured by firms that employed children. Under the *Knight* doctrines Congress could not directly forbid child labor, for the control of production was vested exclusively in the states; but the legislators evidently assumed that they could strike at the product of such labor *after* it entered interstate commerce, for they had often been told that Congress' power over that commerce was plenary. In fact the Supreme Court had previously upheld national laws that seemed clearly analogous, such as the Mann Act, which barred prostitutes from interstate commerce, and the Pure Food and Drug Act, which barred adulterated food.

The hearts of the judges were troubled, however. If the Congress could exclude from interstate commerce any article it chose to exclude, then it could in effect control production, for most firms were dependent upon interstate commerce for their market. Therefore, the Court in a triumphantly negative mood announced that the power to prohibit goods from moving through interstate commerce was subject to limitations previously unknown. Congress could bar such goods if their transportation was followed by "harmful results" (for example, immorality in the case of prostitutes, ptomaine poisoning in the case of adulterated foods). But since the evil aimed at here, child labor, occurs *before* interstate commerce begins, and since the product transported (for example, a can of shrimp) is in itself harmless, the law must fall. The act is repugnant to the Constitution "in a twofold sense."

> It not only transcends the authority delegated to Congress over commerce but also exerts a power as to a purely local matter to which the federal authority cannot extend. . . . if Congress can thus regulate matters entrusted to local authority . . . the power of the States over local matters may be eliminated, and thus our system of government be practically destroyed.

Here then, it might be thought, was a whole set of criteria, of legal rules, that could be used by the Court to mitigate the headlong advance toward public control of the nation's economy. But there was a fly or two in the ointment. For one thing, it was becoming increasingly apparent to those of even modest political sensitivity that the public demand for some form of economic regulation was rising and could not be altogether gainsaid. The first decade of the twentieth century had witnessed after all "the progressive era"; the revelations of the muckrakers had stirred the popular consciousness; one president had publicly chided "the malefactors of great wealth" and another had spoken eloquently about "the new freedom." For another thing, as has been suggested earlier, the members of the Court were not simple obstructionists. Most of them were flexible enough to realize that Herbert Spencer's ideal order was not literally attainable, that in some circumstances government interference with economic activity could serve a useful end. And the case for such interference was likely to seem especially strong when the challenged statute was designed to protect and promote commerce rather than to shackle it, or was designed to stamp out evils that the judges themselves regarded as objectionable, morally or otherwise.

As a consequence of such considerations, the Court proceeded to qualify and attenuate the negative doctrines of the *Knight* and *Dagenhart* cases in a long series of decisions that exude a quite different spirit. But it is both characteristic and significant that these affirmative doctrines were created, not to replace the negativisms just described, but to exist side by side with them as alternative formulations.

This process is illustrated in two fields involving two of the most awesome problems of modern American industrial society—the trusts and the railroads. It will be remembered that the *Knight* decision had gravely crippled the Sherman Antitrust Act, since it amounted to a judicial veto of the program to control the trusts. Within a very few years, however, the judges began to have second thoughts, and they upheld antitrust proceedings in a number of decisions that seemed to reflect a mood of tolerance toward the necessities of government control. The sharp distinction of the *Knight* case between local and national affairs had indeed the merit of clarity, but it had the defect of impracticality. It made no sense to insist that an activity was "local" in character when its effects were unquestionably national; a tidal wave may originate in mid-ocean yet flood the shores of New York.

These realities were trenchantly acknowledged by Justice Holmes in 1905 in a case involving prosecution of the "beef trust." The packers had conspired to control the sale of meat in Chicago, which was of course the "hog butcher of the world." These sales agreements were evidently as local as the manufacturing agreements of the *Knight* case, but the Court's approach to them was very different:

> Commerce among the States is not a technical legal conception, but a practical one, drawn from the course of business. When cattle are sent for sale from a place in one state, with the expectation that they will end their transit, after purchase, in another, and when in effect they do so, with only the interruption necessary to find a purchaser at the stock yards, and when this is a typical, constant recurring course, the current thus existing is a current of commerce among the states, and that purchase of the cattle is a part and incident of such commerce.

In short, the whole "stream of commerce" including sales is subject to federal control; the Court, as Chief Justice Taft was to remark in a later case, would not frustrate antitrust policy by indulging in a "nice and technical inquiry" to distinguish between the local and the national. Indeed it was precisely such a "nice and technical" excursion which the Court had allowed itself in the *Knight* case, but a petty consistency, as Emerson said, is the hobgoblin of little minds.

As for federal railroad regulation, the Court here displayed an acquiescent temper that was often shocking to the proponents of laissez faire and is most difficult to reconcile with the dogmatisms of the *Knight* and *Dagenhart* decisions. The statutory interpretations of the 1890's had shorn the Interstate Commerce Commission of effective power, but Congress duly repaired the damage, endowing the Commission with ample authority, including control over rates. It might be expected that the Court would greet these developments coldly and would assail them with all the resources of the constitutional armory. But in fact the judges cheerfully upheld the laws and approved Commission orders that deeply impaired the supposedly sacred reserved powers of the states.

Perhaps the high point of such judicial toleration was reached in the *Dayton-Goose Creek Railway* case of 1924, which upheld the Transportation Act of 1920. This law required railroads which earned more than a certain fixed "fair return" to turn over one-half of the excess to the Commission and to hold the rest in a reserve fund to be used as the Commission directed. Even worse, the requirement applied to income earned on wholly intrastate business. But the provisions gave the Court no constitutional qualms. The power to regulate commerce, said Chief Justice Taft for a unanimous Court, is a power "to foster, protect and control the commerce with appropriate regard to the welfare of those who are immediately concerned, as well as the public at large, and to promote its growth and insure its safety." In exercising this wide authority over interstate affairs, Congress may also control intrastate commerce, if state and interstate operations are "inextricably commingled." In short, the whole national railway system is subject to federal control, and the "nice and technical" distinctions based on the Tenth Amendment have little or no bearing in this field.

The contrast between the *Knight* and *Dagenhart* doctrines on the one hand and these antitrust and railway doctrines on the other would be bewildering if it were not for the hint the Chief Justice drops in the words just quoted. Congress, he tells us, may "foster, protect and control" commerce to its heart's content; that is, it may do things that are "good" for commerce, but not (so the implication runs) things that are "bad" for it. This point is comparable to the one made in the *Dagenhart* case: that the law can bar "bad" things from interstate commerce, but not "good" things. The translation of both dicta is this: that the Constitution forbids those departures from laissez faire that the Court disapproves, and permits those departures that the Court thinks reasonable and proper. And obviously this is not a legal "rule" in any understandable sense of the word, but a statement of social policy, or rather an assertion of the power to determine it. Under these loose standards the Court can either uphold or overthrow almost any commercial regulation it encounters, depending on whether the judges approve or disapprove the economic policy the law represents. The advantages of this arrangement is that it enables the Court to choose discreetly the dragons it will fight and the maidens it will rescue. But the disadvantage, as in the tax cases, is that it becomes harder and harder to sustain the illusion that the judicial yes or no is based on inexorable constitutional commands, and it becomes easier and easier for observers to see that judicial review is operating as a subjective and quasilegislative process.

DUE PROCESS AND THE COURT'S REARGUARD ACTION

In the tax cases and in the commerce cases, as we have seen, the Supreme Court had conducted only occasional and rather limited forays against the welfare state. America had been notified that there were limits on these two great powers, and this in itself was important, for it preserved the idea of judicial sovereignty, and the knowledge that the Court was keeping an eye on things might discourage some socialistic ventures before their start. But the actual negative decisions of importance were few, and the march toward regulation had been at most deflected slightly and, here and there, somewhat delayed. However, the sharpest weapon in the judicial panoply, as the last chapter suggested, was the due process clause. That clause was available as a limit on both federal and state government. In its modern form it allowed the Court to reach not only procedural but also substantive questions. If the Court was to control American economic policy in any significant way, due process was obviously its major resource.

The feats that were accomplished with this clause in the 1900–1937 period are by no means unimpressive. B. F. Wright has counted some 184 decisions between 1899 and 1937 which invalidated state laws on the basis of either the due process or equal protection clause (the two were frequently used by the judiciary in tandem; it is often, though not invariably, true that a denial of equal protection is also regarded as a denial of due process). Those involving federal laws were far fewer. But according to accepted doctrine, the term "due process" has the same meaning in both the Fifth and Fourteenth Amendments, and it follows that the prohibitions announced against state action were usually presumptively applicable to national laws as well, if Congress might venture to enact them. There is no way of estimating reliably the restraining effect of this cloud of negativisms on state legislators and congressmen who might otherwise have made haste more speedily along the road to the welfare state. No doubt the pace of social change was moderated; a respectable number of "excesses" were prevented; a respectable amount of money was saved for the businessman; a good many laborers were left a little hungrier than they might have been if the Court had not been there to defend economic liberty.

Yet it is highly questionable that the due process clause was a major factor in determining the drift of American economic policy during this period. Most of the important legislative measures that were really demanded by public opinion did pass and did manage to survive the gauntlet of judicial review. In some conspicuous areas, like maximum hours legislation, the Court found a delaying action for a few years and then, when the trend of public demand became unmistakable, gave in. In only a few instances was its position really adamant, and even here the restraining effect of judicial pronouncements is conjectural. Laws are not automatically invalidated because they happen to conflict logically with the doctrine of a previous Supreme Court decision; a case must be brought against each one, and that case must often be carried through extensive labyrinths of the judicial system for years before the law can be pronounced technically dead. Because of such circumstances a great mass of regulatory legislation survived untouched even in these halcyon days of due process. The fact that there was not more such legislation, the fact that Americans during the 1920's tolerated so great a measure of social injustice—this is to be attributed to public apathy amounting to callousness, not to the Supreme Court. To be sure, the Court did its bit to generate and encourage that public mood. But this is very different from saying that the Court rather than the nation was primarily responsible for the failures of public policy.

The virtue of the modern concept of due process was its remarkable flexibility. It allowed the Court to invalidate any law that struck a majority of the members as "arbitrary" or "capricious." These wonderfully ambiguous definitions brought practically the whole world of regulatory legislation within the potential reach of a judicial veto. But, even better, their ambiguity permitted the judiciary to exercise or withhold that veto in any given case, subject to no guiding principles except the judges' own sense of discretion.

The network of "ayes" and "nays" that they fashioned with the help of this carte blanche is too complex for brief summary. A great variety of regulatory measures were scrutinized. Tax laws were queried and sometimes overthrown on the ground that the state had no "jurisdiction to tax" the source in question, or simply on the ground that the tax was arbitrarily administered. State legislation regulating the weight of loaves of bread, prohibiting the use of "shoddy" in quilts, requiring a railroad to construct an underpass for a farmer's personal convenience, were held to deny due process or equal protection of the laws.

But perhaps the most important and instructive pattern of judicial intervention was developed in connection with the problem of rates—prices and wages. And there is a special significance in this field from the judicial point of view, because rates for goods sold or services performed are the very keystone of the free enterprise system. Any state interference with them impinges vitally on freedom of contract, which is the holy of holies for the knights-errant of laissez faire. It might well be expected that the Court would look hard at legislative innovation in this field.

In *Lochner* v. *New York* (1905) this expectation was amply fulfilled. The case concerned working hours rather than wages, but as Chief Justice Taft was later to say, the one is the multiplier and the other the multiplicand, and the operative point for the Court was that the state was seeking to control the heart of the working contract. The law restricted the hours of bakers in New York to ten per day or sixty per week. To Justice Peckham and the majority, this presented a grave challenge to the principle of contractual freedom, for if bakers' hours could be regulated, then so, presumably, could the hours of all other workers. The Court was prepared to concede that working hours in particularly dangerous conditions could be controlled in order to protect the workers' health. Or it would allow hours regulation if it could be shown that long hours might adversely affect the health of the public at large (for example, by leading to the production of unhealthful bread). But neither of these statements can be made about the baking trade, which is not perhaps "absolutely and perfectly healthy" but is "vastly more healthy than [certain] others." To permit its regulation then would expose all or most occupations to hours regulation, would subject the working contract to "the mercy of legislative majorities." The police power cannot be allowed to reach so far; the law is an example of "meddlesome interferences with the rights of the individual," and it violates due process.

The *Lochner* decision represents one of those moments in the Court's twentieth-century history when the judges temporarily embraced the illusion that the regulatory movement could be halted, rather than merely delayed, by judicial pronouncement. The exceptions they allow to the rule against hours laws—the particularly unhealthy occupation principle—should not obscure the fact that a hard line has been drawn. Hereafter, if constitutional limits are as immutable as the mythology attests, American workmen shall be generally free from restraints on their right to work a twelve-hour day. Departures from the model of Herbert Spencer's *Social Statics* will be permitted up to a point, but at that point they must stop.

But in the actual event the process of judicial governance did not work that way. It seldom has. Justice Holmes, filing one of his earliest and most powerful dissents in this case, said:

> I think that the word liberty in the Fourteenth Amendment is perverted when it is held to prevent the natural outcome of a dominant opinion unless it can be said that a rational and fair man necessarily would admit that the statute proposed would infringe fundamental principles as they have been understood by the traditions of our people and our law. It does not need research to show that no such sweeping condemnation can be passed upon the statute before us.

The majority opinion had stated, or implied, that "dominant opinion" does not matter, that the criterion of constitutionality is not traditional fundamental principles, but the individual conscience of the judge, and that a flat rule against general hours regulation was now laid down. However, when we follow the course of doctrine through the next twenty years, we find that it often runs closer to Holmes' standards than the judges themselves may have realized. Or perhaps it would be more accurate to say that it alternates between Peckham's uncompromising defense of free enterprise and Holmes' extreme permissiveness, with the balance of decisions on the latter side.

Three years after *Lochner* the Court found an exception to the flat rule of that case when faced by a statute regulating the hours of females. The social and physical characteristics of women, said the Court, put them at a special disadvantage in the struggle for subsistence, and it is therefore reasonable for the state to limit the hours they can be worked. And in 1917, a new majority took leave of the *Lochner* doctrine altogether, upholding an hours law for manufacturing establishments as a health measure (*Bunting* v. *Oregon*). The startling thing about this opinion by Justice McKenna was that it seemed to assume the validity of hours regulation and focused most of the argument on an answer to the charge that the law sought to regulate *wages* indirectly. *Lochner* was not even mentioned, though counsel had invoked it repeatedly in the briefs. Plainly the Court was showing itself more sensitive to "dominant opinions" than the pristine view of judicial sovereignty would allow. Yet it should not be thought that the Court was giving up contractual freedom entirely to "the mercy of legislative majorities." Only two years before, the judges had affirmed that the state could not, in order to equalize the parties engaged in collective bargaining, outlaw "yellow dog" contracts (agreements, as a condition of employment, that an employee will not join a labor union). Even in *Bunting* there was a hint that the wage contract was still sacrosanct, though hours regulations were not. The Court had taken advantage of the flexibility of due process to yield an outpost or two; for the moment the counsel of modesty and discretion had prevailed. But the *Lochner* spirit of hostility to social change, the *Lochner* illusion of judicial omnipotence, were not dead; they only slept. And a new majority, confronted by new threats to the wage-price nexus, might at any time call them to action again.

A rather similar pattern of judicial outlook and behavior can be traced in the cases involving the doctrine of "business affected with a public interest." This doctrine, it will be remembered, enjoyed its modern rebirth in *Munn* v. *Illinois*, in which Waite had used it to distinguish between rate regulations that would violate due process and those that would not. A business affected with a public interest or "devoted to a public use" was subject to rate regulation. This emphatically did not mean that the state could impose such rates as whimsy dictated; and after 1895 the Court records are dotted with decisions holding that the rates prescribed for a railroad or other public utility were unreasonably low. But if a business could be judicially classified as falling within the rubric of "public interest," its rates could be subjected to some measure of government control.

The problem, of course, was what criteria to use in making such a classification. One possibility would be to adopt the commonsense idea that any business important to the public was "affected with a public interest." But this would legitimize rate regulation on a vast scale, and rates were so crucial to the capitalist system as the judges understood it that they could not in conscience make so unqualified a concession. (Compare their reluctance in *Lochner* to accede to a similarly general ratification of hours regulation.) Yet as the complexities of commercial life multiplied in the twentieth century, it became evident even to conservative judges that there were many businesses whose prices could not be allowed to run wild.

The judicial solution was to allow rate regulation of a variety of businesses under the public interest principle, but to avoid commitment on the question of just what the principle meant, and thus to retain a potential veto. Franchise industries (those enjoying special, government-granted privileges) and public service industries like railroads and electric power companies, clearly fell within the charmed circle. So did certain traditionally regulated occupations like hotel-keeping and taxicab service. Finally, as Chief Justice Taft was to explain, there is another group of industries which have come to be public because "the owner, by devoting his business to the public use, in effect grants the public an interest in that use and subjects himself to public regulation. . . ." The Court so classified, for example, the business of fire insurance and the business of renting real estate in the District of Columbia during the war-engendered emergency. In fact, before 1923, the doctrine of public interest was never used restrictively, to hamper the development of the regulatory movement. But the rhetoric itself implied the possibility of restriction; the Court in making its concessions had been careful not to rule that possibility out. The affirmations of the past in this field were no more binding on the future than the acceptance of hours legislation in *Bunting* was a guaranty against judicial concern for the labor contract.

Normalcy and Judicial Laissez Faire

With the advent of the 1920's the tone of judicial decisions, especially under the due process clause, was subtly altered. We have seen that the modern Court had developed in this area, as in others, an elaborate set of both negative and affirmative doctrines, thus establishing for the judiciary what Benjamin Cardozo called "the sovereign prerogative of choice." And we have further seen that the Court had so far been disposed to wield that prerogative discreetly, upholding many regulatory and welfare measures and using the veto more as a salutary threat than an instrument of continuous control.

In the 1920–29 period the number of negative decisions under the Fourteenth Amendment was almost double the number in the preceding decade. These figures themselves suggest some change in the constitutional climate, and the suggestion is confirmed by examination of individual decisions. True, a great many economic statutes still survived the judicial ordeal; prudent self-restraint was still an important Court theme. But the temper of the times, signalized by conservative Republican electoral triumphs and by the withering of the progressive spirit in public policy, was infectious. The spread of the infection was made somewhat more likely by the coming of men like Taft, Sutherland, and Butler to the bench, for all of them were deeply convinced foes of the welfare state. Now the judges were more confident that they spoke for the nation when they defended laissez faire. And the tension between modesty and boldness became greater; the illusion that the judiciary could really govern became a little more obtrusive, was reflected a little more often in actual decisions rather than mere rhetoric.

The spirit of the *Lochner* case, with its jealous concern for the sanctity of the labor contract, revived impressively in *Adkins v. Children's Hospital* (1923). Congress had established a board authorized to prescribe minimum wages for women and minors in the District of Columbia. The approval by the Court of hours regulation in *Bunting,* and of the Adamson Act (which controlled both wages and hours in the railroad industry in the war emergency) in a 1916 decision, had nourished reformist hopes that wage control would now be upheld. But the Court had carefully confined itself in those two opinions to the particular situation presented, and the implied reservations were now invoked. Justice Sutherland declared for the majority that the regulatory movement had once again gone too far. His opinion is an extremely able statement of the argument that minimum wage laws are unjust, mainly because they impose on the employer the burden to support partially indigent persons. This burden, he tells us, "if it belongs to anybody, belongs to society as a whole." Furthermore the statute is faulty in that the standard it sets for the board's guidance is impossibly vague. The board is required to set wages that will maintain the woman worker in good health and protect her morals. But no general wage standard can accomplish reliably the first aim for any particular person, because particular circumstances may vary. For example, "to those who practice economy, a given sum will afford comfort, while to those of contrary habit the same sum will be wholly inadequate." As for morals, "it cannot be shown that well paid women safeguard their morals more carefully than those who are poorly paid." Though liberty of contract is not absolute, it is "the general rule and restraint the exception." For the reasons given, the exception embodied in this law overpasses the limits of state power, and it is "the plain duty of the courts in the proper exercise of their authority to so declare."

Here again, then, as in *Lochner*, the Court had chosen a milepost on the road to the welfare state and elected to make a stand; here again was the idea that the judiciary could and should decide by flat decree great issues of economic control. Justice Sutherland's opinion was memorable because it reflected in classic form both the free enterprise position (exemplified in some of the gems just quoted) and the uncompromising conception of judicial authority and duty that never seems quite to die. And as the 1920's proceeded, the reminders that this conception was viable became more frequent.

It is particularly appropriate that that decade saw the negative threats of the public interest doctrine develop into realities. Chief Justice Taft used it in 1923 against a Kansas law that empowered a court of industrial relations to fix wages in the meat-packing industry, among others. Without deciding whether the meat-packing business was affected with a public interest in any sense, the Chief Justice held that it was not so *much* affected as to warrant wage-fixing. At this point the now mature and no longer innocuous doctrine was tendered into the care of Justice Sutherland who produced, in 1927, 1928, and 1932, three Court opinions that developed the negative implications most thoroughly. Theater ticket brokers, employment agencies, and ice companies were all excluded from the magic circle, which meant that their rates could not be publicly controlled and that certain regulations which the Court regarded as excessive were likewise forbidden.

It became plain as the decisions proceeded that their effect was to protect all the "common callings" (the grocer, the dairyman, the butcher) from the peril of public rate control, and this interpretation, if adhered to, would indeed have been a significant restraint on the regulatory movement. But Sutherland's zeal for free enterprise and his absolutist approach to judicial duty were a trifle too extreme for his brethren. These unqualified rulings under the public interest doctrine had the effect of narrowing the range of judicial discretion, and the instinct for a more flexible standard asserted itself at last. In 1934, in *Nebbia v. New York,* the Court upheld a state law fixing minimum and maximum prices for milk, and took the occasion to announce that "there is no closed category of businesses affected with a public interest." The cherished idea that "there is something peculiarly sacrosanct" about prices was shattered by this announcement, and the Court's freedom of action in this field was restored. And simultaneously, of course, another obstacle in the path of the regulatory movement was cleared away.

THE JUDICIAL CHALLENGE TO THE NEW DEAL

The Supreme Court now stood, in 1934, at one of the great crossroads of its history. In the latter part of the nineteenth century it had built up, laboriously and piece by piece, a set of doctrines that could be employed for judicial supervision of the business-government relationship. By 1900 or thereabouts the doctrines were ready for service, but their existence did not settle the question of how the Court would employ them. Economic measures were now subject to judicial supervision, but the supervision could be strict and constant or lax and occasional, as the bench preferred. This freedom of choice was inherent in the tax doctrines, in the commerce doctrines, and above all in the due process doctrines that have been described. The Court could use them to govern marginally, to moderate the pace of social reform, to force the nation to take a second look at extreme programs. It could, in short, operate as one influential factor among others in the process of social decision-making. Or it could alternatively seek to decide all the great political-economic questions that faced America, to halt the trend toward government intervention, to use its veto absolutely rather than suspensively.

The majority of the cases of the twentieth century though 1934 seem to reflect, as has been suggested, the former, modest approach. And this approach, for better or for worse, is surely the one most congruous with the Court's past history and most consistent with the conditions and limitations that were imposed on the judicial power by the peculiar circumstances of its origin in the United States. But a modest stance is often hard to maintain, perhaps especially in a democracy, and even more especially when myth and rhetoric encourage illusions of grandeur. So from time to time during these years, we find the other, monarchical vision emerging in a resounding decision, like *Dagenhart* or *Lochner* or *Adkins,* and we can observe this attractive self-imge becoming stronger in the 1920's as forceful personalities like Sutherland speak for it in bold tones. In 1934, the Court seems balanced almost perfectly between these two conceptions of its role. With the elaborately varied precedents at the judges' disposal, they can swing either way. The regulatory trend that began so long ago in post–Civil War years has culminated in the New Deal; the welfare state, which Field and Cooley and Choate dreaded, seems at hand. The judiciary is bound to respond to it somehow, because for seventy years the judges have been sedulously cultivating the idea that the business-government relationship is, in part, at least, a judicial responsibility. The only question is which form the response will take.

For a time the issue hung in doubt, and there was even reason to believe that the Court would call upon its affirmative precedents, uphold national and state New Dealish innovations, and thus maintain a position on the margin of the political arena. After all, America was now beset by the gravest economic depression in her history, an emergency, as Justice Brandeis had remarked, "more serious than war." The decisions of the past three decades which had presumed to thwart economic legislation had been subjected to trenchant scholarly criticism, and the critics, such as Frankfurter, Corwin, and Powell, had been at pains to dispel the myth that the judges were mere agents of the Constitution, bound by its inexorable commands. Indeed the judges themselves had done their part to discredit that myth by insisting upon doctrinal flexibility in all the major areas of judicial control, by eschewing the objective rule. Most important of all perhaps, the New Deal was at this time enjoying a kind of honeymoon. The swift, decisive actions taken by Congress in the early days of Franklin Roosevelt's leadership were startling, but they seemed, to many at least, an improvement on the policy of stark inaction that had preceded them, and it was some time before doubts, even among the business community, were hardened into staunch opposition. The Supreme Court, despite protestations to the contrary, has seldom been insensitive to such considerations.

The *Nebbia* decision of 1934 had strongly suggested an acquiescent judicial temper. In the same year, the Court sustained a Minnesota law allowing courts to postpone mortgage foreclosures during the economic emergency. The law seemed to impair the obligation of contract, but Chief

Justice Hughes held for a five-man majority that, in view of the emergency, some restraint on the enforcement of contractual rights was reasonable. The idea appeared to be that the states could now violate the contract clause so long as they were "reasonable" about it, and the existence of an emergency would be recognized as reflecting on the judgment of reasonableness. It is not surprising that the exponents of economic reform legislation began to hope for judicial approval of their programs. If the Court was willing to ratify departures in a field like the contract clause, where orthodoxy was fairly well defined, then the commerce clause, the tax power, and due process fields, where the precedents themselves pointed both ways, should create little trouble.

But the balance in favor of the laws in such cases as these was precarious. The affirmative judgments were made possible in both decisions by a bare majority of five including the Chief Justice and a new appointee, Owen Roberts. The four other judges had joined in bitter dissents, rejecting the idea that emergency can affect constitutional results (the Court must not "yield to the voice of an impatient majority when stirred by distressful exigency") and warning of "the far more serious and dangerous inroads upon the limitations of the Constitution which are almost certain to ensue as a consequence naturally following any step beyond the boundaries fixed by that instrument." Such a call to arms was not likely to have much effect on Stone, Brandeis, and Cardozo, the three firm "liberals," for they had no great regard for the laissez-faire order they were being solicited to protect and at all events they doubted that the constitutional boundaries had ever been as clearly fixed as the quoted sentence implies. But Roberts was considerably less settled in his views, and as the New Deal was revealed in all its terrifying dimensions to the conservatives of the nation, he became ready for persuasion. As for the Chief Justice, he was neither clearly liberal nor stubbornly conservative, but he seemed to be much concerned for the Court's own dignity and was likely sometimes to swing with a conservative majority to avoid the criticism that might follow a five-to-four decision.

In 1935, therefore, the majority shifted, and for two busy terms the Court waged what is surely the most ambitious dragon-fight in its long and checkered history. The tension between modesty and temerity was temporarily resolved; the autocratic instinct was triumphant. Negative doctrines that had been accumulating for a century were brought to bear on the New Deal program and on kindred heresies; the affirmative doctrines that might have been invoked to produce contrary results were conveniently ignored or distinguished. And throughout the holocaust perorations from the bench and applause from outside the courtroom made it plain that the myths of judicial supremacy had been translated into reality in the minds of the Court majority. The idea of a changeless Constitution, the idea of judicial review as an exact science, the idea that "dominant opinion" is irrelevant, the idea that a nine-man Court can and should save society from itself and the past from the present—these ideas were no longer rhetoric; they had become the wellsprings of action.

With a salvo of decisions during 1935–36, the Court tore great holes in the New Deal program of recovery legislation. The doctrine of "direct-indirect effects" derived from the *Knight* case was used to help dispose of such major laws as the National Industrial Recovery Act and the Bituminous Coal Act. The distinction between production and commerce, stemming from *Knight* and *Dagenhart,* was used against the Agriculture Adjustment Act, which had sought to regulate farm production. The same law ran afoul of the rule of the Child Labor Tax Case that taxes must not operate as penalties to control what is otherwise beyond congressional reach. The due process clause was present in several decisions though sometimes only murkily visible, and the "sovereign prerogative of choice" which the Court had established in interpretation of that clause was of course here seized upon to negate the legislation. The Tenth Amendment, interpreted as a limit on Congress' delegated power rather than as a prohibition against the exercise of powers not delegated, acted as a makeweight wherever it seemed remotely applicable. Even a doctrine which had never been employed negatively before—and has never been since—had its fleeting moments of effectiveness during those years. The NIRA and the Bituminous Coal Act were condemned because, among other things, they had delegated legislative authority to the executive and thus violated the principle of separation of powers.

The final barrage was fired in June of 1936 as the Court reached the close of its two-year joust with the New Deal, and it was directed against a state law. New York had dared to enact a measure providing minimum wages for women. The legislative draftsmen had tried to meet one of the major objections raised by the Court against the law struck down in the *Adkins* case—that the wage-setting board need not consider the value of services rendered. The New York board was authorized to consider this factor, and it was hoped that the law might thus be saved. But the intransigence of the majority seemed to wax rather than wane with the passing months. Justice Butler now announced as a flat rule "that the state is without power by any form of legislation to prohibit, change or nullify contracts between employers and adult women workers as to the amount of wages to be paid." The argument of the Chief Justice, who dissented, that the *Adkins* precedent need not be followed because of "material differences" in the two laws; the argument of Stone, Brandeis, and Cardozo, also dissenting, that precedent since *Adkins* and "what is more important, reason" support state power to control wages, had no weight for five men now thoroughly deluded by the notion that the welfare state could be judicially throttled and the brave old world of their youth restored.

This New York Minimum Wage decision is a fair example of the judicial attitudes that characterized those two years, and it is an example that merits some reflection. By this time—the spring of 1936—the Court's assault on the New Deal had produced a tempest of antijudicial criticism, and as the presidential campaign of that year whetted political feeling, the critics, and of course the defenders as well, became angrier and more extreme (though the President himself said little in the campaign). Much of the criticism simply reflected the bad old American propensity to traduce the law whenever it conflicts with immediate interests, and perhaps the only thing worth saying about this is that, like most deplorable facts, it cannot be safely ignored. Another line of attack, not always distinguishable but with some claim to respectability as a separate point, was to challenge the Court's right and competence to hinder the democratic will, especially in the economic field. However, the Court had made it plain to the nation long ago that it proposed to play some part in defining government-business relationships, and the nation had tacitly acquiesced. It seems a little hard that the judiciary should now be assailed merely for participating in affairs that had been regarded for almost fifty years as judicial business.

But a telling and legitimate criticism of the Court's attitude can nevertheless be made out. The fault was not that the judges meddled in economic affairs at all, but that they meddled with them on a level too high for judicial governance, and imposed constitutional restraints so rigid that no popular government could tolerate them. As Robert Jackson has said, the anti–New Deal decisions had not:

> . . . been confined to the limited issues actually involved in the immediate controversies and the way left clear for the Congress to improve and perfect its remedies. . . . [I]n striking at New Deal laws, the Court allowed its language to run riot. . . . In overthrowing the A.A.A. the Court cast doubt upon all federal aid to agriculture; in laying low the N.R.A., the Court struck at all national effort to maintain fair labor standards; and in out-

lawing the New York Minimum Wage Law . . . the Court deliberately attempted to outlaw any form of state legislation to protect minimum wage standards. The Court not merely challenged the policies of the New Deal but erected judicial barriers to the reasonable exercise of legislative powers, both state and national, to meet the urgent needs of a twentieth-century community.

The historic Court (as distinguished from the Court of myth and rhetoric) had very seldom behaved this way, and the exceptions in the record seemed hardly calculated to inspire imitation. Even in the modern period the dominant tendency had been to moderate the regulatory movement without attempting to destroy it, to nudge and advise democracy rather than to frustrate it. The majority had for the time being forgotten this, had forgotten that the Constitution's strength was its flexibility and that the Court's own strength rested on a tradition of judicious self-restraint.

The price of forgetfulness threatened to be a high one. Franklin Roosevelt was re-elected in November, 1936, by a stunning majority, and, after the dust of the campaign had settled a little, he turned his attention to the hostile Supreme Court, just as Jefferson had in 1801 trained his sights on Marshall and his Federalist brethren. Roosevelt, with characteristic indirection, presented Congress with a judiciary plan that purported to cope with the supposed problem of overcrowded federal court dockets. It would have enabled him to appoint a new judge to supplement any judge over seventy who failed to retire (retirement could not of course be made compulsory, for the Constitution protects judicial tenure "during good behavior"). The significant fact was that the plan would permit the President to appoint six new Supreme Court justices, and thus to insure approval of the New Deal program. It was, as it was called, a "court-packing plan," and its passage would set a precedent from which the institution of judicial review might never recover. It is not too much to say that the ambiguous and delicately balanced American tradition of limited government was mortally endangered by this bill. And it was offered by a President who had just received an overwhelming popular vote of confidence and who had not yet been denied in Congress any of his important demands. Even the five or six judges who had provoked this threat must have slept rather uneasily for a few months.

ECHOES OF THE FUTURE: THE EMERGING PROBLEM OF CIVIL RIGHTS

Like the scenario writer who leaves the heroine hanging from a cliff while he takes up another thread of the narrative, we must now digress for a time in order to touch on a development contemporary with the events so far described in this chapter. It is a characteristic of history, often noted, that the present bears the seeds of the future; and it is therefore hardly surprising that the Court of this era, even at the height of its concern for economic matters, should have devoted a small but increasing portion of its time to a widely different subject which was destined to loom very large in the judicial world yet to come. The subject was "civil rights," that is, the liberties of man as man and not primarily as an economic animal.

During most of its history, the court had paid comparatively little attention to this problem. The Bill of Rights, it will be remembered, had been held inapplicable to the states in 1833. That meant that free expression (Amendment I) and the personal procedural rights connected with arrest and trial (Amendments IV–VIII) could be abridged by the states without raising a federal constitutional question. The ratification of the Fourteenth Amendment in 1868 had created some doubts on this score, but the *Slaughter-House* decision in 1873 had rejected the contention that the privileges or immunities clause protected such rights.

Ten years later it was held in *Hurtado* v. *California* that the due process clause did not require the states to conform to the Bill of Rights in their criminal procedures, and as late as 1922 the Court denied that the Amendment restricted the states in dealing with freedom of expression. As for the equal protection clause, it had been used a few times to invalidate explicit racial discrimination in state law, but its effectiveness in deterring Jim Crow had been at best marginal. Like the due process clause it had been chiefly important in this era as a shield for business enterprise.

The states, then, were for some time relatively unconfined by constitutional doctrine in the civil rights field. On the other hand the national government had so far had little occasion to encroach on civil rights except in wartime, for police regulation that raised questions of this kind was left almost exclusively to the states. Given these facts, it is easy to see why civil rights cases had been a minor item on the Court's docket.

But now logic was working on behalf of civil rights. And although Justice Holmes was no doubt right when he once remarked that logic is not the "life of the law," still logic must not be thought of as irrelevant to the judicial process. The Court had provided the businessman with a generous measure of protection under the Fourteenth Amendment, and particularly the due process clause. Could it really be successfully contended that the "liberty" mentioned in that clause meant the liberty of economic man, and that only? Was there any rational basis for setting economic freedom so high above such basic rights as the right to a fair trial or liberty of expression? And if not, was it possible to maintain a constitutional discrimination against those rights for very long? In a way the development of the due process clause to protect economic rights made the ultimate protection of other rights logically inescapable.

The force of this logic was strengthened, it should be said, by certain personal factors in the 1920's and 30's, notably the presence on the Court of such brilliant libertarians as Holmes and Brandeis. And the First World War and the Russian Revolution played their part in precipitating the growth of constitutional doctrine, for they led to an assortment of state and federal laws infringing on freedom of expression, and the enforcement of these laws thrust the whole question into the judiciary's hands.

The free speech story properly begins in 1919 when the Court was presented with a constitutional claim brought by a man being punished under the federal Espionage Act of 1917 for mailing antidraft pamphlets to draftees. The defendant argued that his right to distribute such pamphlets was protected against national action by the First Amendment, but Justice Holmes for the Court rejected the claim. This speech is not protected, said Holmes, because it is used in such circumstances and is of such a nature as to create "a clear and present danger" of "substantive evils that Congress has a right to prevent" (that is, obstruction of the draft and mutiny in the armed forces). It followed of course that the Constitution *did* protect speech which did *not* present such a clear and present danger. Thus, although the individual conviction was here upheld, Holmes had scotched an old and persistent idea that the protection of the First Amendment was very narrow, and had committed the Court to an essentially libertarian formula for determining when speech may be abridged (*Schenck* v. *United States*).

The *Schenck* case involved a federal law, and the question of whether the free speech guarantees applied to the states by way of the Fourteenth Amendment was still comparatively untouched. However, the Court in 1925, confronted by a New York law punishing "criminal anarchy," declared "we may and do assume" that freedom of speech and press "are protected by the due process clause of the Fourteenth Amendment from impairment by the States." This was said with an offhandedness reminiscent of the concession in 1886 that corporations are persons in the meaning of the Amendment; and it was to be no less important in the long run. Again, as in *Schenck*, the particular prosecution was upheld, and the majority in fact repudiated the clear and present danger rule, holding that speech could be punished even if the danger of evil results was remote and conjectural. Nonetheless, the principle was now established that state action infringing free expression raised a federal constitutional question, and cases began making their way to the Court in increasing number. In 1931 the Court made its first important ruling against a state law in this field. Evidently a whole new dimension of constitutional jurisprudence had been opened up.

Meanwhile a somewhat similar development had been running its course in connection with the procedural rights of fair trial for accused persons. Although it had been held that the states were not bound by the specific procedural mandates of the Bill of Rights (for instance, they need not provide grand jury indictment as required by Amendment V) the Court had never quite gone so far as to say that the Fourteenth Amendment set no restrictions on state criminal procedures. The formula, stated in 1908, was that a procedural right was protected against state action only if it was "a fundamental principle of liberty and justice which inheres in the very idea of free government." This might seem an empty incantation, particularly since for a long time no decision upholding such a right was handed down. But in the 1920's the Court began to pour some content into it, for much the same reasons that prompted the concomitant drift toward protection of free expression; and in the early 1930's it was clearly held that state denials of the right to counsel and state use of forced confessions had offended this canon of due process. "The rack and the torture chamber," remarked Chief Justice Hughes, "may not be substituted for the witness stand."

As for the problem of racial discrimination in this period, it is hard to find the signs of doctrinal growth that are discernible in the fields of free expression and procedural rights (though it is perhaps worth remarking that the right-to-counsel case and the forced-confession case just mentioned, involved Negroes in the South). The Court had not yet challenged the doctrine that state law could require separation of races in schools, parks, and other facilities, so long as the accommodations provided were substantially equal. Indeed the standard of equality required was still very loose. The states had encountered a judicial setback or two in their attempts to exclude Negroes from the election process and from white residential areas, but by a modest amount of ingenuity they were able to evade these rulings with the acquiescence of the Court. Jim Crow was still constitutional.

But anyone able to think analogically might predict that he would have his judicial troubles before long. The logical process that had helped impel the Court to move from protection of economic liberty to protection of free expression and fair trial was equally relevant to the next step—the judicial defense of the right to racial equality. It would be too much to say that any of these developments became factually inevitable simply because the natural trend of logic supported them. Indeed the constitutional protection provided for these crucial rights was still, in spite of logic, skimpy and occasional. But the path was now open, in case the course of other historical events should provide a stimulus, for the Court to tread it more frequently.

THE CONSTITUTIONAL REVOLUTION OF 1937

In fact the occasion was already in the making, and, as it turned out, the time was nearly ripe. Having constructed with the greatest of pains a doctrinal tradition that allowed judicial intervention in economic affairs, and having administered those doctrines with reasonable discretion for some years, the Court had finally and dangerously overstepped the line that marks the limits of its authority. At a moment when the political pressure for economic legislation was greater than ever before, the Court had chosen to call a halt; at a moment when the Constitution's famous flexibility was most required, the Court had chosen to regard judicial review as the automatic application of static principles. The depression, and the New Deal which was its reflex, were forces too cosmic for those Canutes to withstand. Finally, the waves dislodged even the partial and contingent grip on economic affairs that the judiciary had once enjoyed. If the judges had stood firm in the position they assumed in 1935–36, there seems a good chance they would have been submerged altogether.

But they did not stand firm, or at any rate Justice Roberts did not, and he was the man who most mattered. The Roosevelt electoral victory in the fall of 1936 was impressive enough to convince all but those who would not listen that the American people wanted the New Deal. An outbreak of labor-management disputes, some of them accompanied by violence, had graphically illustrated the grim fact that the national economic dilemma was still very acute. On February 5, 1937, the President's "court-packing plan" had been set before Congress. No one, perhaps not even Justice Roberts, could say which of these circumstances was decisive for him; but it is hard to doubt that they played a part in the new tone of judicial decision that began to be sounded in the early months of that year.

It was first heard on March 29, 1937, less than two months after the Court plan was submitted and while the war of words over it was raging.

The Court was presented with a state minimum wage law applying to women and minors, a law not materially different from the one overturned in the New York Minimum Wage Case only nine months before. But now, by a vote of five to four, the judges upheld the law, rejecting both the *Adkins* precedent of 1923 and the New York decision. Chief Justice Hughes for the majority denied that freedom of contract was especially sanctified in the American system of constitutional restraints, declared that the Court must take judicial notice of the depression prostrating the nation, and found without difficulty that a minimum wage law was reasonably related to the legitimate end of preserving the workers' health. Justice Roberts, who had seen the matter differently nine months earlier, silently concurred.

Observers were still recovering from their surprise two weeks later when the Court astonished them again. This time the law in question was one of those major statutes that Congress had passed to cope with the national economic impasse—the National Labor Relations Act. In four decisions the law was upheld in spite of the fact that it controlled labor relations in production industries and in spite of the reiteration only a year before of the doctrine that production affected commerce "indirectly" and was therefore immune from congressional regulation. The direct-indirect distinction was in effect discarded. Again the vote was five to four; again the switch in the position of Justice Roberts tipped the scales.

Finally, on May 24, the Court backtracked dramatically once more. The Social Security Act of 1935 was for most exponents of laissez faire the very symbol of the paternalist theory of government which the New Deal represented and which they found so odious. Moreover, it offended the old negativisms of constitutional jurisprudence in a multiple sense, for it used the tax power to accomplish social ends and induced the states to participate in the plan and conform to nationally prescribed standards. On the authority of the *Butler* decision of 1936, this apparent encroachment on the states' reserved powers was most dubious, but again the Court upheld the law, again by a vote of five to four. Justice Roberts, the author of the *Butler* decision, had again changed his mind.

Meanwhile the controversy over the court-packing plan had been bitterly fought in the Congress and in the forum of public opinion. But although the drive to enact the President's proposal continued after the decisions just described, it had lost much of its force and more of its point. In the long run it failed, and the failure is a significant testimonial to the prestige that attached to the Court's Constitution in the American mind.

Not all the influence of a master politician in the prime of his popularity was quite enough to carry a program that would impair judicial review. Yet the Court's defenders were hardly entitled to be complacent. The Court's recantation had helped save the day; certain fortuitous circumstances relating to legislative strategy had made a difference, too. The danger had been great. Even a close call can teach a lesson.

Constitutional doctrine emerged from those months of crisis profoundly altered. The Court's relationship to the American polity had undergone a fundamental change. Quite probably the judges themselves did not understand how great a withdrawal was portended by their about-face in 1937. But within a few years it would be plain to all that another constitutional era had ended and a new one had begun. As the Civil War had settled the basic question underlying the nation-state conflict, so the Depression and the New Deal had resolved the basic question of economic control. Significant economic issues remained to be decided, of course, even after the nation had made the basic decision against laissez faire, but the Court by its own intransigence had disqualified itself to assist in the process by which those decisions were reached. When the extreme negativist position of 1935–36 was forsaken, as it had to be, the Court could find no stopping place short of abdication.

One aspect of the 1937 judicial revolution then was full-scale rejection of the idea that economic legislation was open to constitutional challenge on the basis of its "unreasonableness." The businessman, so long the Court's darling, was shorn of his constitutional fleece and now faced popular sovereignty protected by nothing save his own ample private resources. The second aspect was judicial acceptance of the idea, almost always implicit in the Court's actual past behavior, that constitutional rules must be flexible within broad limits and that as Justice Stone had put it, "the only check upon our own exercise of power is our own sense of self-restraint." The judicial sovereignty of rhetoric and myth, inexorably holding an irresponsible nation to an objectively ascertainable path of constitutional duty, had died the death with *Lochner, Adkins,* and *United States v. Butler.*

The Court therefore faced a future in which its interests of seventy years past were no longer relevant and in which myths of even longer standing would be deeply impaired. But recent experience, with all its hazards, had not stifled the remarkable institutional vitality that had sustained the Court throughout its stormy history. The old interests and values were gone, but a new set would arise to replace them. It is significant and far from a coincidence that 1937, the year of the great recantation, was also the year in which the Court revived, by implication at least, the clear and present danger test as a standard for judgment questions of free speech (*Herndon* v. *Lowry*). The same year saw the doctrine of judicial control over state criminal procedures stated more explicitly than ever before (*Palko* v. *Connecticut*). One year later the Court for the first time enforced the equal protection clause on behalf of Negro rights in the field of education (*Missouri* v. *Canada*). With or without myths, the future was on its way.

SEVEN

THE MODERN COURT AND
POSTWAR AMERICA: 1937–1959

THE SITUATION OF THE SUPREME COURT immediately after the constitutional revolution of 1937 was in many ways analogous to its situation at the close of the Civil War. Then as now prodigious national events had conspired to decide the question which had heretofore been the main focus of the Court's interest; then as now the nation's decision had left the judges in the status of men who are threatened by technological unemployment. In 1866 as in 1938 the Court was still smarting from wounds incurred by its own rashness. An observer viewing the Court at either of these hours in its history might have felt warranted to predict that judicial review had reached its twilight period, that the Court's career as an important factor in the American political process was drawing to a close.

But such an observer making such a judgment would be reckoning without the durability and elasticity of the institution Marshall and Taney and Field and Holmes had nurtured. He would be leaving out of account the qualities of the American political character that had led to the development of judicial review in the first place and had sustained and encouraged its continuance for so many years. In 1937 the people had again given testimony to the existence of that quality by refusing to abet an assault on the Court even though it was carried on in their name to chastise the Court for thwarting their will. With such a fund of support to draw on and with their august tradition to inspirit them, the judges were not apt to recede into humble obscurity unless they had no other choice.

If they were to play a real part, however, in the modern affairs of the Republic, they needed to evolve a new sphere of interests and a new set of values to guide them within that sphere. The problems of their past— the nation-state problem, the business-government problem—had successively been snatched from their grasp by history. It was necessary once more to reorient the Court's interests, to formulate another system of judicial values, and to develop a role for the Court in these new terms.

The interest that was to dominate this third great era of judicial history was, as has been intimated in the preceding chapter, civil rights. The Court which had once been primarily occupied with the nation-state relationship and, some time later, with the business-government relationship now became more and more concerned with the relationship between the individual and government. And the values that it now chose to cherish and defend were those embraced by Justice Frankfurter's phrase: "the free play of the human spirit."

History, which had displaced the Court's old ideal of free enterprise, was quick to provide material to fill the gap. The rise of totalitarianism created new problems for America and cast a different light on problems that were old. The nation faced mortal threats of a degree it had not known since the Civil War and of a kind that it had never known before. The freedom of political dissent had formerly been preserved without much difficulty simply because there had been little occasion for government to challenge it; but now fear generated repressive political impulses.

Yet at the same time the spectacle of the police state in Germany and Russia and elsewhere caused many Americans to revere freedom of expression more consciously than they had in the past and to resist attempts to inhibit it. The racist doctrines of Adolf Hitler and the frightful implementation of those doctrines in Nazi policy helped provoke a feeling of dissatisfaction and guilt over America's own patterns of race discrimination. The right of fair trial, once taken for granted, assumed new layers of significance in the minds of men repelled by the totalitarian image. For some, the concern for the civil rights issue was enhanced by awareness that America had become willy-nilly the leader of the free world and must set a responsible leader's example. And because these three categories of rights were logically hard to separate, alertness to one tended to stimulate alertness to all, so that they mutually animated one another. This is how self-consciousness about the civil rights problem was heightened in the 1930's and 40's and how the Supreme Court was impelled to focus on that problem. For, as history has repeatedly attested, the members of the Supreme Court are children of their times, and a chronicle of Court doctrine tends to be, in a general way, an intellectual history of America.

However, in the post-1937 period as in earlier periods, the Court's adoption of a new congeries of interests and values created the problem of working out a judicial role that would best serve these new purposes. The doctrines of the past, forged to serve past aims, had to be reconstructed, as the due process clause for example was altered in the 1880's and 90's to suit the circumstances of that era. The judges had to rethink the question of the Court's place in the American polity, to feel their way to a *modus operandi* that would enable the Court to defend its new values with reasonable effectiveness but would simultaneously take due account of the limits of judicial control.

And the problem of role definition was all the more acute, as was suggested at the close of the last chapter, because the Court's own behavior and a generation of criticism by "judicial realists" had undermined the myths of judicial supremacy and objectivity. The Court of the early twentieth century had flagrantly confirmed the thesis of this school of critics by refusing to bind itself to objective standards in any of the great areas of judicial supervision. The judges who came to the supreme bench after the constitutional revolution (Justice Van Devanter was the first of the old guard to resign, to be succeeded by Justice Black) were men who had been reared in that school, and they joined Justice Stone, one of its leading spokesmen. They had reason to be more explicitly aware than perhaps any Court of the past had been that theirs was "not the only agency of government that must be assumed to have capacity to govern" and that "the criterion of constitutionality is not whether [judges] believe the law to be for the public good." Their task of finding a place for themselves in the new order was made more difficult, though perhaps clearer, by this fact that self-deception was no longer so reliable an ally.

THE END OF ECONOMIC SUPERVISION

The first order of business was to convince the informed public, including an almost incorrigibly hopeful legal fraternity, that the Court really meant what it implied in 1937: that economic issues were no longer of much constitutional relevance. Businessmen were so accustomed to the Court's favors that they found it hard to adjust to the new dispensation. Yet the judicial drift quickly became unmistakable, as the old negative doctrines were discarded or refined to the point of disappearance. The restrictive interpretations of the tax power, which had served so well in the Child Labor Tax Case and the AAA case, had been pretty well scuttled in the spring of 1937 by the Social Security Act decisions. Congress could tax and spend for the "general welfare" (Art. I, sec. 8 [1]) and the fact that a tax controlled local affairs would make no constitutional difference so long as the general welfare, as Congress saw it, would be served. Even the ancient ban on "intergovernmental taxation" was drastically moderated in 1939. The Court formally repudiated Marshall's aphorism that "the power to tax involves the power to destroy," and thus wiped out more than a century's accumulation of intricate doctrine. State and nation could now tax each other's instrumentalities so long as the tax was neither discriminatory nor "unduly" burdensome.

In the commerce clause field, too, the hardy old negativisms were mowed down with rude abandon. The second Agricultural Adjustment Act of 1938 was upheld despite the fact that it excluded "harmless" commodities from interstate commerce by establishing quotas on the amount that could be sold, and indirectly regulated production. In 1942 the Court sustained an even more venturesome amendment which imposed limits on wheat grown for on-the-farm uses even though no part of it was sold in interstate trade. A year before it had upheld the Fair Labor Standards Act which prescribed wages and hours for firms engaged in or producing goods for interstate commerce. The idea that production was beyond congressional reach, the distinction between direct and indirect effects were all given the quietus. As Justice Jackson remarked for a unanimous bench in the wheat quotas case: "The Court's recognition of the relevance of the economic effects in the application of the Commerce Clause . . . has made the mechanical application of legal formulas no longer feasible" (*Wickard* v. *Filburn*).

It was now evident that Congress could reach just about any commercial subject it might want to reach and could do to that subject just about anything it was likely to want to do, whether for economic, humanitarian, or other purposes. The decisions, it is true, offer a hint that some regulations might go too far, that some local activities might be exempt from federal control because their effect on interstate commerce was not substantial. But these hints were small comfort to businessmen appealing for present relief; and business was thoroughly warranted in inferring that the constitutional distinction between intrastate and interstate commerce was no longer a practical limit on federal power.

This was a bitter pill to swallow for those who had benefited from the Old Court's solicitous jurisprudence, but the enfeeblement of the due process clause as a substantive limit on economic legislation was even more dismaying. The post-1937 Court in effect adopted the criterion urged by Justice Holmes in his classic series of dissents during the first three decades of the century. It was authoritatively expressed in 1938 by Justice Stone in *United States* v. *Carolene Products:*

> . . . regulatory legislation affecting ordinary commercial transactions is not to be pronounced unconstitutional unless in the light of the facts made known or generally assumed it is of such a character as to preclude the assumption that it rests upon some rational basis within the knowledge and experience of the legislators.

It is hard to conceive a law so patently unreasonable that it would fail under this test, and it is therefore not surprising that the Court since 1937 has never encountered one. And the Court showed itself ready to make a loose standard even looser by stretching its imagination to the limits to find *some* sensible reason for the law and impute that motive to the legislative authors. Not even the most optimistic litigant could persuade himself for very long after 1938 than an economic statute would be held unreasonable on substantive grounds.

Of course the Court had always paid lip service to the principle that a law should be presumed valid "until its violation of the Constitution is proved beyond reasonable doubt" (*Ogden* v. *Saunders,* 1827). But the judges had breached this precept in such decisions as *Lochner, Adkins,* and the anti–New Deal cases, for the very good reason that compliance with it would have forced them to uphold the questioned laws. Now this "presumption of constitutionality" was reinstated with a vengeance, and the extreme form it took is a measure of the Court's determination to have done with economic affairs in the due process area. A state law forbidding women to work as barmaids; another forcing employers to pay employees for hours not worked on election day; still another in effect restricting the river-boat pilot profession to relatives and friends of present pilots—all these were upheld against due process and equal protection attack. The ghosts of Field and Peckham and Sutherland must have stirred restlessly to see freedom of contract so hardly used. But it was not their shades, but those of Holmes and Brandeis that now dominated the course of decision. Constitutional laissez faire was as dead as mutton.

This is not to say that the post-1937 Court was able to ignore the economic world altogether. Though substantive due process in this area was virtually abandoned, the older and historically more legitimate concept of procedural due process survived, and a businessman could still hope for constitutional recourse if, for example, a law took his property without notice or fair hearing. And although the commerce power of

Congress was no longer subject to serious constitutional question, the problem of whether state action impinged on interstate commerce (the old problem of the *Cooley* case) still absorbed a respectable share of the Court's attention. The principle seemed to be that such a state law was acceptable if it did not discriminate against interstate commerce (that is, if it treated the state's own commerce and that of the nation equally) and if the Court felt that the state interest served by the law outweighed "whatever national interest there might be in the prevention of state restrictions." But this form of supervision over economic matters, though not insignificant, is a far cry from the sovereignty once claimed over the whole business-government relationship. And the crucial point is that the Court's doctrines were no longer set up as a barrier against regulations as such. The question of whether America should become a welfare state was now referred strictly to the political branches of government.

Humility versus Pride: International Agreements and Executive Power

All this suggests a judiciary overwhelmed by considerations of modesty and resolved to interfere as little as possible in the conduct of government, particularly when national power is involved. And the impression seems confirmed by certain other doctrinal tendencies of the era. The rule against undue delegation of legislative power, invoked by the Old Court to help extinguish the New Deal, was now so attenuated that it took on the quality of a moral admonition rather than a legal limitation. In a case involving the validity of federal price control legislation, for example, the Court upheld the law even though it empowered the administrator to issue price regulations subject only to the requirement that they tend to effectuate the very broad purposes of the Act (essentially to prevent inflation), that they be "fair and equitable" (whatever that may mean), and that the administrator "so far as practicable" give "due consideration" to the prices prevailing in October, 1941. The arguments of the judges in the NRA case almost ten years before, that executive discretion under the recovery act was "virtually unfettered" and not "canalized within banks that keep it from overflowing," seem equally apposite here. But now only Justice Roberts dissented from the holding that the standards provided for the administrator's guidance were constitutionally adequate. Even before the 1937 revolution the Court had approved the delegation of very broad discretion to the President in the field of foreign affairs (*United*

States v. *Curtiss-Wright,* 1936). Now it appeared that the rule was similarly permissive when applied to domestic administration.

Nor was the conduct of foreign policy hampered by other sorts of judicially contrived restraints. As long ago as 1920, Justice Holmes, speaking for the Court, had declared that a treaty might accomplish results that a mere act of Congress could not, that the limits of the Constitution applied "in a different way" when the treaty-making power was called into question (Art. II, sec. 2 [2]). In view of this decision and in view of the fact that no treaty had ever been held to exceed constitutional bounds, some alarmed observers have suspected that no such bounds exist as far as the judiciary is concerned. And their apprehension about the danger of arbitrary government in the foreign affairs area was hardly quelled by a 1942 decision holding that an "executive agreement" made by the President with a foreign government (without the concurrence of the Senate, which is required for a treaty) was paramount to state laws.

It is a pretty safe bet that the Court would invalidate a treaty or executive agreement that bartered away all or part of the Bill of Rights; the power to make such international compacts could not avail to deprive Americans of free speech or fair trial. But aside from such an unlikely eventuality, it must be conceded that the chances of judicial interference with this authority are very remote. In connection with the power over foreign affairs, as in connection with national power over economic affairs, the modern Court has for practical purposes abandoned the concept of judicial control and has thrust the responsibility for worrying about constitutional limits on the shoulders of the President and Congress. The argument for this policy of abnegation is that government must have great leeway to act effectively in these two intricate and technical fields, and that judicial review is too restricted in its sources of information and too cumbersome in its procedures to supervise such action adequately. The danger is of course that the other branches of government will fail to assume the constitutional responsibility which the Court has tendered to them, and will interpret the assignment as a license to act arbitrarily. But for better or for worse the fact remains that these two great and increasingly important areas of public affairs are now subject to constitutional limits only in the sense that the British Parliament is constitutionally limited, that is, by legislative and executive self-restraint and by the force of public opinion.

Yet in spite of all these evidences of judicial humility in these areas, it would be an error to assume that the judiciary had lost self-confidence altogether as a result of its chastening experience in the 1930's. One of the best single illustrations of the fact that it had not is to be found in the Steel Seizure decision of 1952. In order to avert a nationwide steel strike which he thought would imperil America's defense, President Truman had seized the steel mills on behalf of the United States government by executive order. Mr. Truman's authority to take such action was not specifically granted by statute, and his right, if any, to seize the mills, therefore, had to rest on the old idea that the President possesses certain "inherent powers" to act for the national welfare even without specific statutory authorization. The Court had tacitly recognized some such prerogative in a few opinions during its history, but in general the concept of inherent power had developed extra-judicially as a result of presidential practice and congressional acquiescence. The Court of the past had seemed to feel about this question the way the modern Court felt about the commerce power and the treaty power—that it was best left to the political branches of government.

But now the Court of 1952, otherwise so skittish about intruding in economic affairs, undertook to mediate this hot dispute between the President and one of the great economic forces of the nation. The "opinion of the Court" by Justice Black boldly held that the President had no authority to act as he did because the subject was within the sphere of Congress' authority; when the President entered that sphere without congressional permission, he violated the principle of separation of powers. Some of the other majority judges did not concur in this definition of executive power that would confine it to matters outside Congress' range (what those matters might be would be hard to say considering the modern scope of legislative power). But they did argue that the President had erred in this instance because, said they, certain federal statutes forbid Mr. Truman to do what he did, and surely inherent executive power, even if there is such a thing, does not license the President to violate statutes.

To that proposition all the judges agreed, and so would most observers, including President Truman (who contended that the supposedly prohibitory statutes were being wrongly interpreted). But such a consensus should not obscure the very real question of whether the Supreme Court should have tried to resolve a controversy so heatedly fought at the bar of public opinion, so loaded with immediate and grave national consequences. At all events the decision reminds us that judicial self-restraint is not the only theme of the modern era. The modern judges have been torn, as were their predecessors of the early twentieth century, between the impulse to wield the scepter and the impulse to remain "lions under the throne." A similar tension has been set up; similar lines of division have been drawn. And the Steel Seizure case represents, as *Adkins* did, a breaking-out and temporary assertion of the old urge to monarchize.

THE COURT SEEKS A ROLE:
THE PROBLEM OF FREEDOM OF EXPRESSION

The tension between the instinct to dominate and the instinct to forbear has been most clearly evident in connection with the subject the modern Court seems to care most about—civil rights. And the competing considerations that have helped to generate the tensions here have been by no means easy to resolve. On the one hand, there has been the feeling, more or less deeply shared by all the modern judges, that "those liberties of the individual which history has attested as the indispensable conditions of an open as against a closed society come to the Court with a momentum for respect lacking when appeal is made to liberties which derive merely from shifting economic arrangements." The words are those of Justice Frankfurter and some of the reasons for the rise of the sentiment have already been discussed. It can be judicially implemented, as Justice Stone once intimated, by subjecting to "more exacting judicial scrutiny" legislation "which restricts the political processes which can ordinarily be expected to bring about repeal of undesirable legislation" and which reflect "prejudices against discrete and insular minorities" (*United States v. Carolene Products Co.,* 1938). Coupled with and supporting this modern concern for civil rights as a value, has been the tradition, running back to Marshall and beyond, that the Court has the power and duty to right wrongs, to translate its moral convictions into constitutional limitations.

On the other hand, of course, there were ranged all the notions about judicial humility that had been generated by the iconoclastic movement of the preceding decades, and an awareness—on the part of at least some of the judges—that the historic Court had usually accomplished more by moderation than by arrogance. These notions, well-grounded enough in any event, could be reinforced in the post-1937 era by a special circumstance of the times: the fact that *crisis* seemed to have become a chronic condition. The concept of constitutional limitation had never functioned very well in emergencies. In moments of great peril, when the temper of the populace was likely to be superheated, the judicial tendency had been to withdraw and wait for more auspicious, normal times. This had been Marshall's policy in the dangerous years after the Jeffersonian revolution, and it had been adopted by the Court with varying degrees of frankness in critical periods that followed. The exceptions have not made very pleasant readings for the Court's friends. Judicial attempts to control policy in such times have seldom been ultimately very successful. In the years after 1937, as wars hot and cold posed awesome problems and frayed public nerves, the case for judicial modesty was not easy to refute. But neither was it easy to dismiss the argument that civil rights are the essence of democratic government and that the Court must do its best to preserve them. The difficulty was to decide what its best was.

The Court's erratic pattern of response to the issue of free expression illustrates these judicial perplexities with special force. In the first few years after 1937, the judges seemed inclined to stand the old constitutional order on its head, and to assert a power of review over free speech statutes that was unmodified by considerations of judicial self-restraint. Holmes's clear and present danger principle, ignored by the majority since 1919, was now revitalized and put forward as a talismanic standard to be applied to all categories of free speech problems. Moreover the Holmesian rubric was strengthened in its negative implications by an amendment that had been proposed by Justice Brandeis in a 1927 concurring opinion. In order to sustain a statute inhibiting freedom of speech, he had suggested, the Court must find a clear and present danger of a *serious* evil; "prohibition of free speech and assembly is a measure so stringent that it would not be appropriate as the means for averting a relatively trivial harm to society" (*Whitney* v. *California*).

Now the rhetoric of clear and present danger in this form expresses well enough some of the factors that might guide the citizen or his legislative representative in deciding whether free expression should be restrained; and it is no doubt advisable that the judicial process take account of these factors, too. But in some of the early decisions of this era the Court gave the impression that its opinion about clear and present danger was the only one that counted and that the "presumption of constitutionality," once denied in *Lochner* and *Adkins* to statutes touching freedom of contract, was now denied to those infringing freedom of speech. The doctrine seemed to be, pressing Justice Stone's *Carolene Products* logic hard, that free expression (including of course religious expression) occupied a "preferred position" in America's constellation of constitutional rights, and that government action impinging on it was presumptively invalid. Armed with these concepts and attitudes, the Court disapproved a considerable number of state actions, including a law forbidding peaceful picketing, another requiring union organizers to register, state court contempt holdings against those who were accused of using the press to influence judicial proceedings, and a state law requiring school children to salute the flag in spite of their contrary religious convictions.

Most of the state measures invalidated in this period were foolish or pernicious, and some of them might well have been overthrown even by a judiciary fully alive to the virtue of modesty. But the decisions nevertheless were vulnerable to criticism on at least two grounds. In the first place the opinions that accompanied them were barren of evidence that the Court was taking adequate account of the legislature's claim to share in "the power to govern." It is one thing to decide that a state action exceeds the bounds of reason and quite another, as Sir Frederick Pollock once said, to treat the legislature "like an inferior court which had to give proof of its competence." The judges had long ago been powerfully admonished by Justice Holmes: "It must be remembered that legislators are the ultimate guardians of the liberties and welfare of the people in quite as great a degree as the courts." Now, with respect to free speech statutes, that reminder seemed to be forgotten.

But second, and in practical terms even more important, the opinions assumed a role for the Court and a rigidity of constitutional limits that could not be sustained in the face of real adversity. The idea seemed to be that the Court would hold government action aimed at free speech to the same kind of strict substantive limits that had been applied, in *Adkins* and similar cases, to inhibitions on freedom of contract. This failed to reckon with the possibility of extreme public need or (what is pretty much the same thing as far as the Court is concerned) extreme public demand for repressive legislation. The doctrines and assumptions of these cases proved no more tenable as the totalitarian threat became acute than the similar doctrines and assumptions of *Adkins* had been tenable in the Great Depression.

What was especially unfortunate about all this is that it left the Court unprepared to cope with adversity when it did come. Instead of working out a viable judicial attitude toward infringements on free speech, the Court had enunciated a policy of flat negation; and when that policy had to be abandoned, there was nothing to take its place except uncritical acquiescence to the legislative will. Growing national awareness of the totalitarian threat in the years after 1945 generated a national mood toward "subversion" that sometimes approached hysteria. Government action in response to that mood was often savagely hostile to freedom of expression. If the judges had been thinking their problem through in the years just preceding, they might have been ready with an approach that could have moderated the tempest and contributed usefully to the resolution of a grave national quandary. But since most of them had been orating rather than thinking, and since the uncompromising policy set forth in the oratory had become impossible, the only alternative seemed to be judicial collapse. At no time in its history had the Court been able to maintain a position squarely opposed to a strong popular majority. There was no reason to expect that it could do so now. In contrast to the negativism of the first few post-1937 years, the Court now became so tolerant of governmental restriction on freedom of expression as to suggest that it was abdicating the field.

The two decisions that exemplified this phase of modern judicial history were *American Communication Ass'n v. Douds* (1950) and *Dennis v. United States* (1951). Both involved national statutes visiting penalties on Communists, and in both the Court upheld the government actions, painfully swallowing its brave libertarian protestations of a few years before. However the most troubling thing about the decisions was not so much that they sustained the government, but that they came close to abandoning altogether the concept of judicial limitation. The *Douds* opinion by Chief Justice Vinson suggested, about as strongly as words might, that Congress could use the commerce power to interfere with free speech and association without fear of *any* constitutional hindrance. In *Dennis* the language was somewhat more guarded, but the result was not very different. The clear and present danger doctrine, put forward in recent opinions as a kind of universal rule, was now redefined in such a way as to make it meaningless and, for practical purposes, useless. The Court's role as the uncompromising defender of liberty against all comers, also so recently asserted and reasserted, was likewise abandoned. The implication was that judicial review could contribute nothing to the solution of America's "subversion problem" and that the Court's only course was to stand aside while the winds howled on Capitol Hill and elsewhere.

However, it turned out that another phase in this history of judicial responses was already taking shape at the very time that these spectacularly acquiescent decisions were handed down. For one thing, though shying off from the issue of subversion, the Court had continued to widen the area of freedom in cases involving what might be called "nonseditious free speech." For the first time in history, for example, the Court had overturned state laws censoring magazines and motion pictures. These decisions were couched in careful language; they did not condemn all censorship per se. But they made it clear that censorship does raise a constitutional question and thereby opened up a whole new area of judicial supervision. A comparable development was meanwhile taking place in cases involving both the "free exercise of religion" and the "no establishment" clauses of the First Amendment. The substance of those clauses had been held to be binding on the states by way of the Fourteenth Amendment. Now the Court struck down state aid to religion on the ground that it breached the "wall of separation" between church and state and on the ground that it infringed religious liberty. Again the decisions were so framed as to leave some leeway for state policy; but again it had been made plain that a subject highly relevant to free expression was subject to constitutional control.

In the second place, as public enthusiasm for domestic red-hunting subsided somewhat, and as the Court had a chance to take new bearings, the outlines of a mature policy in the subversive field began to emerge. In the stormy times of the *Douds* and *Dennis* cases, the judges seemed to have forgotten that there is more than one way to skin a cat. Awed by the dimensions of the subversion problem and loath to challenge the substantive power of Congress on an issue related to national defense, they had chosen to do nothing. As their history should have informed them, however, there is a middle way between over-assertiveness and abdication even when congressional statutes are concerned. National laws must be *interpreted* by the federal courts, and judicial misgivings about the wisdom or necessity of such laws can be expressed through "the alchemy of construction." In short, the Supreme Court can often so interpret a law invading free speech as to moderate its virulence. This serves to remind Congress and country that a zone of doubt has been entered and encourages them to take a second look at their problem. Yet it leaves Congress free to correct the judicial gloss if convinced, after reflection, that a harsher interpretation should prevail. A further advantage from the viewpoint of democratic values is that the approach focuses responsibility by requiring Congress to speak unmistakably when it wishes to impinge on freedom of expression.

In the 1950's the Supreme Court rediscovered this item in its bag of tricks and began to use it to exert a significant influence on national policy relating to subversion and allied phenomena. Perhaps the most far-reaching case in point was *Pennsylvania v. Nelson* which involved the jailing of a Communist party member under a state sedition law. By this time (1956) the national government had added three major peace-time sedition statutes to its books, and most of the states had been stirred by the postwar excitement over such matters to elaborate and intensify their own antisubversive programs. This added up to a bewildering number and variety of governmental restrictions on freedom of expression, and in the *Nelson* case the Court simplified the situation by wiping the state laws, temporarily at least, off the slate. The Court argued that Congress, in passing the national sedition laws, had superseded the state laws by implication. Since the problem dealt with by the laws—national defense—is obviously national in character, there could be no doubt that Congress *could* override state laws if it chose to do so. By holding that the Congress *had* so chosen, the Court threw its weight on the side of rationality and liberty, yet avoided the heavy responsibility of an irrevocable constitutional pronouncement against such state activity.

With respect to free expression, then, the modern Court seems to have established, temporarily at least, a balance between the extremes of judicial supremacy and judicial abdication. Doctrines have been reshaped and jurisdiction widened so as to bring a new range of subjects under potential constitutional control. This development of a jurisprudence of free expression has been in many ways comparable to the development of a jurisprudence of laissez faire in the closing decades of the nineteenth century. And now, as then, the Court, having evolved the tools of judicial supervision, has been faced by the problem of how to use them. The current answer seems to be twofold: government is held to a fairly strict but not inflexible standard in fields unrelated to subversion; in fields that do involve the subversion issue, Congress is left free within wide limits, and the Court employs the device of statutory interpretations to mitigate the asperities of repressive laws and insure that the legislative will is clearly expressed. This adds up to a comparatively modest version of the doctrine of judicial supremacy. It constitutes the judiciary as a significant but not dominant partner in the American governmental enterprise. Throughout the modern period there have been members of the bench who chafed under the limitations of this role and yearned to play a greater part in shaping the decisions of the nation. It remains to be seen whether they will ultimately succeed in launching the Court on one of those campaigns of derring-do that have from time to time marked its history.

JUDICIAL SUCCESSES AND FAILURES:
THE PROBLEM OF PROCEDURAL RIGHTS

The modern drive to harry subversives by inhibiting their freedom of expression has also been hampered to some extent by the Supreme Court's insistence that the procedural guarantees of the Constitution must be observed. Like the approach to statutory interpretation just described, this procedural fastidiousness represents a nice compromise between too much judicial review and too little. When Congress is told that it must respect the procedural rights of persons even though they are suspected of subversion, this preserves the substantive power of Congress to accomplish its basic objects and at the same time acts as a reminder that the idea of constitutional limit still lives.

The Court's zeal in enforcing procedural standards has been tempered by an awareness that government needs elbow room to operate effectively, and it is arguable that this spirit of judicial tolerance has sometimes been overdone. During the Second World War, for example, the military authorities (backed, it should be said, by the President and Congress) decided that some 112,000 Japanese-Americans must be moved out of the West Coast military area as a security measure. The decision was carried out in spite of the fact that about 70,000 of the victims were United States citizens and that no crime could be charged, much less proved, against them. The Supreme Court upheld this wholesale invasion of procedural rights, arguing that it could not second-guess the military on a question relating to national defense and calling for swift action. The case provides another illustration—if one is needed—of the proposition that judicial review is likely to be weakest during grave national emergencies. It also illustrates the curious tendency to polarized thinking that occasionally besets the American judiciary. The idea that the Court must either uphold a governmental policy in all respects or disapprove it altogether was controlling in the *Milligan* case in 1866 and in this case almost a century later. Yet the Court's whole history is a refutation of that black-and-white idea.

Procedural rules were sometimes interpreted rather generously in other areas as well. The right against "unreasonable searches and seizures" (Amendment IV) did not avail, for example, to prevent federal officers from searching the premises of an arrested person even though they bore no warrant to conduct the search and there had been ample time to get one before making the arrest. Evidence obtained by wiretapping was not admissible in federal tribunals because wiretapping was forbidden by federal statute, but the Court steadily refused to hold that wiretapping violated the Fourth Amendment, and it allowed the admission of evidence obtained by various hidden listening devices like radio transmitters.

The procedural protection of those threatened by such grave penalties as deportation was not all that it might be. The Court permitted the government to hold a man in prison without bail while deportation proceedings were pending, even though no deportable offense had yet been proved against him and the proceedings might well drag on for years. A federal law of 1954 required witnesses to answer questions that might ordinarily incriminate them and granted them immunity from prosecution on the matters disclosed. The Court upheld the law against the argument that it impaired the privilege against self-incrimination guaranteed by the Fifth Amendment. The statutory immunity from criminal prosecution could not of course protect a man from the other penalties of his testimony, such as loss of employment and "infamy" but the Court declined to extend the right so as to cover such hazards.

Yet the procedural rights that the Court did secure or enlarge during the modern period were by no means insignificant, particularly in their bearing on freedom of expression. In spite of the Immunity Act decision and others which construed the Fifth Amendment narrowly, the Court approached the right against self-incrimination, as Justice Frankfurter said "in a spirit of strict, not lax, observance of the constitutional protection of the individual." The Court made it clear for example in 1950 that the right was available to those who were asked about Communist activities by courts, congressional committees, or any other federal agency. The refusal to enlarge the privilege into a general right of silence or to extend it otherwise by interpretation reflects unwillingness to go forward, not a disposition to go back. And in the field of deportation and denaturalization, although the Court did sometimes uphold rather arbitrary government behavior, it also established in the modern period the important principle that a man threatened by deportation or denaturalization was entitled to *some* procedural rights under the due process clause. The old doctrine, arguably supported by some court decisions, had been that constitutional limits did not apply at all in these areas of governmental power.

Furthermore due process in the procedural sense was increasingly held to be relevant to statutes directly inhibiting freedom of expression. The vice of "vagueness" in a legal prohibition can always be challenged on due process grounds, for a man cannot be fairly punished unless he has a reasonable basis for knowing that his act was forbidden. But vagueness was regarded as particularly objectionable in free speech statutes, and this judicial stand helped to overthrow or discourage the kind of shotgun enactments that legislators sometimes pass, because it takes time and knowledge to draw a statute carefully.

In a similar vein, a "loyalty oath" requirement applied to public college teachers was held invalid on the essentially procedural ground that it penalized innocent as well as knowing membership in "subversive organization" and thus violated due process. The opinions emphasized that such thoughtlessly broad statutes affected not only the immediate litigants but the atmosphere of freedom generally, because they may "chill that free play of the spirit which all teachers ought especially to cultivate and practice." This decision (*Wiemann v. Updegraff*, 1952) was important, too, because it flatly rejected the old, bad idea that "there is no constitutionally protected right to public employment." The government may not exclude a public servant from employment on arbitrary or discriminatory grounds.

This attitude toward procedures, combined with the policy of interpreting free speech laws strictly, enabled the modern Court to reconcile its feelings of modesty with its modern solicitude for individual rights, and to contribute to the solution of the subversion problem. The realm of procedure is after all the judge's special domain; the construction of statutes is a peculiarly judicial art; and the Court's ipse dixit seems more authoritative in these areas than it might if substantive issues of policy were being decided.

Like considerations might seem to have a bearing on another great question in the modern jurisprudence of civil rights—the extent to which the *states* are bound by a federal constitutional standard in their general criminal procedures. But here the problem has been complicated by the Court's respect for a value that ranks very high in the lexicon of some of the judges—the value of federalism. Justice Holmes once said (though not, as it happens, in reference to a procedural issue) that he deprecated the use of the Fourteenth Amendment to prevent experiments "in the insulated chambers afforded by the several States." The modern Court has been troubled by the fear that overly strict constitutional supervision of state law enforcement would impede the evolution of new and more effective methods and would dampen the state's sense of responsibility for policing its own standard.

These misgivings help account for the fact that the Court has advanced more slowly in this field than some libertarians might wish. It will be remembered that by the 1930's the Court had clearly accepted the idea that some procedural rights protected against national action by Amendments IV–VIII, were also protected against state action by the Fourteenth Amendment. The problem then was to determine what those rights were and how they should be applied to limit the states. In 1937 in the *Palko* case Justice Cardozo laid it down that the rights protected were those principles of justice "so rooted in the traditions and conscience of our people as to be ranked as fundamental." Unhappily however this principle, like others that have been encountered in this chronicle, was not quite self-explanatory. Suppose it is decided that the right to counsel is fundamental in the sense intended by the *Palko* doctrine. Does that mean that the right must be granted in every kind of proceeding even down to traffic court cases? Does it mean that the state is obliged to provide counsel for the indigent even in those cases? Or is it necessary, once a right has been identified as worthy of protection, to discriminate between denials of it that are offensive and those that are not?

The modern Court met these difficulties, or attempted to meet them, by developing the "fair trial rule." The right to counsel, for example, *had* been recognized to be protected by the Amendment as long ago as 1932. But, said the Court ten years later, in determining whether a *given* denial of counsel is a denial of due process, we will ask whether "the totality of facts" in the case "constitute a denial of fundamental fairness." Thus an indigent farm laborer was not deprived of due process when the state refused his request to supply counsel in a trial for robbery, because the Supreme Court reading the printed record felt that the trial had been fair.

One trouble with this rule, apart from its possible harshness to the defendant, was its extreme uncertainty. If the totality of facts in a given case was the only basis for determining fairness, it seemed impossible to predict whether a conviction would be upheld unless the predicter could anticipate the thought processes of five members of the Supreme Court. This objection, together with a strong disposition to favor the individual in cases of doubt, led to a series of powerful minority dissents in cases following 1942, and finally in *Adamson* v. *California* (1947) the judges engaged in a full-dress verbal conflict. Justice Black argued eloquently and at length that the Court should take leave of the *Palko* doctrine and its subsidiary, the fair trial rule. Both the intent of the Fourteenth Amendment's framers and considerations of sound judicial policy suggest, he said, that Amendments IV–VIII should be incorporated *in toto* in the Fourteenth. Thus the Court would be deprived of the "boundless power" to expand or contract procedural guarantees; the course of the law would be more certain; and the Court would "extend to all the people of the nation the complete protection of the Bill of Rights."

But Justice Black's assault failed to carry the Court majority. Five members joined in reaffirming the established rules. Justice Frankfurter sharply queried the Black interpretation of the framers' intent, denounced the "incorporation" proposal on the ground that it would imprison the states in eighteenth-century legal concepts, and denied that the *Palko* standard was unduly subjective. On the historical point Frankfurter later received valuable extra-judicial support from Professor Charles Fairman, whose researches into contemporary documents raised serious doubts that the framers had a clear-cut intention to embody the Bill of Rights in the Amendment. The suggestion that the states should be allowed leeway to experiment with reforms has obvious force, but one's ultimate assessment of it will depend on a judgment of whether the leeway is likely to be used for good or ill. And that judgment in turn is related to the weight that is assigned federalism as a value: does state autonomy work against individual liberty or tend to promote it?

As for the charge of subjectivity, perhaps the best answer is what lawyers call a plea in confession and avoidance. The question of subjectivity versus objectivity is as old as the Supreme Court (in fact, of course, a great deal older). Critics have perennially urged the Court to abolish uncertainties by pronouncing a sweeping rule, but historical experience suggests that such advice is dubious, however well intended. The broadly generalized dogmatism has usually created more mischief than it has cured, both from the Court's own viewpoint and from the viewpoint of public policy. It is reasonable therefore to expect that the rules will emerge gradually as inferences from a multitude of decisions, and to hope that they will be well adapted to reality by the nature of their evolution.

But on the other hand the fair trial rule with its emphasis on the "totality of facts" in each discrete situation seems a barrier to the development of any rule at all, and the Court does have an obligation to make the law as understandable as reality permits. The all-out incorporation principle espoused by Black seems to have provoked a similarly extreme contradictory doctrine. It is not the first time in this history that we have seen wisdom fall between two opposite poles. The list of decisions since 1937 in which procedural rights have been defended against state action is a long one. Here as elsewhere during the modern era the Court has been more vigilant to protect the individual than it was in the past. But it has failed to develop in this field a criterion of decision that seems intellectually defensible or practically tenable.

RACIAL DISCRIMINATION AND THE BOUNDARIES OF JUDICIAL POWER

In connection with free speech and procedural rights, as we have seen, the modern Court has pursued a somewhat irregular course, alternating between modesty and self-assertion, retreating and advancing by turns. But the third great civil rights problem—racial discrimination—has been handled quite differently. Here the Court has been more venturesome, more confident in announcing its proscriptions. Moreover the doctrinal direction has been consistently (though not unhesitatingly) forward toward a more generous view of the rights of racial minorities and a more daring assessment of the Court's capacity to protect them. And the radical conflicts of opinion among the judges themselves, so frequent in the other cases discussed, have in this field been far less common.

The explanation for this contrast is not hard to guess. With one or two possible exceptions all of the judges appointed to the bench since 1937 shared a general civil rights ethos. Their commitments to it might vary in degree, and the judges might differ in their ideas for implementing it, but they shared it nonetheless. And in that mutual value system the goal of racial equality assumed a special place for several reasons. Partly, no doubt, it was because persecution on the basis of race seemed the most gratuitously evil of totalitarian malignancies. Partly it was because America's primary racial minority, the Negroes, lagged so patently and woefully behind the rest of the nation in their privileges: this problem seemed the greatest because it involved the most glaring injustice. There is usually an arguable justification for restrictions on speech or denial of procedural rights—the state must be defended, the "war against crime" must not be hindered unduly. For racial discrimination there is no such generally commended rationale, but only prejudice. Add to these considerations the fact that Amendments XIV and XV were passed originally to secure Negro rights, though the former amendment had been diverted to other uses. And further add, as has been suggested earlier, that the modern judges were pervasively conscious of America's position as a symbol of the free world and of the new importance of the "non-White" nations in the world arena. The judicial impulse to act forthrightly in this field is easy to understand.

But, however grievous the wrongs and however strong the will to right them, the problems of judicial governance remain problems still. The Court was spared in this field the old self-questioning about whether the challenged state policy was actually justifiable—were the rights of employers to untrammeled economic freedom really superior to the rights of scrubwomen to a living wage? No such baffling calculus need be conducted here, for the side of justice seemed to the Court unarguably manifest. But another question, the sheer issue of judicial power, was not to be similarly bypassed. The authority of the Court is supported (in theory at least) by the force of the national government, and especially the President. But if such support is not accorded, the judiciary's only remaining mainstay is its own prestige. The nation's respect for the judiciary has been great enough, as we have seen, so that the Court can affect policy in marginal ways. It has not usually been so great that the Court can bank on it against a clear-cut and deeply felt political impulse of the majority of the people. In assailing the problem of Negro rights, the Court challenged a significant segment, not a majority, of the nation. But the strain on judicial capacities was not, as it turned out, to be taken lightly.

The modern chapter of the narrative begins in 1938 with *Missouri* v. *Canada*. It will be remembered that the nineteenth-century Court had diminished the possible effect of the Fourteenth Amendment by denying that Congress could reach private persons under the enforcement clause, and by upholding state-required segregation of races (*Civil Rights Cases*, 1883, and *Plessy* v. *Ferguson*, 1896). The first of these doctrines was fairly well supported by the language of the Amendment: "no *State* . . . shall deny to any person . . . the equal protection of the laws." This means, or has meant to the Court, that the Amendment has no bearing on private discriminatory behavior and that Congress' "power to enforce . . . the provisions of this article" extends only to states and to state officials acting under state law. This confining interpretation is not entirely inevitable; Justice Harlan suggested a plausible contrary gloss in his *Civil Rights Cases* dissent. But the Court has never been disposed to follow these suggestions, perhaps feeling that the majority doctrine, whether right or wrong to begin with, was now unshakably established in the constitutional tradition. There seemed then little room for maneuver on this point; private persons could discriminate at will if their own states would tolerate it.

Moreover, as has been remarked earlier, even the states themselves were not seriously embarrassed by the Amendment for some time after *Plessy*'s announcement of the doctrine that the races could be legally separated so long as facilities were equal. The facilities did not have to be *very* equal to pass the Court's mild inspection. However, the "separate but equal" doctrine, even with its dubious acceptance of segregation as a principle, did contain a restrictive potential, in case a libertarian-minded Court should be inclined to turn it into a reality by insisting on true equality.

In the *Missouri* case that note was finally sounded loud and clear. In accordance with the casual standards acceptable in the past, Missouri had never bothered to establish a Negro law school, although it did maintain one limited to whites. Now a Negro student, duly qualified except for his color, sought entrance to this University of Missouri law school and was of course denied. The state argued that there were too few Negro applicants to warrant the setting-up of a special school; and that, pending the day when the number of such applicants would be substantial, Missouri had done its constitutional duty by offering to pay this Negro's tuition at a university in another state. But these evasions, though once serviceable enough, did not impress a Court now coming alive to the problem of civil rights on many fronts. It was held that the right to equality does not "depend upon the number of persons who may be discriminated against," that the discrimination was not excused by its supposititiously "temporary character," and that Missouri could not pass on to some other state its own obligation to provide equality. In short, equal means equal.

The *Missouri* decision signalized a new judicial mood toward Negro rights. It was followed in the next twenty years by the development of an elaborate jurisprudence of equality extending into a large variety of fields. For example, the Court applied the hoary *Cooley* rule to forbid segregation on interstate transportation, this being a subject that required a uniform national rule; and the Interstate Commerce Act was also construed to outlaw segregation. Attempts to discriminate on racial grounds in the real estate field were seriously undermined by the judicial decision that "restrictive covenants" (agreements that a buyer will not resell to Negroes, Jews, etc.) cannot be enforced in state courts, since such enforcement would be "state action" forbidden by the Fourteenth Amendment. Even the enforcement clause of that Amendment was to some extent revitalized by a holding that a state officer who used the power of his office to encroach on an individual's constitutional rights could be punished by federal law (*Screws* v. *United States,* 1945). The Court still adhered to the "state action" limit on the Amendment's range, but it was evidently prepared to interpret that interpretation as generously as reason would allow.

These were important developments; and there were others. But there were two kinds of race discrimination that mattered more than any of the rest: denial of the voting right and denial of adequate education. Inequality in these fields not only deprived the Negro of his present rights, but impaired his chance to improve his lot in the future. And therefore the Court moved in these fields with special determination.

The constitutional problem of voting rights was complicated. The Fifteenth Amendment forbids the states to abridge the right to vote on account of race or color. A state law directly denying Negroes the right would be overthrown as a matter of course, and in 1915 the Court had invalidated a so-called "grandfather clause" which required literacy tests of those who were *not* descendants of those who could vote in 1867. But two difficulties arose. For one thing, the primary was of course the only election that mattered in the one-party South, yet primaries had not been known by the Constitution's framers, and in 1920 the Court had seemed to say that they were, therefore, not elections in the meaning of the Constitution. For another thing, although the state was prohibited by the equal protection clause of the Fourteenth Amendment from excluding Negroes from primaries by law, the Democratic party (a "private" group and therefore untouched by the Amendment) could accomplish the same result by denying them party membership. This indirect abridgment of the voting right was allowed by the Court in a 1935 decision, and the White Primary seemed securely entrenched against Court interference (*Grovey v. Townsend*).

But the tide of civil rights sentiment in the country and on the bench could not be checked long by such sophistries. A constitution, intended as Story said to endure for ages, cannot be confined by static definitions that ignore changing realities. In 1941, the Court recognized this, upholding Congress' right to prevent fraud in a primary election for congressional representatives, and conceding that primaries are elections in the constitutional sense. Then in 1944 the White Primary question once more reached the Court (*Smith v. Allwright*). Texas had barred Negroes from participation in the Democratic primary by the simple expedient of denying them party membership. Indeed the membership resolution here drawn in question was the same one upheld in 1935. Now, however, the Court was in a different mood, and the recognition that primaries were elections had made the *Grovey* doctrine seem all the more anomalous. The judges therefore held that the action of the party was constitutionally forbidden, because the association between state and party stamped the party's doings as state action:

> If the state requires a certain election procedure, prescribes a general election ballot made up of party nominees so chosen and limits the choice of the electorate in general elections for state offices, practically speaking, to those whose names appear on such a ballot, it endorses, adopts and enforces the discrimination against Negroes, practiced by a party entrusted by Texas law with the determination of the qualifications of participants in the primary. This is state action within the meaning of the Fifteenth Amendment.

In other words, the mere fact that the state makes use of the primary results brings the primary procedures within the scope of the Constitution. In the face of this reasoning it became impossible to devise a White Primary arrangement that would not be technically unconstitutional, and the Court made it clear in subsequent decisions that the Fifteenth Amendment "nullifies sophisticated as well as simple-minded modes of discrimination." To be sure, the Court alone could not insure Negroes access to the ballot box; discriminatory administrative practices and the tactics of terror are not always within judicial reach. But the Court had done its part to preserve the idea that the United States is a constitutional democracy.

While these decisions in themselves did not solve the problem of racial disfranchisement, they helped stimulate a movement in that direction, and Negro voting substantially increased in southern states after *Smith* v. *Allwright*. The white Southern reaction was far from joyful of course, but neither was it in general militantly antagonistic to the Court. The truth is that the new doctrine was hard to criticize without challenging the Constitution itself, and the habit of venerating that document was strong. The Constitution does after all enjoin equality in the election process; and no person could rationally deny that the White Primary abridged voting equality. The Constitution and reason were on the judges' side, and these were potent allies.

A similar point can be made concerning *Missouri* v. *Canada* and the question of educational segregation. Not even Justice McReynolds, who dissented in the *Missouri* case, could contend that the state was granting the colored applicant equality of treatment. The best he could offer was his argument that the state had made a "fair effort" to do so. The majority could serenely answer that the Constitution required not efforts but results.

This continued for some time to be the Court's answer. The equality requirement was progressively tightened notch after notch, though segregation itself was not yet queried. In 1950, it was held that Texas had violated the equal protection clause when it denied a Negro entrance to the University of Texas, even though a separate law school for Negroes had been established. The separate school, said the Court unanimously, was not equal to the University of Texas "in those qualities which are incapable of objective measurement but which make for greatness in a law school." By logical extension this opinion certainly condemned all segregation in public professional schools and probably colleges as well. Indeed it can be argued that public school segregation of any kind was inferentially outlawed by the decision. But the Court itself did not draw the inference; it merely decided the instant case. And again, as in the White Primary Case, its position was rationally powerful. For equality *is* constitutionally commanded, and no fair observer could believe that the special Negro school matched the University of Texas.

However, the judges were continually being pressed, by liberal commentators, by counsel, and no doubt by their own consciences, to take the further step of declaring explicitly that segregation per se violated the equal protection clause. And in 1954, they did so, again speaking unanimously. The opinion of Chief Justice Warren was to be, as all members of the Court surely knew, a state paper of enormous importance; inevitably it would be exposed to the most searching criticism. Yet it does not seem in perspective to have been very well thought out. The Chief Justice was forced to admit that the historical intent of the Amendment's framers was inconclusive on the specific question of segregation. He was compelled to reject the contention that the *Plessy* doctrine was currently binding. But he might have made out a strong argument that the framers intended to create an elastic general standard, which could alter and grow with the times; and this argument would help to justify a Court interpretation based on conditions in 1954 rather than 1868. Further, the opinion might have claimed powerful support in precedent both before and after *Plessy*, and thereby undermined in advance the criticism that the decision "was sheer judicial legislation."

Instead the Chief Justice chose to go, almost without preliminary, to the question of whether segregation necessarily involved inequality in contemporary America and to rest his affirmative answer heavily on psychological and sociological literature. If one of the aims of a judicial opinion is to persuade the persuadable, this selection of citations was, to say the least, uninspired. The decision called for the argumentative talents of Marshall and Story rolled into one, and that ideal is rather a lot to hope for. But it is not unfair to wish that the opinion had come a little closer to it.

However, the impact of the opinion, whatever its deficiencies, was not to be mistaken. "Separate facilities are inherently unequal." For the time being the judges postponed any judgment about how the decision should be implemented, but a year later the lower federal courts were ordered to fashion their desegregation decrees in the light of the principles that guide the law of equity (that is, flexibility in the shaping of remedies and due consideration for the problem of adjusting public and private needs). Although this order was obviously designed to permit the states some leeway, the Court was undeviating in its insistence that the states concerned must make "a prompt and reasonable start" toward desegregation and that "the vitality of these constitutional principles cannot be allowed to yield simply because of disagreement with them."

The reaction of the white South to this judicial onslaught on its institutions was noisy and stubborn. Certain "border states," which had formerly maintained segregated school systems, did integrate, and others permitted the token admission of a few Negro students to schools that had once been racially unmixed. However, the Deep South made no moves to obey the judicial command, and in some districts there can be no doubt that the Desegregation decision hardened resistance to integration proposals. The moral support of the President, which might have helped to muster obedience, was accorded too grudgingly and tardily to do much good. The situation settled down into a quasi-stalemate in which the Court steadily reiterated its doctrine as specific cases arose, and the South passionately vowed that it would never yield. The decision had done much good and no doubt some harm. Whether it would ultimately achieve the moral end it contemplated was a question locked, in Justice Story's words, "in the inscrutable purposes of Providence."

The final effect on the judiciary of the decision's backlash is also a matter for conjecture. For the southern foes of the Desegregation doctrine were not content with passive resistance; they mounted a counterattack against the Court. At first the attack was largely rhetorical: the Calhounian slogan of "interposition" was heard in the land once more, with states earnestly proclaiming their sovereignty and impeaching the nation's, as if *Cohens* v. *Virginia* had never been decided and the Civil War never fought. This kind of thing was no cause for perturbation except among those who were already perturbed.

But then, ironically, the Court itself provided an element that made the situation more serious. In 1956 and 1957 it handed down a group of decisions hopefully calculated to moderate the venom of certain "antisubversive" measures. These judicial pronouncements have been touched on earlier in this chapter and their general drift described. They manifestly were not direct challenges of government's power to deal with subversion. The emphasis was on statutory interpretation and procedural caveats throughout. But they furnished the necessary ingredient for an alliance between Southern segregationists and Northerners fearful of domestic subversion and made it possible to shift the attack on the Court from the realm of mere polemics to the much more dangerous arena of Congress. The judgments in the subversive field were catechized as denying the nation the right of self-preservation and Congress the right to function as a co-ordinate branch of government; and the fact that these charges were wildly incongruous with the actual decisions was conveniently ignored. Southerners who frankly favored segregation and Northerners who welcomed a pretext to join them, eagerly supported proposals to "curb" the Court by modifying its appellate jurisdiction.

If the Courts of John Marshall and Morrison R. Waite could have been on hand to observe this development and the twenty-odd years of constitutional history that preceded it, they might well have experienced the shock of recognition. They, too, had been faced by the problem of enforcing a value system that was still a subject of popular controversy. Like the judges of the modern era, they had taken up constitutional clauses of vague and seemingly limited content and had shaped them into the tools of a new jurisprudence. They, too, had struggled to evolve a role for the Court that was adequate to the tasks it faced, yet not beyond its capacities. They, too, had seen the Court assailed and defended for its acts and its failures to act. They, too, were often reminded, as the modern Court has been, that the Constitution's meaning is never quite settled, that the judicial tasks can never be quite done, that the ordeal of self-appraisal is never quite over, and that the challenges to the Court's authority can never quite be stilled. These are the prices that they paid—and the modern judges pay—for maintaining a tribunal that is a vital factor in the American political system.

EIGHT

CIVIL LIBERTIES, CIVIL RIGHTS, AND THE SUPREME COURT

As ROBERT McCLOSKEY finished his book in 1958, he could reasonably believe that the Court, with some dramatic exceptions such as the Steel Seizure and School Segregation Cases, had indeed learned the lesson he believed taught by history: The Court maximized its impact on the actualities of American life by limiting itself to relatively modest efforts to affect for the better (according to the Court's scheme of values) the course that history was in fact already taking. Should, however, the Court instead engage in sweeping programmatic pronouncements designed to fend off powerful political currents and to keep them tightly channeled within the Court's conception of a proper course, it would only make trouble for itself. At best, the Court would emulate King Canute, who pathetically commanded the tides to come at his convenience. At worst, the breaking of judicially constructed levees would lead to a floodtide of popular discontent over the Court's clumsy attempts to thwart popular will, which might well lead in turn to attacks on the Court's role as the instantiation of constitutionalism and of the rule of law themselves. And McCloskey, for all of his criticism of the Court's past performance, left no doubt that he viewed the Court as a vital actor in the epic of constitutionalism.

The two cases mentioned, however dramatic, could be shoehorned with only some distortion to fit his thesis: The Steel Seizure Case was in many ways a "one time only" decision; it struck down the action of a notably unpopular President and had no immediate doctrinal aftereffects. No one other than President Truman was required to do anything as a result of *Youngstown Steel,* and he in fact complied immediately with the decision. As for *Brown,* the Court in 1955 announced that "all deliberate speed" would be its operative decision rule and that federal district judges, who, after all, owed their appointments to close association with the senators from their home states—and were thus unlikely to be far in advance of the dominant political culture—would be the agents of enforcement. As shall be seen in the next chapter, astonishingly little change of behavior took place in the states of the old Confederacy between 1954 and 1960, and the Court gave little sign of genuinely trying to transform this situation.

By 1965, however, McCloskey would write that "the Court of the past dozen years has developed judicial activism to a degree that at least matches the record of the Old Court of the 1920's and 1930's and that certainly exceeds the record of any other Court in our constitutional history." More particularly, he described the four-year period between 1961 and 1965 "as one of the most creative and daring periods in constitutional history," during which "the remarkable extent of the Warren Court's will to govern bec[ame] fully manifest." Whatever lessons of history it was purporting to follow were surely those not elaborated in the earlier part of this book, and McCloskey concluded his 1965 article by wondering if the American people genuinely had "a so-far unsatiated appetite for government by judiciary." It is not so much that the Supreme Court had taken on a dramatically new role—its primary concern at this period continued to be civil liberties and civil rights—as that it displayed a willingness to confront a host of important issues head-on and become, in some important ways, a primary constructor of the domestic policy agenda.

It is worth mentioning that the unfortunate proclivity to identify Courts by reference to their Chief Justices not only overestimates the importance of many of these denizens, but also, and more importantly, underestimates the importance of their colleagues. Even the redoubtable John Marshall was only the first among equals, and no Chief Justice since Marshall has enjoyed anything close to his measure of domination over the Court. Earl Warren's replacement of Fred Vinson clearly made *some* difference to the Court prior to 1960, but it would not be an easy matter to specify it. Some believe that Warren's personal skills helped to account for the crucial achievement of unanimity in the *Brown* decision; others point to his providing the fifth vote in some liberal civil liberties decisions. But, as McCloskey pointed out, the Court had scarcely struck out in systematically bold new courses by the end of the 1950's. No one would have viewed the Court circa 1960 as a mere tabbycat, but no one either would have confused it with a tiger.

What happened? One might point to changes of membership: By

1962 Byron White and Arthur Goldberg had been appointed by President Kennedy to replace Charles Whittaker, a nonentity, and Felix Frankfurter, the titan of judicial restraint. Both were considerably more liberal than their predecessors. But, it should be said, Eisenhower's appointees, save for Whittaker, had not been particularly conservative. Potter Stewart and John Marshall Harlan (the grandson of the author of the immortal dissents in the *Civil Rights Cases* and *Plessy* v. *Ferguson*) were both relatively moderate—indeed, from the perspective of the post-Reagan Republican Party, extremely liberal—Republicans. The last of Ike's picks, William J. Brennan, was a New Jersey Democrat appointed by Eisenhower during the 1956 election campaign in an effort to appeal to Northeastern Catholics, and he proved to be the anchor for the next 30 years of the liberal coalition within the Court. The Court between 1958 and, say, 1981 might well be denominated "the Brennan Court" in recognition of his impact.

But the Court, of course, is embedded within a wider political context, and one can scarcely ignore the fact of Kennedy's election itself. To the astonishment of many, the United States had been willing to elect a 42-year-old Roman Catholic from Massachusetts, who had run on the theme that the United States must be ready to "move" toward bold new courses. Not the least important moment of the campaign—some commentators at the time ascribed his extraordinarily narrow election to it— was a telephone call to the family of Martin Luther King, Jr., the leader of the Southern civil rights movement, expressing Kennedy's concern over King's having been arrested and jailed by Georgia authorities for participating in a civil rights demonstration. The country, however tenuously, seemed to endorse a liberal resurgence after the perceived quiescence of the 1950's, and the Supreme Court seemingly enlisted to do its part.

THE CIVIL RIGHTS MOVEMENT AND THE CONSTITUTION

The civil rights movement of which King was one of the acknowledged leaders furnished many occasions for the Court to decide what role it wished to play in the struggle for racial justice. One form the movement took, for example, was "sitting-in" at restaurants that refused to serve African-Americans. This led, not surprisingly, to the arrest of many persons, both African-American and their white allies, for violating the property rights of the restaurant owners. Would the Court uphold such prosecutions? Or would it interpret the Fourteenth Amendment to ban them because the property owners were so clearly trying to use the state to reinforce their own racial discrimination? In a series of decisions from

1961 to 1964, the Court at once reversed on a variety of strained technicalities the convictions of those who had been arrested while resolutely avoiding deciding the basic underlying issue.

Congress, by passing the Civil Rights Act of 1964 that outlawed racial discrimination in such public accommodations as restaurants, relieved the Court of having to decide this most delicate issue of constitutional law—and to run the risk of yet another spate of headlines throughout the South about overruling an eighty-year-old precedent like *The Civil Rights Cases*. To be sure, many Southerners, led by Senator Ervin of North Carolina, argued that Congress lacked the power to pass the Civil Rights Act, that it was not the genuine "regulation of commerce" that its supporters described it as being. When the Act came before the Court in 1964, in *Katzenbach* v. *McClung*, it was unanimously upheld as well within the post-1937 understanding of Congress's expanded power under the Commerce Clause.

Perhaps the most significant doctrinal development that can be traced to the civil rights movement was *New York Times* v. *Sullivan* (1963), in which the Court had to consider the constitutionality of a $500,000 damage award assessed by an Alabama jury against the *New York Times* for its having published an advertisement that had concededly contained some errors about the conduct of the Montgomery Police Commissioner in regard to the local civil rights movement. Like many other plaintiffs in libel actions, Sullivan claimed that relatively minor errors in the reporting of their actions harmed his reputation, and many states allowed juries to find newspapers liable for damage on proof of error alone. Not even "negligence" needed to be demonstrated. Truth was always a defense, but the problem was that often errors had in fact been published.

The Court unanimously reversed the Alabama jury. Justice Brennan wrote an opinion for the majority that envisioned the First Amendment as providing breathing space for "open and robust" public debate, and this in turn required the legal toleration of error, especially in regard to "public officials." Indeed, Brennan analogized the situation to old attempts to punish sedition—criticism of governmental officials—and he declared that the First Amendment simply prohibited any punishment for seditious speech. Thus, according to the majority, a newspaper could be liable for misstatements involving public officials only if they were published "knowingly" or in "reckless disregard" of the possibility of their being false. Otherwise, the newspaper would be free from liability. Justices Black and Douglas would have gone further and freed media from liability under any and all conditions, including the knowing publication of harmful lies. In subsequent cases, the Court extended the "*New York Times* rule" to "public figures," whether or not officials of government.

It is, of course, possible that the Court would have gone down this path had the *New York Times* been found liable by a New York jury after falsely reporting that the local parking commissioner had engaged in financial misdealing. But it seems impossible to understand *New York Times* without acknowledging its origin within the context of the civil rights movement, surely the most important domestic social struggle since at least the great union organizing drives of the 1930's. The particular case considered in *Sullivan* was simply the tip of an iceberg; at the time the Supreme Court heard it, there were, throughout the South, libel claims totalling more than $300 million brought by white Southerners against various largely Northern media. Local juries, almost invariably all white, seemed more than happy to send a message to the interloping media that they entered the Southern states at their peril, with bankruptcy a possible result of any misstep. It was absolutely clear that the media needed protection, and the Court provided it, to the great applause of liberals in general and newspapers in particular. The newspapers, of course, were the big winners from the case. One can say with confidence that few decisions ever received as much editorial support as did *New York Times*. In later decades, though, newspapers would complain that the *New York Times* test still allowed too much extremely expensive litigation in contrast to the approach desired by Justices Black and Douglas, which would have eliminated the libel action entirely. Needless to say, victims of media misrepresentation criticized the Court for giving too much freedom to the media to be careless in checking facts. Both sides are correct.

THE SUPREME COURT AND FREEDOM OF SPEECH

New York Times was only one among many cases of the 1960's testing the resolve of the Court to protect unpopular dissenters from conventional norms. As the typical defendant shifted from a member of the Communist Party—the norm during the late 1940's and the 1950's—to a civil rights activist, whether African-American or white, the Court indeed was far more willing to protect what local authorities deemed "subversive" speech. Indeed, by 1969, in *Brandenburg v. Ohio,* a case involving, ironically enough, a member of the Ku Klux Klan, the Court delivered the most speech-protective opinion in American history. It held that a speaker could be punished only if (a) he was inciting an audience to commit an unlawful act *and* (b) there was in fact an "imminent likelihood" that the act would be committed by the affected audience. This test has in fact survived the significant changes of membership throughout the 1970's and the 1980's, and in the quarter century since *Brandenburg* there were no prosecutions similar in character to the *Debs* and *Dennis* cases that blighted earlier periods of American history.

The Court was also willing, by and large, to turn "freedom of speech" into a more general "freedom of expression." For example, it protected the wearing of a black armband by a student who wished to protest the Vietnam War. Even more dramatic, perhaps, was its 1971 decision, *Cohen* v. *California,* that protected Paul Cohen's wearing a jacket containing the words "Fuck the Draft" on its back in a courtroom. Ironically enough, Justice Black dissented in both cases, on the basis that neither genuinely involved "speech." The Court did not, however, extend its protection to David O'Brien's burning his draft card in protest of the Vietnam War; it upheld a conviction under a statute passed by an angry Congress that wished to suppress draft-card burning as a form of protest.

Later Courts, even when dominated by political conservatives, would continue to be relatively protective of unpopular "expression" in general. Thus the Court in 1989 and 1990 struck down Texas and federal laws, respectively, that in effect barred the burning of an American flag as a form of protest. Although the liberal Justice Brennan wrote the decisions in both cases, he was joined by the arch-conservative Justice Scalia, who adopted Justice Black's view that the First Amendment really did mean, with almost no exceptions, that "no law" could be passed that directly abridged speech. Scalia, unlike Black, was quite willing to agree that speech included almost any "expression" of ideas. Similarly, Scalia wrote a majority opinion in a 1992 case, *R.A.V.* v. *St. Paul,* that involved the punishment, under an "offensive conduct" ordinance, of someone who burned a cross across the street from the home of an African-American in St. Paul, Minnesota. The Court reversed. According to Scalia, St. Paul was simply without the power to pick and choose among forms of expression on the basis of their "offensiveness" to the population.

The Court also proved far more willing to protect a variety of "nonpolitical" speech that had traditionally been given far less protection than "political" speech directed at public issues. For example, although the Court had in 1957 held that "obscene" speech was totally unprotected by the First Amendment, it also stated that sex was not synonymous with obscenity, thus undermining the basis of existing obscenity law. A number of decisions in the 1960's offered protection to literature and movies deemed pornographic by authorities if the material in question, however sexually explicit, had at least some "redeeming social value." Later decisions in the 1970's would offer communities more leeway in regulating pornography, but, relative to the legal standards existing prior to the Warren-Brennan years, communities remained vastly more constrained in regulating pornography than they had been. For better or worse, sexually explicit material was far more available than had ever been the case before in American history. One can obviously not give too much credit (or blame) to the Supreme Court; the United States as a whole was undergoing what many described as a "sexual revolution," and the Court could scarcely have stopped it even had it wanted to. Nonetheless, at key moments of the "revolution" during the 1960's, the Court appeared to ally itself with the partisans of new sexual freedom against the denizens of more traditionally repressive culture.

Similar latitude was revealed by the Court in another area of traditionally regulated speech, that dealing with advertising. In 1941, the Court almost casually dismissed the claim that "commercial speech" was protected by the First Amendment. By 1976, however, it would find such speech protected, even if somewhat less so than core "political speech." That is, whereas both the *Brandenburg* and *New York Times* tests allowed regulating politically related speech only in extreme circumstances, the state could prohibit false advertising entirely and could subject even accurate advertisements to significant regulation. But "unreasonable" regulations were now regularly struck down by the Court. As a consequence, for the first time in American history major businesses became warm partisans of the First Amendment; this was no small advantage inasmuch as many of the decisions of the post-1937 Court in general, and the Warren-Brennan Court in particular, had cost it the support of its traditional allies within the economic elite.

By the 1970's the major focus of "free speech" litigation had shifted away from the unpopular dissenters who had been the subjects of classic earlier cases. Three issues now predominated: the financing of political campaigns; the regulation of non-print media; and access to public property to convey one's views.

In 1972 Congress passed a number of laws limiting the amounts that could be contributed to, or spent by, political campaigns. In addition, presidential campaigns would, for the first time in American history, be eligible for public financing. The Court considered these new regulations in *Buckley* v. *Valeo* (1976) and made absolute hash of the legislation. A majority of Justices held first that spending money on speech is the constitutional equivalent of speech itself and, therefore, subject to the constraints of the First Amendment. Shifting majorities of Justices, who could not agree on a single majority opinion, treated the different aspects of the 1972 legislation quite differently. Thus the contribution limits were upheld, while the spending limits were struck down. Finally, it upheld a public-financing scheme for presidential elections that patently discriminated in favor of the established Democratic and Republican parties (by paying them in advance of the elections) and against third parties (who had to gain at least 5 percent of the national vote before being compensated for any of their expenditures). One consequence of the Court's decision was that millionaires, constitutionally protected in spending as much as they wanted on their own campaigns, were given significant advantages over less wealthy opponents, who could ask for only limited contributions from their supporters. And, of course, the existing two parties were provided significant advantages against possible third-party competition, unless, of course, the third party was headed by someone like the Texas billionaire Ross Perot.

Though one should be wary of overestimating the influence of any given Supreme Court decision, including *Buckley,* it is hard, nonetheless, to avoid blaming the decision, which eventuated in a scheme of electoral-finance law that never received the formal support of a single legislator, for the increasing prominence of many unusually wealthy candidates who were able to swamp less affluent opponents. The issue of the role of money in politics is a basic issue of democratic politics, and it is impossible to view the Court as having contributed to any kind of cogent resolution of the problem in *Buckley* or, indeed, a variety of subsequent decisions—sometimes upholding regulations, sometimes striking them down—involving election regulation.

As *New York Times* itself revealed, the print media were a special object of solicitude of the Court. But what about the increasingly important non-print media, including radio and television? The Federal Communications Act of 1934, one of the basic New Deal regulatory measures, authorized the Federal Communications to regulate the electronic media—which at that time, of course, consisted only of radio—in "the public interest." This led fairly rapidly to FCC requirements of "fairness" in programming, including a "right to reply" by persons who had been attacked in a program. Moreover, stations were required to provide "equal time" to all other candidates for a political office if they gave any time (excluding news coverage), to one of the candidates.

The first major test of such requirements took place only in 1969, *Red Lion Broadcasting Co. v. FCC,* which challenged the order by the federal agency that a religiously conservative radio station offer a "right to reply" to a secular liberal who had been accused of "communist affiliations." A unanimous Court (though the libertarian Justice Douglas did not participate in the decision), which implicitly recognized the illegitimacy of any such regulation if applied to newspapers, nevertheless upheld the FCC. (Indeed, in the 1974 *Tornillo* case, the Court unanimously struck down a Florida "right-to-reply" law that applied to newspapers.) The Court focused on the alleged "scarcity" of places on the electromagnetic spectrum used by radio and television stations. Although the Court has been justifiably subjected to withering criticism—there are, in most cities, far more radio and television outlets than there are newspapers—it has never repudiated *Red Lion;* indeed, only Justices Douglas and Stewart questioned it at all.

During the Reagan-Bush era, the FCC itself rejected *Red Lion's* view of its own powers and declared that "fairness" and "right-to-reply" rules violated the First Amendment. The Clinton Administration, though, has indicated its desire to reinstate some of these regulations, and the Court will undoubtedly have a chance to revisit the issue. Moreover, the so-called "cable-revolution" and "information highway," which include, among many other things, getting one's "newspaper" on a computer, has exploded completely any coherent distinction between "print" and "non-print" media. Which way the Court will go in resolving the issues attached to regulation of these new media is anybody's guess.

The final issue dominating the contemporary free-speech docket of the Court involves the state's power "indirectly" to regulate speech through exertion of its power as a property owner. Several cases in the 1960's, during the heyday of the civil rights movement, had protected civil rights demonstrations occurring even in such venues as public libraries. Building on decisions going back to 1939, the Court seemed to be on the verge of placing a significant burden of proof on the state to demonstrate strong reasons justifying prohibitory regulation of speech on public property. Otherwise, the Court seemed to suggest, citizens were to be entitled to access to the property. Indeed, in the 1968 *Logan Valley* case involving the prosecution for trespass of union leafletters within a privately owned shopping mall, the Court described the malls as performing a basically "public" function and thus controlled by the First Amendment, which in turn protected the leafletters. (Justice Black wrote the dissent, describing the decision as an assault on the rights of private property.)

Once again, however, the Court backtracked. It increasingly accepted governmental arguments that the fact that the "public" owned property did not amount to a right of any member of the public to use it as a "public forum" for unregulated speech. The Court distinguished between "traditional" public forums, such as public parks and streets, and other forums such as post offices, airline terminals, military bases, and the like. The state was given far more latitude in regard to the latter than the former. Similarly, the Court by 1972 limited, and by 1976 flatly overruled, the shopping center case, and it has subsequently offered no succor to anyone seeking access to private property (though it did uphold a California decision that granted such access under the *state* constitution against the claim of a shopping mall owner that it violated his constitutionally protected property rights). Some critics charged that the meaning of the Court's decisions between 1970 and 1990 was that it was willing to protect more and more speech in fewer and fewer places.

THE COURT CONFRONTS THE CRIMINAL JUSTICE SYSTEM

Many of these cases illustrate, among other things, the extent to which the Warren-Brennan Court was a *nationalist* body, exhibiting relatively little respect for states' own decisions as to how to arrange their affairs. To be sure, much of this disdain for "states-rights" arguments was triggered by the traditional use of such arguments as a justification for racial oppression or the harassment of those with unpopular views about politics or culture. But Felix Frankfurter, among others, had insisted, even as he endorsed the constitutional power of Congress to pass sweeping legislation deemed necessary in the national interest, that the Court respect the values of localism and diversity that federalism at its best could be said to protect. The Court would, during the 1960's, exhibit little respect for such points of view. Indeed, the Warren-Brennan Court was probably the most truly nationalist Court in American history, save, perhaps, for the Marshall Court in its first two decades.

Dramatic illustrations of the actively nationalist Court are provided by its decisions involving the procedures used by states in enforcing their criminal law. States were, as never before, put under a sharp microscope in regard to their practices of catching and convicting alleged criminals. Between 1953 and 1960, the "Warren Court" had decided fifty-five cases testing these practices. It had upheld the states twenty times, ruling against them thirty-five times, which indicates that even then, as Bob Dylan put it, "the times, they were a'changin.'" After all, in the five years before Earl Warren's arrival, the Court had decided only twelve of thirty-three claims against the state. But in the five years following 1960, the states would be successful only about 15 percent of the time, eleven times out of seventy-five cases. And far more important than the sheer numbers was the Court's abandonment of its practice of fact-bound case-by-case scrutiny in favor of the enunciation of sharply defined rules designed to transform the practices of police departments and courts nationwide.

The principal vehicle of change was the "selective incorporation" of most of the criminal-procedure provisions of the Bill of Rights into the Fourteenth Amendment as a limit on the states. Hugo Black had lost the great battle of 1947 in the *Adamson* case, where he made the case for "full incorporation," but he won the more general war. In the spring of 1961, for example, came *Mapp* v. *Ohio,* in which the majority held that states that had seized evidence in violation of the Fourth Amendment (which had been incorporated against them in 1949) would no longer be allowed to offer that evidence in trials against the defendants, as allowed by the 1949 decision. This "exclusionary rule," which had operated against the federal government since 1914, dramatically changed the formal rules of the criminal-law game in most of the states (though empirically oriented analysts raised questions about the actual extent to which the decision changed police practices). Two years later, in *Gideon* v. *Wainwright* (discussed at greater length in the next chapter), the Court ruled unanimously that due process required that indigent criminal defendants be supplied counsel by the state. No conviction resulting in a jail sentence could stand if the indigent was not represented by counsel. Similarly, the Fifth Amendment's protection against compulsory self-incrimination was applied to the states in *Malloy* v. *Hogan,* and prosecutors were later disallowed from even commenting to the jury about the fact that defendants had not testified in their own defense.

Undoubtedly the most controversial decision was *Miranda* v. *Arizona* (1966), in which Chief Justice Warren, for a five-Justice majority, held that anyone arrested had a right to be told that he had a right to counsel and that he had a right to remain silent and, therefore, a right as well to refuse to answer any questions asked him by the police. A distinctive feature of *Miranda* was the Court's legislature-like enunciation of a specific set of "*Miranda* warnings" that the police could literally copy on a card and read off to suspects. The case served as a rallying point for conservatives who argued both that the Court was ignoring the legitimate needs of the police and that it had forgotten the difference between itself and a legislature.

The Warren Court undoubtedly read the Constitution more generously than did prior Courts in terms of the formal legal rights offered
criminal defendants. In other ways, though, the Warren Court was
scarcely generous to defendants. It refused, for example, to examine the
extent to which continued reliance on monetary bail systems meant in
fact that those without significant economic resources would be kept in
jail while wealthier defendants could purchase their freedom at least before trial and conviction. And several decisions in the late 1960's upheld
the practice of "plea bargaining," which in effect allows the state to encourage (its detractors would say "force") criminal defendants to waive
many of their constitutional rights in return for a lesser sentence than
might be received after full trial and enjoyment of one's formal rights. The
United States is unique among nations in its reliance on plea bargaining
to dispose of criminal cases; more than 90 percent of all cases are settled
through plea bargains. Not surprisingly, it is those who are most vulnerable to pressure who must in fact accept the state's offers.

Still, the perception of the Warren Court was that it was unduly solicitous to the rights of criminal defendants, and the specific beneficiaries of
such decisions—the actual defendants whose convictions were reversed—
scarcely had significant political clout that would be useful to the Court
in defending it against its detractors. Indeed, many future presidential
campaigns would be run against this aspect of the Warren Court legacy;
although conservative Republicans were most eager to attack the Court,
liberal Democrats were certainly not eager to offer public defenses of its
criminal-justice legacy. It can occasion little surprise, then, that later
Courts certainly backtracked in regard to legal rights accorded criminal
defendants.

None of the decisions mentioned above was flatly overruled, however.
Instead, later Courts "distinguished" the facts of newer cases or, for example, allowed warrantless searches that would ordinarily be disallowed
by the exclusionary rule if the police in "good faith" believed that they
were legal. The Reagan-Bush Supreme Court of the 1980's, led by Chief
Justice William Rehnquist, also exhibited sometimes extraordinary activism in cutting down the practical ability of those convicted of criminal
offenses to complain before federal courts that they had been deprived of
their federal constitutional rights in trials that occurred in state courts.
Rehnquist could counter, however, that the earlier Court had itself exhibited equal activism in welcoming defendants to federal courts.

But even the far more conservative Court of the 1980's was willing,
on occasion, to forge relatively new paths. Thus it held, in 1986, that the

ages-old practice of "peremptory challenges," by which prosecutors were allowed to keep off a jury a selected number of persons without giving any reason at all, was subject to challenge at least where prosecutors used this power to get rid of all potential minority-group jurors in trials involving defendants of the given group. Within five years, the principle would be extended to defense attorneys as well as prosecutors (and, indeed, to *civil* as well as criminal trials), and it was no longer necessary that the jurors struck be the same race as the defendant. In 1994 the Court applied the same principle to gender, and it will undoubtedly have to ask whether lawyers will be allowed to eliminate potential jurors because of their religious affiliations, national origin, and other attributes that lawyers commonly use in selecting juries.

During the 1960's, the Court also began to scrutinize the imposition of the death penalty; by 1972 five Justices were willing, in *Furman* v. *Georgia,* to declare the procedures by which it was imposed unconstitutional (and Justice Brennan and Marshall, in particular, denied that *any, procedure could legitimize the penalty). Many pronounced the death penalty in America to be at an end, thanks to the leadership of the Court. If, however, the Court believed that it was accurately reading the pulse of the public—as Justice Marshall claimed to be doing when he argued that capital punishment violated the norms of contemporary American culture—it was disastrously wrong. Many states passed new death penalty laws, and by 1976 the Court began to pull back significantly from its abolitionist posture. Still, a majority in *Coker* v. *Georgia* (1977) ruled that the death penalty for anything less than murder—including, most importantly, capital punishment for rape—was unconstitutional.

With subsequent changes of membership, by the mid-1980's, a firm majority of justices supported the constitutionality of the death penalty; indeed, they seemed positively disdainful of those who continued to register constitutional opposition to its infliction. The Court upheld its imposition on minors and the mentally retarded. And it found irrelevant, in *McCloskey* v. *Kemp* (1987), the fact that Georgia juries were far more likely to impose capital punishment on black murderers of whites than on white murderers in general or black murderers of blacks. Interestingly enough, no state in the 1980's tried to test the new flexibility of the Court by reimposing the death penalty for anything other than murder. In this respect, at least, liberal abolitionists may have won a significant victory, even as they were otherwise routed.

EQUAL PROTECTION COMES INTO ITS OWN

Justice Holmes in 1927, with characteristic acerbity, described arguments based on the Equal Protection Clause of the Fourteenth Amendment as "the usual last resort of constitutional arguments," offered only (and almost invariably unsuccessfully) when nothing better was available. If equality means that like cases should be treated alike, then it seems logically entailed that unlike cases can legitimately be treated differently. Thus Holmes cautioned against being seduced by arguments that "introduc[e] a factitious equality without regard to practical differences that are best met by corresponding differences of treatment." Given that one of the central meanings of 1937 was the adoption of a Holmesian stance of judicial deference toward legislative decision making, it is surely no surprise that his disdain for the Equal Protection Clause was reflected in the Court's jurisprudence, at least where the treatment of racial minorities was not at issue. State legislatures were basically given *carte blanche* to classify as they wished.

Whether because of the pressure of the race-relations cases, including *Brown* v. *Board of Education*, or because of a more general cultural interest in egalitarianism, the Court in the 1960's would engage in the most systematic exploration in American history of the meaning of equality. It would move well beyond the racial dimension, which had, after all, been a steady part of the Court's docket ever since the addition of the Fourteenth Amendment, and confront issues that had not theretofore been accepted by the Justices as fit for judicial resolution.

Perhaps the most dramatic symbol of the Court's newfound willingness to confront—and to try to resolve from Washington—basic issues of American political life was its 1962 decision in *Baker* v. *Carr*. There a sharply split Court, in an opinion written by Justice Brennan, overruled several prior decisions, including one as recent as 1946, and declared that the issue of legislative districting was "justiciable." This meant that the Court would now assess the fairness of the electoral schemes undergirding representation in state legislatures by reference to the Equal Protection Clause of the Fourteenth Amendment. In the particular case, Tennessee had not redrawn political boundary lines for its state legislature since 1901; as a consequence, the urbanites in Memphis received far fewer representatives than an equal number of farmers spread out among several districts. Had earlier decisions been followed, the suit would simply have been dismissed as raising a "political question" inappropriate for judicial resolution. Now, instead, the Court ordered the Tennessee federal court in which suit had originally been filed to consider the merits of the claim.

Justice Frankfurter, in his last great opinion before a stroke forced him to leave the Court, denounced the majority not only for deviating from precedent, but also for taking the Court into a "political thicket" that could easily ensnarl it in partisan political conflicts and rob it of the legitimacy derived from public perception of a body above such conflicts. Frankfurter summarized the thought of a lifetime in declaring that "[i]n a democratic society like ours, relief must come through an aroused popular conscience that sears the conscience of the people's representatives" rather than through judicial mandate.

No one could doubt that *Baker* represented a bold departure for the Court. One should note, though, that the departure was warmly supported by the new administration of John F. Kennedy, elected in 1960, and his Solicitor General, Harvard law professor Archibald Cox. Almost by definition, one was unlikely to find enthusiastic majority support for a system of representation that entrenched minority rule. By no means, therefore, could the Court be accused of gratuitously seizing new power or standing steadfast against the wishes of newly empowered majorities, as had presumably been the case during the *Lochner* era.

Robert McCloskey, in a 1962 article in the *Harvard Law Review* on *Baker,* noted that it had received widescale applause from the public, but he cautioned the Court against moving too boldly in implementing its decision, which, after all, said only that the Court would address, rather than dismiss, issues raised by political districting. In particular, he expressed great fears that the Court's prestige would be significantly diminished as angry politicians and voters who opposed judicially mandated reapportionment would go on the attack. As political scientist John Roche put it, 'Power corrupts, and the prospect of losing power corrupts absolutely.'' The struggle about legislative districting was precisely about the ability of established political elites, usually rural, to maintain power, and there was no reason to believe that they would go gently into the political night of loss of power. Many other writers, however, saw Frankfurter's appeal to politicians' consciences or McCloskey's expression of prudential fears about the consequences of judicial assertion as representing an almost willful blindness to the reality of a political pathology that mocked the majoritarian underpinnings of the American political system.

Baker's limitation to the issue of justiciability allowed McCloskey to hope that the Court would confine its intervention into legislative districting to a relatively few, particularly egregious, incidents. Any such hopes (or fears) were dashed in *Reynolds* v. *Sims* (1964), when the Court, this time through Chief Justice Warren, almost blithely struck down the state legislative systems in most of the states insofar as they had adopted some form of "little federalism" that, as in the United States Senate, apportioned representatives by political subdivisions (usually counties) rather than by population. "Legislators represent people," wrote Warren, "not trees or acres. Legislators are elected by voters, not farms or cities or economic interests." The mandate, then, was for "one person-one vote," and the Court later extended this principle to almost all popularly-elected multimember decision-making bodies within states. And an earlier decision that same year had required strict equality of population in regard to congressional districts.

To a remarkable extent, however, little of the strong counterattack feared by McCloskey in fact took place. To be sure, the House of Representatives, whose members stood to face future political instability because of the necessity to redraw electoral districts, passed a bill that would have withdrawn jurisdiction over legislative apportionment from the judiciary. And some members of Congress promoted a constitutional amendment that would have had the same consequences. Liberals were, however, able to stave off such attacks on the Court, and "one person-one vote" quickly became accepted by the public as the new status quo.

One result of these decisions is that legislative districting has now become a permanent part of the Court's docket, particularly in the immediate years following the constitutionally required decennial census that reveals which among the states (and which regions within the states) have been the gainers or losers of population. Although the Court has remained almost rigidly devoted to a strict equipopulation standard in congressional districting, it has adopted a somewhat more relaxed attitude about districting in regard to state institutions.

Increasingly important on the Court's docket are cases involving gerrymandering, the drawing of electoral districts designed to promote desirable political outcomes, whether defined as the victory of a given political party or, quite commonly, the protection of incumbent politicians. Not until 1986 did the Court formally hold that gerrymandering was justiciable. Although gerrymandering usually evokes oddly shaped single-member districts, it can also include the adoption of "multi-member" districts that offer the majority of the district the opportunity to elect all of the district's representatives and, concomitantly, the opportunity to deprive the minority of the ability to elect any representatives sympathetic to their own views. The Court held in the 1970's that nothing in the Constitution forbids such multimember districts, even if breaking down the district into single-member entities would allow the minority to prevail in at least one of the new districts. The Court has, however, invalidated multimember districting motivated by the desire to limit the practical ability of a *racial* minority to elect a representative. That is, a Democratic or Republican legislature could do almost everything it could to reduce the likely electoral success of their partisan opponents, but it could not act to reduce the prospects of racial minorities. Indeed, under the Voting Rights Act of 1965 and subsequent amendments passed by Congress, state legislatures appeared to be under a duty to *enhance* the prospects of African-Americans and other victims of racial discrimination.

In *Shaw* v. *Reno* (1993), however, the Court called into question (but did not declare unconstitutional) the ability of states to take race into account when drawing electoral districts, even if the motivation was to assure the election of minority representatives. Not surprisingly, *Shaw* occasioned heated dissent from four of the justices, who found it almost perverse to hold that states might be barred from taking measures designed to increase the presence of minorities in legislatures or Congress. It remains to be seen whether *Shaw* announced a full-scale attack by a conservative-dominated Court on the use of racial criteria in districting (and much else) or simply a warning shot across the bow that states shouldn't believe that they can get away with just anything when drawing districts. (The Court had described the North Carolina district in *Shaw* as a writhing "snake" that extended sinuously approximately 250 miles in order to make sure that an African-American would be elected to Congress, as in fact occurred in the 1992 election.)

GENDER AND EQUAL PROTECTION

In 1948 the Court almost casually upheld a Michigan law that prohibited women other than bar owners' wives from tending bar. It clearly had no interest in seriously examining the legitimacy of gender classifications. States could, practically speaking, do as they wished.

Interestingly enough, there were no great cases involving women's rights during the 1960's. It was left to Earl Warren's successor, the considerably more conservative Warren Burger, to write a 1971 opinion in *Reed* v. *Reed* that ushered in the age of scrutinizing with some care legislation that classified on the basis of sex. Justice Brennan was able to gain three other allies in 1973 for the proposition that gender classifications should receive the "strict scrutiny" (described by Gerald Gunther as "fatal in fact" to the legislation being scrutinized) given racial classifications, but he could not get the key fifth vote. Finally, in *Craig v. Boren* (1976) the Court coalesced around an "intermediate" test, in which the state would have to show a "substantial" interest to justify gender classifications. In the case under consideration, it struck down an Oklahoma law that allowed women under 21 to drink stronger beer than males under 21. Over the next fifteen years the Court would sometimes uphold gender classifications—Congress was allowed to require only men to register for the draft—and would sometimes strike them down—Mississippi was disallowed from prohibiting men from taking nursing classes at the Mississippi University for Women.

Far more important in fact than anything the Court said were rapid changes in the surrounding American culture, ranging from the "sexual revolution" to the increasing entry of women into the job market. And far more significant legally was antidiscrimination legislation passed by many state legislatures and by Congress. The Civil Rights Act of 1964, for example, had included, almost by accident, a prohibition against sex discrimination, and the Court was reasonably vigorous in enforcing the statute.

One of the major controversies of the 1970s concerned the Equal Rights Amendment, which had been proposed in 1972 by Congress and provided that "Equality of rights under the law shall not be denied or abridged by the United States or by any State on account of sex." Although it was quickly ratified by 30 of the 38 needed states, it thereafter was successfully blocked by vigorous opponents. Although some of them could easily be described as opposed to gender equality, at least some of them based their opposition on a mixture of plausible doubt about the meaning of the language and, more to the point, an unwillingness to trust the Supreme Court to give acceptable specific meanings to the Amendment.

ENTER PRIVACY: A SECOND ERA OF "SUBSTANTIVE DUE PROCESS"?

What Justice Stewart termed an "uncommonly silly law" triggered perhaps the most controversial set of "individual rights" decisions of the Court during the last third of the twentieth century. Connecticut made it criminal to sell, use, or counsel the use of contraceptives for the purpose of birth control. (One could sell and use contraceptives for the purpose of preventing disease.) Participants in a Planned Parenthood organization working out of New Haven, Connecticut were charged with violating this law. The majority of the Court struck down the conviction in *Griswold* v. *Connecticut* (1965). Justice Douglas wrote for the majority that the written text of the Bill of Rights contained "penumbras and emanations" that protected marital privacy against the invasion represented by Connecticut's law. Justices Harlan and Goldberg, in separate concurrences, more unabashedly endorsed the Court's ability to identify "unenumerated rights" as part of the Constitution.

Stewart made his comment about Connecticut's law in a dissent, and he argued that the meaning of the post-1937, post-*Lochner* Court was that it would forego attempting to identify "unenumerated rights" in the Constitution. "Privacy" was, he said, just such an "unenumerated right." Hugo Black, the great textual absolutist of the mid-twentieth century, agreed. Though he described the Connecticut law as "offensive," he went on to argue that the Constitution just did not include the requisite language that limited a state's right to regulate contraception however it wished. He, too, accused the majority of returning to the discredited era of *Lochner*.

Had the issue been confined to the "silly" and "offensive" Connecticut law, it is hard to believe that anyone besides law professors would really have cared. *Griswold* was widely popular, as demonstrated vividly some twenty-two years later when the appointment of Robert Bork, the conservative nominee of President Reagan for a seat on the Supreme Court, was derailed in large part because of his derision of the case. What made the situation entirely different was the Court's willingness to extend the protection of "privacy" announced in that decision first to the distribution of contraceptives to unmarried adults and even to minors and, most fatefully, to the issue of abortion.

There can be almost no doubt that *Roe* v. *Wade* (1973) is the most important decision at least since *Brown,* especially if measured by consequences for the American polity. In that decision the Court, in an opinion written by Justice Blackmun and joined by two of the three other Nixon appointees to the Court, struck down the antiabortion laws of forty-six states. The Court held that protected "privacy" included the basically unhinderable right of a women to procure an abortion from a doctor in the first trimester of pregnancy. States were allowed to exercise some measure of regulation in the second trimester and to prohibit abortion entirely in the third trimester. "Privacy" had replaced "freedom of contract," and there could be little doubt that the Court was stunningly willing to read the Constitution as containing rights not obvious from reading the text. Justices White and Rehnquist heatedly dissented. Stewart, interestingly enough, concurred, saying that the Court had clearly decided to get back into the substantive due process business and that he agreed that abortion should be protected.

Justice Blackmun mentioned in his opinion that many states were in fact liberalizing their abortion laws, and it is possible that neither he nor his colleagues in the majority had any inkling of the firestorm they were about to ignite. One message of the 1960's, after all, had been what Mc-Closkey had called the remarkable willingness of the public to accept government-by-judiciary. To be sure, criticisms had been voiced, and Blackmun owed his own place on the Court to the election of a Republican President who had in many ways run against the Court. (And Blackmun was in fact, at least early in his judicial career, quite conservative in regard to the issues of criminal justice that were the focus of Nixon's concern.) But, when all was said and done, the level of resistance to the Court could be dismissed as relatively minimal, especially given the scope of the changes promoted by the Court during the 1960s. Fulminating members of Congress could not in fact gain the support necessary to mount a genuine assault on the Court's citadel.

Abortion rights could well be seen as widely supported by the national political and cultural elites to which the members of the Court were likely to be most attentive. Blackmun himself had served as counsel to the Mayo Clinic, the world-famous medical facility in his home state of Minnesota, and he clearly had imbibed its attitude of sympathy to the plight of women who wished to terminate unwanted—and possibly dangerous—pregnancies. Indeed, whatever the cogency of the Court's adoption of "privacy" as its legal rationale, the decision quickly became part of the debate about the role of women and, concomitantly, the role of the state in making it easier or harder for women to forego "traditional" burdens of childbearing and instead to enter the workforce or, at the least, to time their pregnancies for maximum convenience.

Whatever the perceptions of the Court about its ability to control public response, opponents of the decision, many of whom saw it basically as offering constitutional protection to the mass murder of innocent fetuses, mobilized against it. Although it is not self-evident that one's views on abortion would necessarily correlate with more typical measures of "liberalism" or "conservatism," the antiabortion movement in fact quickly allied itself with the Republican Party, especially that wing of the Party that was sharply critical of the permissive cultural trends of the 1960's. By 1978 several Democratic supporters of abortion lost their seats in the United States Senate, and there can be little doubt that the rise to power of Ronald Reagan and the Republican capture of the Senate in 1980 was considerably helped along by the energies of the "right-to-life" movement. The Republican Party platform by 1980 included specific opposition to *Roe* and the promise that Justices would be appointed who would overrule it.

In fact, that never occurred, even though by 1991 a majority of the Court had been appointed by Presidents Reagan and Bush (and White and Rehnquist remained on the Court). Although the Court throughout the 1980's in fact allowed much more state regulation than would have been upheld by Justice Blackmun and other partisans of *Roe*, it always "distinguished," rather than overruled, *Roe*. Finally in 1992, in the *Casey* case, the most direct test of the vitality of *Roe*, a five-Justice majority that included Justices O'Connor, Kennedy, and Souter—all conservative Republican appointees—announced their refusal to overrule the decision insofar as it offered basic support for the right of a woman to choose abortion and a concomitant protection against the state's placing "undue burdens" on the exercise of this right. Writing for the three Justices named above, O'Connor wrote a remarkable opinion that, without once ever suggesting that *Roe* had in fact been rightly decided, said that the Court would suffer institutionally if it overruled the case in effect simply because of changing membership. Precedent had its claims, the three said. Justice Scalia wrote a mocking dissent, joined by Chief Justice Rehnquist and Justices White and Thomas. Justices Blackmun and Stevens also dissented, though from the opposite direction; they would have struck down a number of Pennsylvania's restrictions that were upheld by the majority. With the 1993 retirement of White and his replacement by Ruth Bader Ginsburg, who had argued many of the classic women's rights cases for the American Civil Liberties Union and who clearly supported the right to choose, it is unlikely in the extreme that *Roe* will be overruled.

Whatever the claims of precedent evoked by Justice O'Connor, it seems relevant as well to note that some version of a right to choose abortion is supported by a fairly wide majority of Americans. The fairly clumsy compromises, at least from a traditional doctrinal view, made by the Court in this period might well gain the support of that majority. This might also suggest that Reagan and Bush, who had in fact supported abortion rights earlier in their political careers before aligning themselves with the antiabortion movement in the 1980's, in fact had mixed feelings about returning abortion to the full-scale political process. When abortion rights were directly tested in the political marketplace, Democratic supporters, especially if "moderate," tended to prevail over hard-line Re-

publican opponents. There was no reason to believe that the political interests of the Republican Party would be served by the overruling of *Roe,*
however much they were served by incessantly denouncing the decision
and promising to seek its overruling. One doubts that Reagan and Bush
put O'Connor, Kennedy, and Souter on the bench in order to preserve
abortion rights, but it is certainly possible to believe that these presidents
were less than zealous in applying a "litmus test" of opposition to *Roe*
on the part of nominees to the Court and that, at least in private, they
might be well satisfied with the intermediate position between Blackmun
and Scalia taken by the Court's majority.

Another issue generated by *Griswold* and *Roe* was the protection to
be accorded unconventional sexual practices. By far the most important
was gay and lesbian sexuality, which was criminalized in many states under the rubric of antisodomy laws. (Some states prohibited sodomy *only*
by homosexuals or bi-sexuals, while allowing it between married couples
or even unmarried heterosexuals.) In *Bowers* v. *Hardwick,* a bitterly split
five to four Court rejected the argument that the Constitution protected
what Justice White for the majority insisted on calling "homosexual sodomy" and what Justice Blackmun in dissent labeled instead rights of personal sexual intimacy. The crucial fifth vote was provided by Lewis Powell, who gave a speech several years later, following his retirement from
the Court, indicating that he wished he had voted with the dissenters
(who would, therefore, have comprised a new majority). *Bowers* is, in its
way, almost as offensive as *Dred Scott,* with its notorious emphasis that
blacks simply were not part of the American political community and,
indeed, were "so far inferior, that they had no rights which the white man
was bound to respect." If one takes seriously a constitutional vision that
offers "equal concern and respect" to the members of the American polity, then *Bowers* betrays it.

It must be noted, though, that anyone adopting the general approach
articulated by Robert McCloskey might well stress the unwisdom of the
Court's taking the lead in granting full-scale legal rights to a minority that
continues to be highly unpopular among much of the public. Indeed, the
storm of controversy in 1993 that defeated President Clinton's attempt to
lift the ban on open gays and lesbians serving in the armed forces indicates the extent of antipathy on the part of much of the public to accepting gays and lesbians as full members of the American community.
The Court is already unpopular with many elements of the public, and it
should be concerned, according to a McCloskean analysis, with carefully
nurturing what capital it retains rather than profligately spending it in a

venture that is likely to spark far more opposition than support. Finally, it must be acknowledged that in many ways the criminalization of sodomy is more a symbolic than a "real" issue. Anyone even minimally familiar with American culture and society in the 1990's knows that gays and lesbians are increasingly a visible part of the American political community, earnestly solicited by many politicians as part of their political coalitions and increasingly elected or appointed to public office. Least of all, it might be argued, should the Court invest its scarce resources in basically symbolic gestures. Victims of very real homophobia would, of course, dispute that the issue is "merely" symbolic and would emphasize the Court's role—which it rhetorically embraced after 1937—of protecting vulnerable minorities against majority tyranny. And so the argument goes on.

"When a Nation Is at War":
The Supreme Court, Hot War, and Cold War

No survey of the Court's willingness to protect individual rights can ignore the fact of war. As Justice Holmes wrote in 1919, "When a nation is at war many things that might be said in time of peace are such a hindrance to its effort that their utterance will not be endured so long as men fight." Whether or not one agrees with Holmes as a normative matter, his description seems accurate enough. And the previous chapter certainly made clear the willingness of the pre-1960's Court to enlist in the Cold War struggle against communism and the Soviet Union by upholding the criminalization of much communist speech and conduct. It is, therefore, all the more remarkable that the entrance of the United States into the distinctly "hot" Vietnam War during the 1960's provoked astonishingly little official suppression of speech as such, and the Court generally, though not always, protected protesters. Earlier paragraphs mentioned the black armband worn by Mary Beth Tinker to school to protest the War and the vivid jacket worn by Paul Cohen to protest the military draft that fed citizens to the jaws of war.

Many of the Court's most significant war-related cases involved the administration of the Selective Service System, and it generally cracked down on local draft boards that sped up the induction of war protesters or otherwise seemed to be making its decisions on blatantly political grounds. As noted earlier, though, the Court, through Chief Justice Warren, did uphold in 1968 a prohibition against burning one's draft card.

The Court also had to decide several cases involving the meaning of "religion" in statutes that offered conscientious objector status to those who opposed all war on the basis of their "religious" beliefs. The Court read "religion" extremely expansively to include, basically, any kind of belief that functioned similarly to ordinary religious belief as the foundation of one's stance toward life. However, the Court refused to grant conscientious objector status to a traditionally religious man who denounced the Vietnam War as immoral under the classical just-war theory, but conceded that he would in fact participate in a "just" war.

Surely the most remarkable protection of speech by the Court during the Vietnam War era was in the so-called Pentagon Papers case of 1971. It was triggered by the decision of the *New York Times* and other newspapers to publish secret documents compiled by the United States Defense Department concerning the major escalation of the War by the United States in 1964 and 1965. Although the documents dealt only with the Kennedy and Johnson Administrations, the Nixon Administration, citing the general importance of the Executive Branch's being able to preserve the secrecy of its materials, sought an injunction against further publication of any of the documents. Since 1931, the Court had read the First Amendment as being especially weighted against "prior restraints," which prevented speech, through licensing requirements or otherwise, from being delivered at all. The majority thus refused to issue the injunction and protected initial publication, though several of the Justices suggested that the United States could criminally prosecute the newspapers subsequent to publication. (In fact no such prosecutions were filed.) Three Justices, including Chief Justice Burger, wrote heated dissents.

The Vietnam War clearly divided American society, especially at the elite level, as no foreign war had before in our history. Lyndon Johnson, elected in an overwhelming landslide in 1964, withdrew from the 1968 campaign after being challenged in the New Hampshire primary by antiwar Democratic Senator Eugene McCarthy of Minnesota, and the 1968 Democratic Convention in Chicago was literally the most riotous such gathering in history. The very willingness of America's leading newspapers, such as the *New York Times* and *Washington Post*, to publish the Pentagon Papers illustrated their own disinclination any longer to be cheerleaders for American foreign policy even in time of war when many Americans (not to mention Vietnamese) were dying in the battlefield. The Court deserves credit for protecting the newspapers, but it can scarcely be described as climbing far out on a limb to rescue truly unpopular and vulnerable dissenters.

What the Court exhibited no interest at all in doing was accepting any of the challenges to the very legality of the Vietnam War itself. The War was never formally "declared" by Congress. Instead, its legal basis was the so-called Gulf of Tonkin resolution in 1964 that authorized the President to take such measures as he deemed necessary to rebuff purported attacks on American forces then in South Vietnam. The legal argument against the War was scarcely frivolous. Although there were many episodes of military conflict that had not been preceded by any official declarations of war (including the Korean "police action" of 1950–1953), the Vietnam War, which left over 50,000 Americans dead, was of significantly greater magnitude. And one of the enduring issues of American constitutionalism, going back to the initial debates about the 1787 Constitution, was the power granted the President regarding the disposition of American armed forces. All of this being said, the Court, over consistent dissents by Justice Douglas, decided to avoid taking any of the cases raising such fundamental issues.

Again, one can have no doubt that McCloskey would have been appalled had the Court done otherwise. Imagine, for example, the Court's issuing an injunction ordering the President or the Secretary of Defense to withdraw American armed forces from Vietnam. That might have worked with Harry Truman and the steel mills, though McCloskey was scarcely an enthusiast even in those circumstances. It is inconceivable to contemplate its working when the lives of soldiers are at stake and, just as importantly, the society is sharply divided about the underlying merits of the war itself. After all, millions of Americans, led by the President of the United States, defended American participation in what others perceived as a Vietnamese civil war, and the Court could scarcely have expected general public approbation had it chosen to adjudicate the legal merits of the Vietnam War.

Although the Court would sometimes set up barriers to the unfettered Cold War state—in 1972 a unanimous Court (Justice Rehnquist not participating) rejected the Government's claim that it could wiretap individuals without warrants in "national security" cases—it scarcely was eager to address the constitutional problems posed by such a state. It refused, for example, to accept a challenge to the constitutionally dubious practices of Congress in regard to the secret funding of intelligence agencies like the CIA, holding that no one had "standing" to invoke the Court's jurisdiction. And a sharply divided Court in 1972 refused to enjoin the Army from engaging in the surveillance of lawful civilian political activities. The decision was based on a legal technicality, but the message was that the Court would not stand in the way of the executive's being able to ferret out information about its domestic antagonists, even if it presumably could not punish them for having their oppositional views.

Even more striking in its way was *Dames & Moore* v. *Regan,* a 1981 case in which the Court upheld an agreement between President Carter (defended by President Reagan) and the Iranian government that had been holding over four hundred Americans hostage in Tehran for well over a year. In return for releasing the hostages, Carter agreed, among other things, to suspend certain legal claims that had been filed in American courts by private businesses against the Iranian government. The Court exhibited no qualms about accepting the President's authority in effect to deprive these businesses of their legal rights. What distinguishes the Iranian and Steel Seizures cases, of course, is not only that the latter involved a politically vulnerable president and the former a brand-new chief executive, but also that a contrary decision in the Iranian cases might well have triggered an international crisis.

By the end of the 1980's, and, even more so, after the Persian Gulf War of 1991, it was hard indeed to view the Court as interested in playing any role at all in curbing executive power relative to the basic conduct of American foreign policy and engagement in foreign hostilities. That, for better or worse, would be left up to Congress, with its own power of the purse and other political resources.

One other case involving the President must be mentioned, though: *U.S.* v. *Nixon* (1974), in which the Court in effect delivered the final blow to Richard Nixon's efforts to retain his shattered presidency by ordering him to disclose to the Special Prosecutor tapes of conversations in which Nixon had discussed the Watergate break-in and its subsequent coverup by operatives of the Republican Party and of the President himself. Even there, though, the case was mixed in its messages, for it found, for the first time, a constitutionally based "executive privilege" of the president to withhold material from senatorial or judicial scrutiny, even as the Court held that the privilege was overridden in the specific circumstances of the Nixon case. Although Nixon had hinted that he would refuse to comply with an adverse decision by the Court, he in fact immediately bowed to the decision and, within days, resigned his office. However dramatic the *Nixon* case is, it surely tells us little about the true power of the Court. At the time of the decision, Nixon was clearly on the brink of impeachment, deserted even by rapidly increasing numbers of Republicans. The Court's decision undoubtedly enhanced its own popularity, though it is difficult otherwise to draw much in the way of a message from the episode.

NINE

JUDICIAL MONITORING OF THE
NEW AMERICAN WELFARE STATE

B
Y THE TURN OF THE TWENTIETH CENTURY, government was increasingly accepting responsibility for assuring the welfare of its citizens. It is crucial, however, to recognize that the particular means most often chosen to enhance their welfare was the *regulation* of the private sector. Rarely did the state take on direct responsibilities, including raising the necessary monies through taxation, for the supply of goods and services to a citizenry not adequately served by the existing market system. Many important cases in the next thirty years or so after 1937 continued to address the basic question of regulation and the existence of limits, if any, on the Congress's or a state legislature's ability to regulate the private market. The message of almost all of the post-1937 cases is that the state is unconstrained, subject only to such limits as the inability to order racial segregation and the like.

The only exception to the general rule that the post-1937 Supreme Court is willing to give Congress a green light when regulating economic relationships arises in regard to the imposition of certain requirements on states themselves. Thus the Supreme Court in *National League of Cities* v. *Usery* (1976), for the first time in four decades, held that Congress had exceeded its powers under the Commerce Clause when it extended federal wages-and-hours requirements to state employees. This, said the Court, imposed on the "core" interests of the states and thus violated the principle of federalism. Although the case generated a flurry of scholarship wondering whether the 1937 settlement was being challenged by newly empowered conservatives appointed by President Nixon (who, with Potter Stewart, a Republican appointed by President Eisenhower, provided the five-man majority), the Court quickly showed that it had no stomach for a fight. Succeeding cases carefully "distinguished" *Usery* and upheld challenged congressional legislation. Even as a formal matter the case survived only nine years, when it was overruled, by only one vote, in 1985.

Nonetheless, the Court, with conservative justices Souter and Thomas having replaced Brennan and Marshall, in 1992 accepted New York's plea to invalidate a congressional requirement that states assume responsibility for the disposal of certain non-state-created radioactive waste. The majority emphasized that the nuclear waste regulation was not general, as with wage-and-hours legislation that applied to both private and state employers alike, but instead applied only to states. Although some academic commentators once again predict a 1935-like setting up by a confidently conservative Court of barriers to congressional conscription of the states as compulsory partners in social programs, that seems unlikely, if for no other reason than the fact that many statutes include the supply of federal funds contingent on acceding to congressional desire. Chief Justice Rehnquist, who authored *National League of Cities,* wrote for the Court in a 1987 case, *South Dakota v. Dole,* upholding the requirement by Congress, as a condition of receiving federal highway funds, that states raise their drinking ages to twenty-one. The Court did not address the question whether Congress could directly raise the drinking age itself under the Commerce Clause. Instead, it viewed the issue within the framework of Congress's "spending power" under Article I of the Constitution and its freedom to attach conditions to the receipt of federal funds. Although Rehnquist asserted that "Congress' power under the spending power is not unlimited," it is hard, as a practical matter, to divine what those limitations are in regard to states. Such declarations, of course, do reserve the Court's power to invalidate some future congressional program, even if it provides no useful guidance beforehand as to when that might occur.

THE RISE OF THE WELFARE STATE

A *welfare* state, in the sense used in this chapter, involves the active dispensation by the state of funds or services to recipients chosen at least in part on the basis that they have legitimate needs that could not otherwise be supplied through the operation of the standard market, even one subject to the higher level of regulation associated with the New Deal era and afterward. If the earlier part of the twentieth century features the coming to maturity in the United States of the modern *regulatory* state, then the dominant motif of the last third of the century is the remarkable growth of governmental programs, at both federal and state levels, that involve direct expenditures of tax revenues.

First, some facts. The national budget passed the $100 billion point only in 1962, the previous high of $95 billion being reached in 1945, the last year of World War II. During the truncated Kennedy Administration, a "war on poverty" was declared, though it was the successor administration of Lyndon Johnson that won the major legislative victories in this war. Between 1964 and 1966, for example, Congress passed, at Johnson's behest, a plethora of statutes, including the Food Stamp Act and the legislation establishing Medicare and Medicaid. Although Johnson's successor, Richard Nixon, was scarcely thought of as a liberal, his administration consolidated the changes provoked by Johnson and, indeed, in some cases added to them. By 1975 the federal budget was $326 billion. Controlling for inflation, in constant 1972 dollars the federal nondefense budget went from $32.1 billion in 1960 to $60.9 billion in 1969 and fully doubled again, to $125 billion, by 1978. Breaking down these figures functionally, one discovers that federal spending on elementary and secondary education went from $417 million in 1961 to $46.5 billion in 1979, and health care costs climbed from around $150 million in 1961 to $4.9 billion in 1966, immediately after the passage of the 1965 Medicare legislation. Nor did the coming to power of a significantly more conservative antiwelfare state Republican like Ronald Reagan fundamentally change things, except to slow down the almost inexorable growth of the welfare state. By 1988 the United States was spending, in nonconstant dollars, almost $80 billion dollars on medical care alone.

The Court had almost nothing to do with these dramatic developments, other than to get out of the way of the state and national governments. Still, the consequences of these changes in the polity inevitably affected both the business, and ultimately the role, of the Supreme Court during the last third of the twentieth century. Insofar as one of McCloskey's aims was to identify the variation in primary issues confronting the Court—and the different roles the Court would choose to play—it seems legitimate to suggest that the concern about civil liberties and minority rights he identified as the dominant motif of the post-1937 Court began to give way by the 1970s to concern about somewhat new issues linked to the rise of the welfare state. Indeed, the Court has taken on as one of its principal roles that of *monitoring* this new state. Among the central questions that confront the Court are the following:

(1) To what extent, if at all, was government *required* to take account of the welfare needs of the populace and to supply at least some of these

needs to those with inadequate financial resources? This is the problem of so-called "affirmative rights."

(2) Insofar as most welfare programs are limited to those who establish their specific eligibility for benefits, must the state give some degree of "due process" to persons when making decisions of eligibility?

(3) What limits, if any, are placed on the state when it offers to provide public funds in return for a promise from the recipient that he/she will behave, or refrain from behaving, in certain ways desired by the state? This is the problem of "unconstitutional conditions." A linked issue is raised by the vast increase in the number of public employees hired to administer the welfare state. To what extent can the state impose certain conditions—the inability to engage in normal political activity, for example—in exchange for the job?

(4) How much freedom does the state have in defining those general classes of persons eligible to receive benefits? For example, can the state distinguish between citizens and noncitizens, long-term residents and newcomers, African-Americans and whites, men and women? To some extent, these are treated under the Equal Protection Clause of the Fourteenth Amendment (or, for the federal government, the Fifth Amendment). In addition, though, they raise classical questions about the role that ought to be played by the Court in assuring that legislatures strive to achieve some ascertainable "public interest" rather than become mere agents of politically-dominant "private" or "special" interests.

All of these raise obvious problems not only of constitutional doctrine, but also of the effective role that can be played by the Supreme Court as an actor within American politics. In all of these areas, one sees, at least in the period 1963–1993, a Court that has been hesitant to declare (or maintain) any sweeping doctrinal visions, whether because of the political fragmentation among the justices that has made consensus unachievable or because of the intrinsic difficulty of the issues themselves.

THE REJECTION OF AFFIRMATIVE ENTITLEMENT

Generally, constitutional rights within the American system have been viewed as "negative" limitations on state power to deprive its members of certain liberties guaranteed by the Constitution. But does the state have "affirmative" duties to give succor to persons rather than merely not directly "mistreat" them? The American legal tradition has generally rejected any "duty to rescue." It is perfectly acceptable, as a legal matter, for an onlooker to refuse to go to the aid of a drowning person even where giving such aid would be without risk to the rescuer. Should it be different if the state is the onlooker?

The "rediscovery" in the early 1960s of poverty in America led to a host of statutes attempting to alleviate the circumstances of those in need (and thus to "rescue" them from their desperate circumstances). Inevitably, the legislative response was limited, whether by budgetary pressures or the simple political unpopularity of certain groups making claims for aid. Just as inevitably, the Supreme Court, perceived since *Brown* v. *Board of Education* as an ally or reformers, was called upon by political activists to join in solving the plight of those poor unable to win legislative victories.

The first move toward recognizing an affirmative right to economic assistance came in regard to indigent criminal defendants. Although the Sixth Amendment provides that "[i]n all criminal prosecutions, the accused shall enjoy the right . . . to have the Assistance of Counsel for his defense," this had been interpreted only "negatively," as prohibiting the state from interfering with the representation of defendants by lawyers they had hired in the private market (or who were voluntarily contributing their services). It provided nothing to the indigent unable to hire counsel (or to find a volunteer attorney).

Although *Powell* v. *Alabama* (1932) held that indigent defendants in cases where the death penalty was a possibility had to be provided counsel, the Court had carefully refrained from extending any such right to indigent defendants in general. A 1943 case, *Betts* v. *Brady*, did hold that courts should reverse convictions of lawyerless defendants where, because of the complexity of the trial, the lack of representation was "fundamentally unfair." Over the next two decades, Justices were forced to become intimately familiar with trial records in order to determine whether the lack of representation fatally tainted their procedural fairness.

Finally, in *Gideon* v. *Wainwright* (1963), the Court unanimously overruled *Betts* and adopted a *per se* rule to replace the case-by-case general standard of the earlier case. According to Justice Black, "any person haled into court, who is too poor to hire a lawyer, cannot be assured a fair trial unless counsel is provided for him. . . . [L]awyers in criminal courts are necessities, not luxuries." Similar cases arising in the mid-1960s extended this right to counsel to any charge that carried with it the threat of jail, as well as to initial appeals from convictions. Later Courts became significantly more restrained in their reading of *Gideon*. Thus 1974 and 1989 decisions rejected the duty of the state to provide legal assistance in regard, respectively, to appeals to the Supreme Court itself and, far more importantly as a practical matter, to petitions for habeas corpus filed in federal courts by convicts challenging the fairness under federal constitutional norms of their convictions in state courts.

Nor did the Court exhibit the slightest enthusiasm for supplying state-paid attorneys to indigents faced with *civil* litigation, however important the interests involved. Thus the Court in 1981 rejected claims that "fundamental fairness" required legal assistance to an indigent mother threatened with loss of custody of her child because of charges of child neglect. To be sure, Congress and many states began funding civil legal services for the poor at the end of the 1960's, but this was apparently a matter of legislative grace rather than constitutional necessity.

Although *Gideon* and its progeny, if taken seriously, were significantly redistributive in their implications, the Court was happy to leave the details of how the lawyers supplied the indigent were to be paid. It was quickly agreed, though, that indigent defendants certainly weren't entitled to the level of representation that could be purchased by the well-off; furthermore, it basically refused to hear any of the multitude of "inadequacy of representation" cases challenging the quality of state-provided counsel.

An affirmative right of a quite different sort also seemed to be the result of a 1966 case, *Harper* v. *Virginia Board of Elections,* that invalidated Virginia's poll tax as a condition for voting in elections for state offices. (The poll tax for elections for federal officials had been prohibited by the Twenty-fourth Amendment, added to the Constitution in 1964.) Although Justice Douglas spoke of the specific importance of voting, his opinion for the Court also contained language that suggested that classification by ability to pay would now be treated by the Court as an "invidious discrimination" barred by the Fourteenth Amendment. Finally, in a 1969 case dealing with the ability of states to require a year's residence before providing welfare to indigent new residents, Justice Brennan had suggested, in striking down the requirement, that such welfare was a "fundamental interest" and that the state therefore had to supply a "compelling state interest" before depriving an indigent of the aid in question.

Thus both the general political ambiance of the 1960's and the specific apparent receptivity of a liberal Supreme Court, especially between 1963 and 1969, to egalitarian argumentation spurred many organizations to seek judicial help. They would be frustrated, however, in part, no doubt, because of changes of membership that left the "Warren Court" only a memory. Warren had submitted his resignation early in 1968, to take effect on the confirmation of his successor. President Johnson nominated Justice Fortas to be Chief Justice, but a Republican filibuster prevented confirmation, thus leaving Warren in office after the 1968 election. Its winner, Richard Nixon, had explicitly promised to change the direction of what was described as a dangerously liberal, activist, Supreme Court, and he quickly named Warren Burger, a conservative member of the Court of Appeals for the District of Columbia, as the new Chief Justice. Fortas in turn was forced to resign after disclosure of some dubious financial dealings. The Senate then rejected two Southern conservatives nominated by Nixon; his third choice, the Minnesotan Harry Blackmun, was easily confirmed in 1970. In 1971 Nixon was successful in placing on the Court Lewis Powell, a racially moderate but otherwise conservative Southern Democrat, and William Rehnquist, by far the most conservative nominee for the Supreme Court since the New Deal.

The period between 1970 and 1973 would prove to be a decisive watershed; by the end of this period, it was clear that the Court had repudiated any suggestions that the state might be under any general duty to rescue indigents from their unhappy fate. In *Dandridge* v. *Williams* (1970), the Court upheld a provision of Maryland's law on Aid to Families with Dependent Children that limited the monthly grant to any one family to $250, regardless of its size or computed need. As a result, individual members of a large family received less per capita than the state itself recognized as the minimum required for subsistence. Although Justice Stewart for the majority conceded that the case "involves the most basic economic needs of impoverished human beings," he refused to apply any special scrutiny to Maryland's program. It was, the Court said, just another socioeconomic policy of the state, and the teaching of 1937 is that the state had extensive discretion in establishing or administering such programs. A similar fate met a 1972 claim that the "need for decent shelter" should lead the Court to engage in especially strict oversight over the operation of Oregon landlord-tenant law.

A like pattern can be detected in 1977 and 1980 cases dealing with the right of states and the federal government to refuse to include most abortions in medical benefits provided poor women, even though the state would pay for services surrounding childbirth. *Roe* was interpreted as prohibiting only the criminalization of abortion. It did not require active aid by the state for women unable to purchase abortions through the private market.

Perhaps the most dramatic illustration of the Court's resistance to finding affirmative rights within the Constitution came in the 1989 *De-Shaney* case dealing with a Wisconsin youngster beaten into a permanently brain-damaged state by his father after state welfare authorities had become aware of the possibility of the child's being abused. They had, in fact, temporarily removed the child from parental custody before returning him to the father. Should Wisconsin, then, have to accept financial responsibility for the fate visited upon "poor Joshua" (as he was called by Justice Blackmun in dissent)? No, said the Court. "The affirmative duty to protect"—in effect, to rescue—"arises not from the State's knowledge of the individual predicament"—the state is scarcely unaware that many people are in precarious or even desperate straits—"or from its expressions of intent to help him, but from the limitation which it has imposed on his freedom to act on his own behalf." Wisconsin "played no part in [the] creation of the child's plight, nor did it do anything to render him any more vulnerable to them."

After 1969, then, the Court basically accepted no invitations to declare new rights of the poor that suggested a constitutional duty to rescue them from the dire fate that lack of resources can entail in a market-oriented society, though many of the key decisions were by five to four votes. By a quarter century later, the Court was firmly controlled by conservatives who would certainly continue to be resistant to any such suggestions, and there was certainly relatively little public outcry about the Court's stinginess in this regard. Indeed, if the public wished to rescue those in need, it had only to elect legislators who promised to raise the necessary taxes, and this the public was most definitely unwilling to do.

User Fees, Equality, and the Welfare State

Just as the Court disappointed liberals who hoped that it would require states to fund new redistributive programs designed to alleviate the plight of the less-well-off, so did it reject most of the challenges, encouraged by decisions like the 1966 *Harper* case, to the extraction of fees for public services. *Boddie* v. *Connecticut* (1971) did hold that Connecticut could not constitutionally impose filing fees from indigents suing for divorce. Justice Harlan stressed that the state absolutely monopolized the dissolution of legal marriage; it was, therefore, fundamentally unfair for it to deprive indigents seeking divorce from access to state courts because of their inability to pay the fees. Two years later, however, in *Kras* v. *U.S.* a five-justice majority composed of the four Nixon appointees and the relatively conservative Kennedy-appointee White refused to find constitutional unfairness in the policy of the United States that prohibited access to federal bankruptcy courts by those unable to pay a $50 filing fee.

Perhaps the most visible sign of the Court's unwillingness to expand notions of constitutional entitlement—and, just as importantly, to enter into almost certain political struggle with elected politicians and the publics they represent—was a 1973 case, *San Antonio Independent School District v. Rodriguez*, which challenged the Texas system of school finance. Like many states, Texas relied basically on local property taxes, supplemented by some state funds, to finance the public schools. This meant, among other things, that the amount of money available for the education of students within given school districts, even after the state supplement, depended on the wealth of these districts. This, argued the parents in low-wealth districts, violated the Equal Protection Clause. Four justices—Brennan, Marshall, Douglas, and White, all Democrats—agreed. More importantly, of course, five justices did not. Education was not, wrote Justice Powell, a "fundamental interest," nor was reliance on district wealth "suspect." The Court found that Texas' method of school finance was "rationally" justified by its aim of preserving local autonomy over public schools.

In the ensuing years, many state supreme courts—including that of Texas—have struck down educational finance systems as violations of state constitutions. Almost invariably, such decisions have generated political crises within the states, given the inevitability of significantly increased taxation to pay for the redistribution from the better off to the less well off. The class dimension has also, in many states, intersected with racial and ethnic dimensions: Plaintiffs are often members of racial or ethnic minorities living within America's inner cities who are complaining about the considerably greater resources often available to white suburbanites. State legislatures dominated by suburban members are often less than eager to comply with judicially imposed mandates to equalize school finance, and courts in turn have been tested both as to the extent of their own commitments and, just as significantly, the actual extent of the political resources available to them in regard to achieving their goals.

Whatever the travails of supervising such court-ordered changes as reapportionment or even school desegregation, they only rarely involved spending large sums of money and the concomitant necessity of finding new funding sources. It is inconceivable that anyone who shares even a measure of Robert McCloskey's skepticism about judicial capacity to move beyond the broad mainstream of public opinion could lament the failure of the United States Supreme Court to embark on the kind of political tasks that would have been required by a serious commitment to equalization of financial resources among the literally thousands of American school districts.

One lesson, then, of the first quarter-century of the "modern" American welfare state is that states and Congress are, with few exceptions, given a free hand in the basic decisions of establishing redistributive programs in the first place and then deciding upon the level of funding of those programs. One might explain this simply in terms of the majority of justices during this period being politically conservative and thus likely to be unsympathetic to redistributive transfers of wealth. But one should also acknowledge that even many liberals following the 1960's became more skeptical of the Court's capacity to make the kinds of judgments linked with the construction of a modern welfare state. How, for example, does one really decide what are "fundamental interests" in a modern society, and is there any reason to rely on judges to identify them? It is also clear that any Court that found a significant number of interests to be "fundamental" and thus constitutionally entitled to governmental funding (whatever the wishes of tax-passing legislatures) would be at the same time establishing itself as precisely the kind of "superlegislature" whose legitimacy was denied by the Revolution of 1937.

DUE PROCESS IN THE ADMINISTRATION OF THE WELFARE STATE

Whatever the minimal constitutional duty to establish any welfare programs in the first place, state legislatures and Congress have in fact chosen to establish many such programs. Many of them, particularly those most likely to be identified by the public as "welfare"—income transfers from better-off to less-well-off—involved the use of so-called means tests, by which access to the programs was limited only to those who could demonstrate their lack of financial resources. A fear surrounding any means-tested programs is that cheaters will try to take advantage of state largesse by falsely claiming to be eligible. Almost immediately, questions arose regarding the procedures regarding determinations of eligibility.

Perhaps the quintessential "Brennan Court" case was the 1970 case *Goldberg v. Kelly*. Could New York, in administering its Aid to Families with Dependent Children (AFDC) and Home Relief programs, terminate public assistance payments to those it thought to be cheaters without first giving them a hearing at which the recipient would be informed of the charges and given a chance to respond to them? New York in fact offered *post-termination* hearings, but it saw no duty to offer *pre-termination* ones. They would, it argued, not only increase the costs of administering the welfare program, but also ultimately result in less overall money being distributed to deserving recipients, unless legislatures added the money necessary to finance the pre-termination hearings without taking it from other programs serving the poor. The Court disagreed, emphasizing that welfare payments provide "the means to obtain essential food, clothing, housing, and medical care."

Once again reflecting the crucial changes in membership, the Court in *Mathews* v. *Eldridge* (1976) considerably cut back on *Goldberg* in a case involving the termination of desirability benefits under the Social Security Act. The formality of procedures depended on balancing the importance of the individual need for a government benefit, the state interest in expeditious action, and the likelihood of the state's actually committing error in its (pre-hearing) process of decisionmaking. Reasoning that "a disabled worker's need is likely to be less than that of a welfare recipient," the Court found post-termination hearings adequate. *Goldberg*, which had been hailed by some as the initial stage of a "due process revolution" in the administration of state and federal welfare programs, thus turned out to be of relatively marginal importance.

"UNCONSTITUTIONAL CONDITIONS" AND THE MODERN WELFARE STATE

Perhaps the central issue raised by the post-New Deal activist state is whether the Constitution places limits on the kinds of conditions placed by the state on its own willingness to deal with the recipients of its largesse. *Dole,* the South Dakota drinking-age case, exemplifies one aspect of the problem, though most of the cases involve private individuals asserting their own claims.

Justice Holmes, then on the Supreme Judicial Court of Massachusetts, established one end of the spectrum in terms of an answer to this question in an 1892 case involving a New Bedford policeman dismissed for violating a departmental regulation against political activity: "The petitioner may have a constitutional right to talk politics, but he has no constitutional right to be a policeman. . . . [H]e takes the employment on the terms which are offered him." The state, then, can in effect require waiver of First Amendment rights as a condition of receiving the "privilege" of a job. Holmes's analysis was extended in many cases to cover almost all welfare-state benefits, which were treated as "privileges" to be extended on practically any terms asserted by the granting state.

If Holmes is one end of the spectrum, Justice Douglas is at the other.

For him "the central question is whether the government by force of its largesse has the power to 'buy up' rights guaranteed by the Constitution." Not at all coincidentally, he delivered this remark in a 1971 case, *Wyman v. James,* involving yet once more the administration of a state's AFDC program. The state conditioned its aid on the agreement by recipients to accept unannounced "home visits" by welfare caseworkers monitoring the program. Such "visits" would ordinarily be barred by the Fourth Amendment, which requires authorities to get search warrants before unconsented-to entries into homes. The Court, in upholding the state's demand, insisted that "the visitation in itself is not forced or compelled. . . . If consent to the visitation is withheld, no visitation takes place. The aid then never begins or merely ceases, as the case may be." Douglas, in dissent, emphasized that the recipient's circumstances made it difficult indeed to reject the state's offer.

The Court has scarcely explained when it will uphold certain waivers of otherwise-protected constitutional rights or, in contrast, describe them instead as illegitimate attempts by the state to compel through the pressure of its own offer of welfare benefits results that it could not legislate directly. Perhaps one explanation for the intellectual intractability of the "unconstitutional conditions conundrum" is the fact that it has no particular political valence, either liberal or conservative, that might tempt a politically sophisticated court to proffer a grand theory designed either to legitimate or to head off something with a predictable political tilt.

An early critique of Holmesian argumentation was offered, for example, by the very conservative Justice Sutherland, in a 1926 opinion invalidating California's attempt to condition the right of a trucking company to use public roads on its agreement to charge its customers California-determined prices. "If the state may compel the surrender of one constitutional right as a condition of its favor, it may, in a like manner, compel a surrender of all." The Court found it "inconceivable that guarantees embedded in the Constitution of the United States may thus be manipulated out of existence." Sutherland, of course, was defending the traditional right of private business to set its own prices; Douglas was defending the privacy rights of poor women. Each, though, could readily adopt the rhetoric of the other.

It should therefore occasion little surprise that the Supreme Court has preferred case-by-case balancing, looking at the importance of the proclaimed state interest and the actual burden placed on the recipients, as an alternative to grand pronouncements designed to cut the Gordian knot. Thus the Court struck down a requirement that noncommercial radio stations that accept any support at all from the United States agree not to engage in any editorializing. The majority, over heated dissent, found this unjustified by a "compelling" state interest, which the Court required because the condition involved a waiver of rights otherwise protected by the First Amendment. The Court also ruled, in a series of cases extending from 1968 to 1989, that the state could not condition unemployment compensation on the willingness of recipients to violate tenets of their religion, such as working on their Sabbath-days or, if they are religious pacifists, working on military weapons.

On the other hand, in *Rust* v. *Sullivan* (1991) a sharply split court upheld a so-called "gag rule" that prohibited doctors in family planning programs that accepted federal funding from informing their patients of the availability of abortion as a possible alternative to carrying a pregnancy to term. The majority did not see this as raising serious First Amendment questions at all. *Rust* is significant not only for its general result, but also because it illustrates as well a remarkable deference by the Court to administrative agencies in their interpretations of congressional statutes. The initial congressional statute, passed in 1970, did not impose the "gag rule" on recipients, unlike, say, the radio editorializing statute mentioned above, which was specified in the statute. The abortion "gag" was the result of an administrative interpretation offered by the Reagan Administration in 1988. The Court nonetheless upheld this interpretation by invoking a 1984 decision involving the Chevron Oil Company in which the Court announced that it would, as a general practice, accept the interpretations of congressional statutes offered by administrative agencies so long as they were at all reasonable. More than a few commentators viewed this as a conservative Court's happy acquiescence to the shift of practical decision-making power from a Democratic-dominated Congress to a conservative-dominated executive branch. (One of President Clinton's first acts was to change the Reagan Administration interpretation, thus eliminating the "gag rule.")

A similar shift arguably was the result of a 1983 decision, *Immigration and Naturalization Service* v. *Chadha,* where the Court invalidated the so-called "legislative veto," by which Congress preserved, in various statutes, the power to override offensive regulations promulgated by administrative agencies. According to the majority, such "vetoes," sometimes requiring resolution only by one house or even a committee of Congress, were in fact new laws and thus required "presentment" to the President. Any glib political analysis is complicated by the fact that one of the two dissenters was Justice Rehnquist (White was the other), and the majority included Justices Brennan and Marshall. At the time, *Chadha* was thought to be extraordinarily important inasmuch as it called into question literally 200 statutes, including the War Powers Act passed by Congress in 1973 to curb presidential power. In its first decade, though, *Chadha* has had little apparent impact.

In any event, both the so-called *Chevron* doctrine and *Chadha* underscore some of the ambiguities involved in the notion of judicial deference to politically accountable decisionmakers. Especially in a political system like that of the United States, which often places different political parties in charge of the legislative and executive branches, "we the people" evoked by theories of popular sovereignty speak in decidedly mixed, sometimes flatly contradictory, tones. A court's decision to favor legislature over executive agency, or vice versa, might as often be explained in terms of political preferences as by any notion of abstract judicial deference to "popular" branches of government.

Rust also illustrates the fact that any full analysis of the American Supreme Court should include recognition of the ever-more important role it plays as statutory interpreter. The modern state is quintessentially a state of statutes and of regulations issued by administrative agencies interpreting these statutes. The constitutional-law docket of the Court may in fact draw attention disproportionate to its actual importance in the modern state. Some of the most important civil rights decisions of the Court during the 1980's, for example, offered restrictive interpretations of legislation passed in earlier decades, which in turn led to bitter struggles both within Congress and between Congress and President Bush before Congress successfully overturned several of the decisions.

BUREAUCRACY AND THE WELFARE STATE

One thing the welfare state has meant is a sharp increase in the number of governmental employees who staff its various bureaucracies. Although the theoretical issues may be the same whether the state employs one person or one thousand, the social consequences are obviously greater the number of persons affected. In 1816 the entire federal government had fewer than five thousand civilian employees; their number reached one hundred thousand only in 1881. It took almost another sixty years, until 1940, to reach a million employees. By 1988 approximately 17.5 million wage earners (out of 115 million overall) received their paychecks from the federal, state, or local government.

General American law had given employers the right to engage in "employment at will"; that is, an employee could be fired without the demonstration of any justifying cause. In fact, civil service laws grant public employees a variety of protections against arbitrary firing. But does the Constitution itself guarantee any particular process beyond what a legislature chooses to grant?

A 1972 decision, *Board of Regents* v. *Roth,* said yes, at least if one had a "justifiable expectation" to continued employment. Whether or not one had a "right to be a policeman" (or school teacher, or social worker, or whatever), one retained a right not to be dismissed from what one could justifiably perceive as a "permanent" position without at least some due process, including hearings. Subsequent litigation dealt with the timing of any hearings, pre- or post-termination.

But due process is certainly not the only issue presented in the governmental-employment context. As noted in an earlier chapter, the Cold War Era of the 1950's provoked much litigation about the ability of the state to deny jobs to persons who were members of the Communist Party or who refused to take loyalty oaths that included promises never to join the Party. Such litigation continued well into the 1960's, when a series of decisions limited the formal power of the state to take political views into account. Perhaps the most remarkable decision was *Robel* v. *United States,* a 1967 decision that struck down a bar on Communists working in defense plants. The Court basically said that only the kind of behavior that would support a criminal conviction—knowing membership in the Party coupled with actual support for any illegal goals it professed— would justify exclusion from routine public employment. Moreover, the Court basically eliminated loyalty oaths as a significant aspect of public employment, though a 1972 decision written by Chief Justice Burger upheld a requirement that an employee pledge fidelity to the Constitution. Far more significant "negative" oaths—"I am not a member of the Communist Party" and the like—continued to be forbidden, and the issue basically disappeared from American politics.

The Supreme Court has been quite tolerant of governments' continued desire to limit the political activity of their employees, even where no one could argue that the activity was "subversive." The federal government especially justified such limitations on the ground that this contributes to the vitally important perception (and reality) of neutrality on the part of the public bureaucracy. The Supreme Court twice, first in 1947 and then in 1973, upheld such rules against attack, finding the loss of employee rights a cheap price to pay for maintaining a civil service divorced from politics.

Equally important was another 1947 decision, in which the Court upheld a federal spending program that conditioned the receipt of highway funds by states on their willingness to prohibit state officials spending these funds from taking "any active part" in political activities. Whatever the response to such decisions by the states, who have complained, much like the individual recipients of welfare payments, of the unfair pressures placed upon them by the national government, the Court itself can scarcely be viewed as foisting them on the hapless states. Here, in a pattern going back at least as far as *McCulloch,* the Court is simply legitimizing ever-more-expansive assertions of federal power by the Congress itself.

Where the Court did take the lead, first in *Elrod* v. *Burns* (1976) and then again in *Branti* v. *Finkel* (1980), was in restricting the traditional role played by political patronage in dispensing governmental jobs. To prefer Democrats or Republicans for nonpolicy-level positions, it said, violated the First Amendment rights of the members of the "wrong" political party. Such positions must be chosen on a nonpartisan basis. Justice Powell denounced the Court's willingness to disregard the value of political patronage for maintaining strong political parties and the presumed contribution to American democracy of such parties.

Similarly, the Warren Court led the way in protecting federal employees against retaliation for engaging in speech critical of the agencies for which they work, though a later Court limited protection only to what it was willing to classify as matters of "public concern." A later decision rather surprisingly protected the job of a sheriff's department clerical employee who had expressed sympathy with the attempted assassination of President Reagan. Perhaps the key to understanding these two outcomes is the realization that both decisions were 5–4; one is analyzing less "the Court" than the refined perceptions of one or two Justices.

RACE AND THE WELFARE STATE

The great civil rights case of the century, *Brown* v. *Board of Education,* was the culmination of a series of cases going back to 1938 testing state policies in regard to public education, which Chief Justice Warren pronounced "perhaps the most important function of state and local government." Nevertheless, the Court was scarcely clear in delineating its position regarding the use of racial criteria in dispensing the goods of the welfare state.

Through heroic efforts of sometimes outright obfuscation, the Court maintained a staunch unanimity in almost all of the major racial segregation cases following *Brown* in 1954. One explanation for this unanimity—beyond its obviously serving the institutional interests of the Court itself—is that the Court in fact did relatively little following the thunderbolt of 1954.

The major act of the Supreme Court, in the ten years after *Brown,* was defense of its self-appointed role as "ultimate interpreter of the Constitution" in *Cooper* v. *Aaron,* a 1958 case triggered by the refusal the year before of Arkansas Governor Orval Faubus to enforce a judicial decree ordering the admission of nine African-American students to Central High School in Little Rock. President Eisenhower ultimately used federal troops to enforce compliance. The Court reaffirmed *Brown* and denounced the refusal of Arkansas authorities to comply with the law. That use of troops was, of course, vitally important in demonstrating that the Court would in fact be supported by the Executive branch, but it also made clear the potential difficulties presented by a resisting South. One way of interpreting the relative quiet of the Court in the decade following *Brown* is as a "testing of the waters" to see if its views would in fact garner necessary support from the electorally accountable branches of the national government (and, though this was a more forelorn hope, even of the affected Southern states themselves).

When *Brown* was decided in 1954, there were only twenty-three African-American school children attending secondary or elementary schools with white children in the Southern States—that is, the states of the Confederacy that attempted to secede in 1860–61. In the 1960–61 school year, during which John F. Kennedy was elected, the number of African-American children in the Southern states other than Tennessee and Texas attending racially mixed schools was 432, approximately .02 percent of the total of African-American school children in these states. (If one included Texas and Tennessee, the number went up to approximately 4,300 and the percentage to .16 percent.) The border states—Missouri, Kentucky, Maryland, Delaware—and the District of Columbia had a better record; by the 1960 school year, almost 50 percent of African-American children in those states were attending school with whites.

What dramatically changed things was not anything the Court did, but, rather, the active collaboration of the Congress and President Lyndon B. Johnson, with a shared sense of political purpose, at least between 1964 and 1966, that has occurred only rarely in American history. These political leaders were in turn heavily influenced by the civil rights movement symbolized by the leadership of Martin Luther King, with its calls for realization of basic American values of equal justice under law. The Civil Rights Act of 1964 not only mandated the desegregation of public accommodations and made illegal racial and gender discrimination in employment; it also gave the Justice Department far more extensive authority to press for school desegregation. Moreover, the federal government was, for the first time in its history, beginning to engage in significant distribution of federal revenue to states for use in public education, and what was then the Department of Health, Education, and Welfare threatened to cut off much-needed funds to school systems that refused to move toward desegregation. Thus by the end of the Johnson Administration, almost a third of all African-American students in the South (including Texas and Tennessee) were attending racially mixed schools, a figure that would leap to over 90 percent by the end of Richard Nixon's first term as president in 1973.

This outpouring of national support for overcoming at least the worst aspects of discrimination against African-Americans undoubtedly encouraged the Court, in *Green v. New Kent County* (1968), to invalidate a so-called "freedom of choice" plan by a Virginia county that resulted in overwhelmingly "racially indentifiable" schools. The "free choice" was likely to be illusory, according to the Court, a manifestation either of traditional (and no longer acceptable) Southern mores about the desirability of racial separation or, even more ominously, of pressures brought by economically and politically powerful whites upon vulnerable African-American parents to make "choices" that maintained this separation. The government's duty, stated Justice Brennan for the Court, was to "fashion steps which promise realistically to convert promptly to a system without a 'white' school and a 'Negro' school, but just schools."

Green concerned a small, rural county, but its principle of "nonidentifiability" of schools as "white" or "Negro" was applied by many judges in urban settings to require the self-conscious assignment of students in ways likely to produce racially mixed schools and the "busing" of many of these students to schools relatively distant from their quite likely segregated neighborhoods. Three years after *Green,* a unanimous Court, in *Swann v. Charlotte-Mecklenburg Board of Education,* upheld a sweeping order by a North Carolina district judge that required extensive busing in order to achieve, in most schools within the system, "racially-balanced" schools. Thereafter, busing became a major political issue, with the Nixon Administration leading the opposition to many of the far-reaching decrees issued by liberal district judges appointed by Lyndon Johnson.

There was, however, an inexorable shift away from busing as a favored remedy throughout the 1970's. By the mid-1980's, the controversy over busing had in effect been resolved via a judicial retreat that saw far less ambitious and controversial remedies imposed on those districts found to have engaged in segregated schooling. One might wonder if the Court would have initially endorsed extensive busing had, first, Congress and the President, seemingly backed by the public, not vigorously thrown their own weight behind the striving for integration, and, second, had many of the busing orders not been issued by district judges who themselves were part of the social and political elites of the communities in question. Moreover, these district judges were often perceived by the Court as unusually courageous in their commitment to enforce desegregation, and the Court was willing to support them. Throughout the 1970's, though, busing became increasingly unpopular, even among many African-Americans themselves; the Court beat a hasty retreat, and many schools thus remain easily identifiable by race.

Busing arose as an issue only after a court had decided that a district was in fact guilty of discrimination in the first place. The Supreme Court had to decide what counted as discrimination triggering the need for any remedy at all. Two sentences in *Brown* exemplified the potential for confusion: "Separate educational facilities," the Court stated, "are inherently unequal." It also declared, perhaps thinking that it was simply making the same point, that "To separate [children] from others of similar age and qualifications solely because of their race generates a feeling of inferiority as to their status in the community that may affect their hearts and minds in a way unlikely ever to be undone." The first sentence suggests that the constitutional harm lies in the very existence of "separate educational facilities," of what the Court in *Green* had called "racially identifiable schools." The second sentence, however, though on the surface a strong denunciation of the harms of racial discrimination, points in a different direction, suggesting that the Constitution prohibits only those racially separate schools that are the result of assignment based "solely" on racial grounds.

The Warren Court did not really have to wrestle with these questions because its race-oriented docket came almost entirely from Southern and border states that had explicitly used race in their public policies as a means of segregating African-Americans or otherwise keeping them "in their place." For the South the question was remedy rather than the existence of the initial constitutional violation.

By the 1970's, however, an increasing number of school cases were arising outside the South, including such cities as Boston, Cleveland, Detroit, and Denver. Plaintiffs usually argued that the "racial identifiability" of the schools was enough to establish unconstitutionality; the defendants, in response, argued that such "identifiability" was irrelevant unless it was the product of a conscious desire to create and maintain segregated schools, as distinguished, for example, from a defensible desire to assign children to "neighborhood schools." In an important 1974 case involving the Denver, Colorado public schools, the Court, though finding the system in violation of the Constitution, nonetheless emphasized that plaintiffs would have to show (and did successfully show in regard to Denver) that the Board "intended" to bring about the separation in question. Thereafter, an increasingly conservative majority became harder to convince that various assignment practices were "in fact" simply subterfuges designed to maintain racial separateness. What this meant is that relatively few Northern school districts were subjected to the radical transformations seen in the South, and "racially identifiable schools" remain an omnipresent reality of most Northern school systems even as they have been significantly limited throughout the Southern and Border states whose practices were struck down by *Brown*.

The Court also assured the practical maintenance of racial identifiability throughout the North when, in *Bradley* v. *Millikin* (1974), it overturned a district judge's decision to force the consolidation of many separate school districts in and around Detroit, Michigan, into one "superdistrict" the size of Delaware for the purposes of achieving desegregation. Many Southern districts, including that of Charlotte, were quite vast "consolidated" city-county districts. The pattern in the North, however, was for urban areas to be subdivided into sometimes literally dozens of separate school districts, themselves often predominantly white or African-American in demographic composition. In a sharply divided five to four decision that signified the final collapse of the Court's carefully maintained emphasis on unanimity in cases involving racial matters, the majority held that federal judges were without power to order the consolidation of these formally separate districts unless they had been drawn with the purpose of maintaining racial segregation, which was almost never the case.

RACE AND "AFFIRMATIVE ACTION"

Much of the debate throughout this period was couched in terms of the validity of Justice Harlan's call, in his *Plessy* dissent, for a "colorblind"

Constitution. Although no justice rejected this as an "ideal" vision of the Constitution (and, more to the point, of American society), the justices were in fact sharply divided concerning the pace at which the Constitution required race to become irrelevant to governmental decisionmakers. The very sharpest conflicts took place in regard to "affirmative action," the use of racial classifications for the ostensibly benign purpose of enhancing the access of racial minorities to education, jobs, and other important social goods. These are, of course, quintessential aspects of the welfare state.

There was, obviously, nothing "colorblind" about such programs. What saved them, according to their supporters, was precisely that they were "affirmative" rather than negative in regard to the treatment of the affected minorities. The debate about affirmative action was foreshadowed in the Court's opinion in the very first case construing the meaning of the Equal Protection Clause in regard to race, *Strauder* v. *West Virginia* (1880). The majority there had had no trouble striking down a state prohibition of African-Americans from jury service. It did not do so, though, on the simple ground that the state had used a racial classification. Instead, the Court several times emphasized the "unfriendly" nature of the classification and defined the Fourteenth Amendment as providing "protection against unfriendly action" directed at African-Americans because of racial animus. This left open the possibility that "friendly action," designed to include rather than exclude, could be legitimate even if based on overt racial classifications. Yet *Strauder* also described the Fourteenth Amendment as "ordain[ing] that the law in the States shall be the same for the black as the white." As with *Brown* 74 years later, the Court scarcely spoke with any great precision.

The first major "affirmative action" case to be decided by the Court was *Bakke* v. *Regents of the University of California* (1978), which involved a program at the University of California Medical School at Davis that reserved sixteen places in its entering class for persons selected from an applicant pool consisting only of African-, Hispanic-, Asian-, and Native-Americans. (*All* groups were entitled to compete for eighty-four "open" places.) Once again the Court was sharply divided; indeed, presaging many of the future "affirmative action" cases, not even five justices could coalesce around a given "majority" opinion. Four justices, led by Justice Stevens, argued that one need not even reach the constitutional issue because of the Civil Rights Act of 1964, which stated that "[n]o person in the United States shall, on the ground of race, color, or national origin, be excluded from participation in, be denied the benefits of, or be subjected to discrimination under any program or activity receiving Federal financial assistance" (as Davis did). The majority of justices, however, agreed, in Justice Powell's words, that the Act "must be held to proscribe only those racial classifications that would violate the Equal Protection Clause or the Fifth Amendment," which had been held, in *Bolling* v. *Sharpe*, the companion case to *Brown* in 1954, to apply equal protection-like limitations to the federal government.

Four Justices—Brennan, Blackmun, Marshall, and White—would have upheld the Davis program in its entirety because of its benign purpose. The ninth Justice, Justice Powell, though taking a wholly idiosyncratic position, wrote what in fact became the most influential opinion in the case. Like the Stevens four, though on constitutional rather than statutory grounds, he invalidated the program. The reason, however, was not that the Constitution required "colorblindness," but, rather, that it prohibited rigid "quotas" of the kind concededly adopted by Davis. Thus Powell agreed with the Brennan four that the Constitution did not prohibit any taking of race into account in the admissions process, at least so long as there was no rigid quota *and* the university could show that a "compelling state interest," such as achieving diversity of backgrounds in a student body, required the use of the racial classification. Alan Bakke was thus admitted to medical school, but the debate continued.

A similarly fragmented court in 1986 struck down a preference adopted by the Jackson, Michigan school board that protected recently hired minority teachers against being laid off, even though the traditional practice was "last hired, first fired." Though apparently willing to accept racial preferences in the initial hiring decision, the Court was unwilling to extend its tolerance to a layoff policy that meant that some whites with seniority would be laid off before more recently hired African-Americans.

The Court's fumbling around on the issue probably reflected quite well the public confusion (and ambivalence) regarding racial preferences. For example, although the Nixon Administration was almost flamboyantly conservative on such issues as busing, that same Administration promoted the establishment of many of the initial affirmative action programs by private businesses in the 1970's. And even though the public elected Republican Presidents in the 1980's who drew significantly on white antagonism to affirmative action, the same public often elected Democratic representatives and Senators—as well as some Republicans—who continued to be, by and large, supportive of racial preferences. Thus the Bush Administration was forced to beat a hasty retreat when one of its officials suggested that it violated the law for universities to offer race-sensitive scholarships. Like Goldilocks, the mainstream of the public seems to be willing to accept some amount of affirmative action that is "just right," even as it finds many actual programs either "too hot" or "too cold."

A majority of the Court was finally able to come together in a majority opinion in *City of Richmond, Virginia* v. *Croson* (1989), which struck down a requirement that at least 30 percent of publicly-financed building projects go to minority contractors. Yet Justice O'Connor in her majority opinion emphasized some of the specific facts about the city, including its having a majority-African-American city council. The program could therefore be viewed less as a "friendly" gesture by the white majority than as a decidedly "unfriendly" effort by a newly empowered African-American majority to direct public funds to its own constituents.

Only a year later, Justice Brennan, in his final opinion for the Court, upheld a minority-preference program of the Federal Communications Commission in the allocation of television licenses (which, if not a direct distribution of funds, has been described as a "license to print money" on the part of the lucky license holders). The Court held that Congress had much more latitude in adopting racial preferences than did state legislatures or city councils.

Sharp divisions on the Court concerning the overt use of race as a classification were reflected as well in regard to controversies involving the differential *impact* of programs on various racial groups. An important 1972 decision, *Griggs* v. *Duke Power Co.* interpreting the Civil Rights Act of 1964, written by Chief Justice Burger, had struck down the use of certain employment criteria by the Duke Power Company on the grounds that their use served to exclude a disproportionate number of African-Americans from the employment pool and that the Company could not show that the use of the tests was necessary to achieve legitimate business goals. This suggested to many that the Constitution itself would be similarly interpreted to bar state practices that disproportionately affected African-American and other vulnerable minorities, at least in the absence of the state's being able to present a "compelling interest" justifying the practices. Such hopes were dashed, however, by another case decided the same year, *Jefferson* v. *Hackney*, in which the Court rejected a suit brought by recipients of Aid for Dependent Children who claimed that Texas was considerably more generous in offering aid to the aged and infirm, who were presumably predominantly white, than to the predominantly African- and Mexican-American beneficiaries of AFDC. Justice Rehnquist rejected the plaintiffs' "naked statistical argument" and rejected as well a potential judicial role of "second guess[ing] state officials charged with the difficult responsibility of allocating limited public welfare funds among the myriads of potential recipients." Later cases underscored the Court's determination to require proof of the state's *intent* to discriminate; it would not, with rare exceptions, be sufficient to point simply to differential *effects*. Indeed, the 1972 *Duke Power* decision was itself significantly modified by the Court in 1989, which helped to trigger the struggle between Congress and President Bush noted above.

GENDER AND THE WELFARE STATE

Many welfare programs have been quite explicitly gender-linked, sometimes explicitly, sometimes only as a matter of social fact. Neither kind of linkage perturbed the Court prior to the 1970s, when the Court began restricting the wide latitude it had traditionally given states to use gender as a classification in making public policy. The change of legal reality in the 1970s had obvious implications for the American welfare state.

A number of provisions of the Social Security Act, for example, specifically gave "widows" more benefits than "widowers," on the assumption that women were less likely to have alternative sources of income because they had probably not worked outside the home. The Court throughout the 1970's struck down a number of such provisions, emphasizing that they rested on outmoded social stereotypes about either a woman's "proper" role or even her likely behavior, given the dramatically greater number of women participating in the compensated workforce.

Inevitably, gender-segregated education would be challenged in much the same way that racially segregated schools had. Ironically, the main such case to be decided by the Supreme Court, *Mississippi University for Women* v. *Hogan* (1982), involved a complaint by a male, Joe Hogan, who wanted to enter the nursing program at M.U.W. In a five to four decision written by Justice Sandra Day O'Connor, appointed in 1981 by President Reagan as the first woman on the Supreme Court, the Court granted Hogan his wish, saying that Mississippi, in order to defend gender-segregated education, had to present a more "substantial" justification than in fact it had done. The dissenters, led by Justice Powell, emphasized the potential benefits to women of being able to choose gender-specific schooling, quoting, among others, the president of Wellesley College. Interestingly enough, none of the proponents of a "colorblind" Constitution seriously suggested that "gender-blindness" was required. Whether the issue involved the propriety of maintaining separate-sex schools or the ability of the armed forces to exclude women from certain combat roles, there was, rightly or wrongly, far more acceptance of gender classifications than of racial classifications by the public and by the Court. No one, for example, seriously mounted constitutional challenges to sexually segregated public bathrooms, though, even by the 1960's, any such racially segregated facilities would have instantly been prohibited.

As with race, the Court must confront *impact* as well as *intent;* the Court fairly quickly determined that it would require the latter and, relatively speaking, ignore the former in regard to gender. Perhaps the most bizarre illustration of the Court's use of an "intent-impact" distinction in the context of gender and the welfare state was provided in a 1974 challenge to California's exclusion of pregnancy from the health insurance provided its public employees. According to the majority, California "does not exclude anyone from benefit eligibility because of gender but merely removes one physical condition—pregnancy—from the list of compensable disabilities." Although it is obviously true that only women can be pregnant, "it does not follow that every legislative classification concerning pregnancy is a sex-based classification." The Court's decision was overturned by Congress, which made it illegal for insurance programs to discriminate against pregnant women.

The Court emphasized the importance of intent in the 1979 *Feeney* case upholding a Massachusetts policy that gave all veterans of the armed forces an absolute lifetime preference for positions in the state bureaucracy. Given the officially mandated exclusion of women from the draft and the relatively small number of women who had, up to that time, volunteered for military service, this operated in effect to exclude almost all women from access to jobs in the Massachusetts bureaucracy so long as a male veteran applied for the job as well. The Court, with only Justices Brennan and Marshall dissenting, upheld the program, which, it said, had been passed in order to help veterans, a traditional object of state beneficence, rather than to hurt women. The fact that it did the latter was simply an incidental effect of its doing the former. And, of course, some women, however few, did benefit from the veterans' preference.

This case only underscores the fact that perhaps the most sustained beneficiaries of the American welfare state have been male veterans (and, in many cases, their widows). One scholar has noted that the national commitment, emphasized by the Republican Party after the Civil War, to take care of veterans of the Union Army and their dependents, meant that "for over thirty years prior to World War I the United States national government ran the world's largest and most expensive disability and pension system in the world," even though it is Bismarkian Germany that is usually given credit for initiating the bureaucratic welfare state.

RELIGION AND THE WELFARE STATE

Few issues presented the Court more problems than determining the intersections of the Establishment and Free Exercise Clauses of the First Amendment with the realities of the modern welfare state. In many of the cases discussed above, one can describe the Court as refusing to read the Constitution to require more in the way of welfare expenditures than state legislatures or Congress was willing to appropriate. But sometimes the legislatures proved to be far more generous than the Court was willing to tolerate, as when they included, as part of general programs involving aid to non-public schools, state aid to religious schools or students as well. The Court frequently struck down such aid as a violation of the Establishment Clause.

The 1947 case that "incorporated" the Establishment Clause into the Fourteenth Amendment as a limit on states, *Everson* v. *New Jersey,* involved a classic welfare-state issue, the payment by the state of transportation fees for students attending parochial schools. The Court upheld such payments, in part because no money went directly to parochial schools themselves. Four justices dissented. It is hard to read some of the dissenting opinions in that case (and opinions in other cases as well during that era) without seeing in them traces of quite traditional Protestant suspicion of Roman Catholics, who were by far the largest group of beneficiaries of the challenged state policies.

One might also see in many of the opinions illustrations of an ever-increasing secularization on the part of the political elites from whom Supreme Court justices tend to be drawn. This might help to explain, for example, the Court's willingness in the early 1960's to strike down state-compelled prayers in the public schools, extremely controversial decisions that triggered much public opposition and not a little defiance in regard to the actualities of classroom behavior. These decisions, however, have survived the transition to a far more conservative Court than that of the 1960's. Thus the Court, albeit divided 5–4, in *Lee* v. *Weisman* (1992) cited them in invalidating prayers offered at the beginning of state-sponsored baccalaureate ceremonies. School prayer is primarily of symbolic importance; aid to parochial schools raises far more basic questions about the nature of a pluralistic state and the ability of government to use public funds to nurture pluralism.

Perhaps the most significant case was *Committee for Public Education & Liberty* v. *Nyquist* (1973), which involved a New York program giving both direct money grants to religious schools and tax credits to parents with children at such schools. To qualify for such grants, schools would have to show that they "serv[ed] a high concentration of pupils from low-income families." The New York legislature had found that a "fiscal crisis in nonpublic education" was leading to severe problems; moreover, it noted that the parents of the children attending these schools had often paid substantial taxes for public education which they were not using and, moreover, that the public school budgets in effect depended on their *not* having to educate the children attending nonpublic schools. None of these considerations was relevant to the majority of Justices, who saw only an interweaving of church and state forbidden by the Establishment Clause.

Subsequent cases were successful only in issuing what one distinguished scholar called "a series of inconsistent and almost inexplicable decisions." Shifting majorities, almost always of the bare minimum of five justices, declared that certain kinds of aid were, or were not, forbidden "establishments." Thus a 1977 decision forbade public subsidy of transportation for student fieldtrips, distinguishing *Everson* on the basis that there were no teachers on the New Jersey buses who might discuss religion with the students. Other decisions upheld the ability of the state to supply textbooks, but rejected the right of state legislatures to loan maps or other instructional materials. While academic commentators poured ridicule upon the Court, politicians expressed frustration not only about specific results but also about the lack of any coherent guidelines.

The coming to the Court of new justices appointed by Ronald Reagan and George Bush, who had made explicit appeals to religious groups critical of secular public schools, did not, contrary to some expectations, lead to dramatic shifts, though the Court allowed states to offer parents tax writeoffs for at least some of the tuition paid to parochial schools. In addition, some other programs of state aid were upheld in the 1980's that might have been rejected earlier, but the decisions upholding them were almost always narrowly written, adhering, at least as a formal matter, to the more restrictive tenets set out years before in *Nyquist*. In *Zobrest* v. *Catalina Foothills School District* (1993), the Court, while upholding state funding of a sign language interpreter for a deaf student attending a religious school, emphasized the minimal nature of the program. Whether this was a heartfelt point or simply a strategic decision by a conservative majority to appear to be moving away only marginally from the generally anti-aid precedents remains to be seen, especially given the replacement by' Ruth Bader Ginsburg in 1993 of Byron White, who almost always voted to uphold programs that included parochial schools or their students as recipients of aid.

If aid to parochial schools required determining the meaning of the Establishment Clause, then other welfare state programs forced the Court to confront the implications of Free Exercise. As noted above, it held that states could not condition unemployment compensation on the willingness to violate religious tenets as to days of rest or participation in religiously offensive jobs. But in 1990 the Court, in an extremely controversial decision, *Employment Division, Department of Human Resources of Oregon* v. *Smith,* upheld the right of the state to criminalize the use of peyote even in Native American religious rituals and, consequently, to deny unemployment compensation to a state employee fired for such use. The Free Exercise Clause, wrote Justice Scalia for the Court, did not protect religious minorities against "general" legislation that did not select them out for special treatment. After a three-year struggle, Congress in effect overturned this decision by passing in 1993 a statute requiring that incursions on important religious interests be accepted only if the state presents a "compelling interest" in their behalf. To put it mildly, there is no agreement on what precisely this means, and there can be no doubt that the Court will have many opportunities to return to this contentious issue.

Most of the education cases looked at earlier involve persons claiming in effect that the state is not adequately meeting their needs for education. One case, *Wisconsin* v. *Yoder* (1972), on the other hand, involved a claim by the Amish community that Wisconsin, by imposing a requirement of compulsory education until the age of sixteen, in effect was forcing too much education upon its children. According to leaders of the Amish community, this violated the tenets of their "withdrawn" agrarian religious community, which required less formal education. The Court upheld the claim, though it was careful to limit its decision to groups like the Amish, with their many-centuries long history and general record of good behavior. Justice Douglas dissented, claiming that the majority ignored the interests of the children in becoming aware of possible alternatives to the lifestyle desired by their parents.

Attempts to build on *Yoder,* such as claiming that it was unconstitutional to force the Amish to participate in Social Security, proved unsuccessful, and it may prove to be what is sometimes called "a sport in the law," having no real general consequences. It most certainly remains on the books, however, and the issues it raises, which go to the heart of the nature of America's pluralism and, indeed, multiculturalism, are scarcely marginal issues.

Defining the Community of Welfare Recipients

The struggle between the Amish and the state of Wisconsin illustrates only one difficulty in defining the nature of the American political community. Should that community be able to limit its beneficence to those deemed part of the community, while keeping it from those deemed "outsiders"? No one has seriously argued that the Constitution entitles the children even of Mexico—let alone Azerbaijan—to welfare provided by California or by the national government of the United States. But what about, for example, foreign immigrants to the United States who reside in the United States? Then things get considerably more complicated. Once more, the Supreme Court has monitored the desire of local communities to dispense their various welfare goods—whether defined as direct cash payments, eligibility for access to state institutions like universities, or certain licenses given by the state, for example, to practice law or operate a television station—only to favored insiders.

The Court first addressed the issue of national citizenship and the welfare state in *Graham v. Richardson* (1971), when resident aliens legally entitled to live within the United States challenged state policies that either limited welfare benefits to citizens or required that resident aliens have lived in the country for a long period of time, such as 15 years. The Court struck them down, arguing that states violated the Equal Protection Clause in distinguishing between citizens and resident aliens. Once the United States as a nation agrees to let persons into the country, then they must be given, by and large, the same treatment as citizens. There are, however, some exceptions. The Court, for example, reached mixed results in deciding a number of cases involving eligibility for public employment or positions requiring state licensure, such as membership in the bar that allows one to practice law.

The Court struck down, in In re *Griffiths* (1971), Connecticut's attempt to limit membership in the bar to U.S. citizens. It also invalidated a similar limitation by New York in regard to eligibility for civil service jobs. On the other hand, later decisions concluded that the state could limit eligibility for "policy-making positions" to citizens. Thus the Court upheld citizen-only requirements to join the state highway patrol or to teach in the public schools.

Undoubtedly the most controversial of all such decisions was *Plyler* v. *Doe* (1982), in which Justice Brennan wrote for a five-justice majority in overturning a Texas law that refused to allocate any state funds to pay for the education of children brought illegally into the United States. The Court provided no particularly cogent analysis as to why conduct that could be criminalized—i.e., illegal entry into the United States—could not also serve as a bar from receiving educational benefits. Justice Brennan primarily pointed to the undoubtedly high social costs attached to tolerating the development within the country of an underclass deprived by lack of education from even the chance of bettering their position. Justice Powell, who had written for the Court a decade earlier in the San Antonio case rejecting a constitutional requirement of equal educational spending, provided the crucial fifth vote; he viewed Texas as in effect depriving the children of *any* education at all. Chief Justice Burger, writing for himself and three fellow conservatives, castigated the majority for its activism. It is difficult to believe that the case would have come out the same way even in 1987, when Justice Kennedy replaced Justice Powell; by 1993, only Blackmun and Stevens remained of the five justices who had come together in *Plyler.*

By the mid-1990's, popular concern about immigration, especially its illegal variety, were finding ever-greater expression within the political arena. It is unlikely that the Court, whether for reasons of its own political preferences or because of its genuine commitment to a more deferential posture to politically accountable institutions, will reach out to protect noncitizens from a resentful electorate composed entirely of citizens. This is especially true if the noncitizens in question are poor.

National citizenship raises the most basic questions of political community, but the United States, as a federal system, continues to be faced with residual questions about the meaning of membership in state communities. Thus another quintessential "Brennan Court" decision, linked both in time and spirit to *Goldberg* v. *Kelly,* was *Shapiro* v. *Thompson* (1969), in which Connecticut (among other states) required that new residents of the state live there at least a year before being eligible for welfare payments. Justice Brennan wrote that such durational-residence requirements violated a constitutionally protected "right to travel" that disallows states from in effect discouraging immigration from one state to another by depriving newcomers of welfare benefits. Interestingly enough, Chief Justice Warren dissented, perhaps because, as the former governor of California (which in 1941 had unsuccessfully attempted to bar indigent refugees from the Oklahoma dust bowl from entering the state at all), he was more sensitive to the potential costs to the state treasury of such Court-mandated generosity. The Court retreated from the more far-reaching implications of the decision by 1971, when it affirmed a lower court decision upholding a Minnesota state law that required that persons live in the state a full year before being eligible for reduced state-university tuition available only to residents. The district court below had noted the lack of "any dire effects" on the students in question, in presumed contrast to the welfare recipients who were the subject of *Shapiro*. Still, the Court adhered to *Shapiro* in striking down an Arizona law that required a year's residence to be eligible for state-provided medical treatment.

Moreover, even after the shift in membership to a considerably more conservative group of justices, the Court continued to look askance at state efforts to differentiate between short- and long-term residences when distributing benefits. Thus only Justice Rehnquist dissented in *Zobel* v. *Williams* (1982), which struck down Alaska's attempt to distribute to its residents the income from its vast oil reserves on the basis of length of residence. Chief Justice Burger, for the majority, found this "irrational."

CONCLUSION

As these words are written, at the beginning of 1994, it is hard to see any prospects for closure in regard to the Court's role as monitor of the welfare state. The principal issue before the American public is an extraordinarily ambitious medical care program widely described as the most transformative piece of legislation brought before Congress since the Social Security Act of 1935. There can be no doubt that, if (or when) adopted, it will raise a host of basic constitutional questions, ranging from questions of eligibility for services, including the "rationing" of health care, to equally fundamental questions of federalism. Will, for example, Congress be able in effect to order the states to pass and administer vast new social programs?

No doubt a future reviser of this book will be able to speak of some new modal role of the Court that will have supplanted its role as monitor of the welfare state. It is, of course, a condition of our being embedded in our own historical situations that these developments are only dimly perceived, if at all, and that we concentrate not on the acorns that might be taking root but, rather, on the existing mighty oaks. But for now, it is the Court's confrontation with the issues raised by the American version of the welfare state that stands out. One suspects that McCloskey would approve of the Court's basic caution in monitoring the welfare state, especially insofar as more assertive decisions might have important impact on public finance and thus, perhaps uniquely, spark public resentment and attack on the Court. But here, as elsewhere, one price of caution may well be acquiescence in basically unjust treatment of those who are most vulnerable and thus in special need of the services provided by a welfare state.

Epilogue: The Court of Today and the Lessons of History

THOSE WHO STUDY HISTORY and write about it have always been attracted by the idea that the present is illuminated by the past. No doubt they tend to magnify the virtues of their muse and to expect without warrant that others will heed her. Patterns of error in the very historical record they read should serve to remind them that their mistress is not everyone's fancy and that the present is likely, in large measure, to make up its own mind.

Yet they cannot be entirely dissuaded from hoping that today will learn a little from yesterday, that—to come back without further ado to the subject of this book—the Supreme Court of the 1960's will be understood and evaluated in the light of what has gone before. True, the case for such optimism is not overwhelming. As recently as the New Deal period, we saw that some judges of the Supreme Court itself did not know the history of the bench they occupied, or had failed to understand it. From first to last the Court has been attacked and defended in terms of a historical performance that was often completely fictitious.

The Desegregation decision and the 1956–57 subversion decisions seem to have set going one of those irruptions of antijudicial spirit that have from time to time enlivened the chronicles of the Court. And as always the attackers have been met and to a degree countered by a muster of ardent champions. In part, as always, this has been a contest between those who happen for the moment to like the Court because it serves their purpose and those who traduce it because it does not. Such clashes by night are not very edifying, but neither are they very novel or alarming. The Court has survived times more perilous than this. An institution that came through the Jeffersonian revolution, the slavery controversy, and the

New Deal is not likely to expire in the face of this latter-day threat, noisy though it may be.

However, the clamor has been accompanied by a strain of much more responsible and thoughtful evaluation. The strident voices of the ill-informed or ill-intentioned have awakened others to realize that the case for (or against) judicial review merits serious reconsideration in the light of modern circumstances.

This realization was long overdue. The critical assault on judicial review that culminated in the Battle of 1937, did not destroy the Court, but it did impair many of the ancient myths which had long served as justifications for the Court's activities. Thereafter it was no longer possible for the judges and their supporters to take refuge from reasoned criticism behind the old incantations—the idea that the Court was merely the passive mouthpiece of an unambiguous constitution; the idea that the nature and range of the Court's power to intervene was settled once and for all by the Constitution itself or by unmistakable inferences from the Constitution. There had grown up a generation of jurists and scholars convinced that the Court's judges were conscious molders of policy and that the Constitution had left open many questions about its own meaning, including the question of the Court's proper role.

Presumably judicial review could be defended even in the light of these insights; presumably a viable definition of its role could still be worked out. But evidently this could not be accomplished merely by invoking the discredited mystique of the past. It required a new defense and a new set of definitions that took account of the "new realism" about the Court's nature.

For a good many years after 1937, this need for rethinking was pretty thoroughly ignored both by the judges and by informed students of the Court. The judiciary doled out the "yeas" and "nays" and onlookers viewed with approval or alarm, but there seemed little disposition for either the Court or its critics to go beyond the *ad hoc* issues of the individual cases and find a reasoned apologia for judicial review in the modern era. Finally, when the 1950's were nearly over, the cries of the anguished South and its allies helped inaugurate a current of sober and scholarly discussion. In particular the participants in this discussion have been addressing themselves to a problem framed by the most venerable of modern judges in the words: "when a court should intervene." That is, under what circumstances can the judiciary feel warranted in disallowing the acts of the other branches of government? What are the proper limits of judicial review?

This development is healthy and hopeful. It may end by greatly illuminating the problem of judicial review in modern America. But it does seem fair to say that much of the discussion so far, though thoughtful and serious, is marred by inadequate attention to the lessons of history. Of course the Supreme Court of the 1960's must be evaluated as a modern institution, not as an antique. But knowledge of the real (not the fictitious) past of the Court is indispensable to any sound estimate of its capacities in the present and future. The child is father to the man in institutional, as well as individual, life.

In concluding a volume that has compendiously reviewed the history of the Court, it may be useful then to ask what light the chronicle sheds on this contemporary debate. History will not provide final answers to the question of "when a court should intervene" and the other questions that trouble today's judges. But it should carry us a few steps closer to those answers by setting the living problems in a living context.

To begin with, judicial history seems to suggest that this great question of the Court's proper role is not susceptible of any single, final answer. One of the main points to emerge from this study is that the interests and values, and hence the role, of the Court have shifted fundamentally and often in the presence of shifting national conditions. The concept of the judicial function that is reflected in some of Marshall's great opinions after 1815 would not have been appropriate to the Court during Taney's early years. The great Chief Justice was cutting new trails, and the task required the judicious boldness that he so amply possessed. The function of the Taney Court was to preserve and consolidate the imperium Marshall claimed, and the role it played had to be correspondingly modified.

Indeed the facts of the Court's history impellingly suggest a flexible and non-dogmatic institution fully alive to such realities as the drift of public opinion and the distribution of power in the American republic. The comparative meekness of the judiciary during the Civil War years, the retreat in 1937 in the face of the election returns—these are only two dramatic examples of a propensity that has been surprisingly constant. As was suggested in the first chapter of this volume, it is hard to find a single historical instance when the Court has stood firm for very long against a really clear wave of public demand. Even the Income Tax law, popular though it was in some circles, was surely not backed by an imperious popular mandate in the 1890's: a constitutional amendment was not even proposed by Congress until fourteen years after the *Pollock* decision.

This is not to suggest that the historical Court has slavishly counted the public pulse, assessed the power relationships that confronted it, and shaped its decisions accordingly. The process in question is a good deal more subtle than that. We might come closer to the truth if we said that the judges have often agreed with the main current of public sentiment because they were themselves part of that current, and not because they feared to disagree with it.

But the salient fact, whatever the explanation, is that the Court has seldom lagged far behind or forged far ahead of America. And the logic of this, as was also suggested at the outset of this volume, was inherent in the conditions of the Court's inception. Judicial review in its peculiar American form exists because America set up popular sovereignty and fundamental law as twin ideals and left the logical conflict between them unresolved. This dualism gave the Court the opportunity for greatness. But it meant that the opportunity was hedged about by reservations and penalties. A tribunal so conceived was not likely to shape its policies without regard for popular sentiment.

It may be deplorable that this is so. There might be something to be said for a Court that imposed loftier ideals and tried to goad the nation faster toward Utopia. But it is at least very doubtful that such a tribunal could have succeeded in holding the scepter it tried to grasp. The American Supreme Court—it should not be forgotten—is the most powerful court known to history. Foreign observers have never ceased to be amazed at the part played by these nine judges in national affairs, and a multitude of students have sought to account for the judiciary's exalted status in this country. The answer I suggest—illustrated over and over in the historical record we have reviewed—is to be found in what has just been said: that the Court seldom strayed very far from the mainstreams of American life and seldom overestimated its own power resources. To put the thing in a different way, the Court learned to be a political institution and to behave accordingly; and this fact above all accounts for its unique position among the judicial tribunals of the world.

All these observations bear directly on the problem of what role the Court should play, or is likely to play, in the modern American order.

For example, the Court's modern shift away from economic rights and toward civil rights can be properly evaluated only when it is seen in historical perspective. There has been a considerable amount of argument over the question of whether the judges ought to have abandoned their old preoccupation with economic matters, should have turned the property-holder as such over to the legislative power to do with as it wished. Perhaps there are still some marginal issues in this area that are open to fruitful discussion, but surely the broad rejoinder is that history, not the Court, made this decision, as it has made similar decisions in the past. Before 1860, America itself was undecided on the question of nation versus states; before 1932, America was undecided about the question of government economic control versus laissez faire. Until those dates the Court could still play a vital part in helping the nation to make up its mind. It happens that the Court's line in the one case was in accord with the final historical decision, and in the other was not. But this makes little difference to the point. If in either case the Court had tried to follow its own course after the Civil War and the New Deal had respectively signalized firm national judgments, the judges would have been talking to themselves. Ethical justifications for these farewells to the past are no doubt still worth seeking, but we should be clear that they are ex post facto.

As for the modern Court's espousal of civil rights as a substitute for the economic rights it once so cherished, this too was less a matter of deliberate choice than of predictable response to the wave of history. As we have seen, the Court has always tended to focus on the great open questions that plagued America as a whole—the nation-state problem from 1789 to 1860, the business-government problem from 1865 to 1937. To be sure, there are some such "great issues" which are probably not meet for judicial treatment. The slavery question in the 1850's seems in retrospect one of these; the question of foreign policy in modern circumstances is, for rather different reasons, another. But within the limits of what it regards as its capacities, the Court can be expected to preoccupy itself with the issues that most preoccupy America. And civil rights is just such an issue—more important perhaps than any modern American problem except foreign affairs, still undecided in spite of what partisans on either side would like to think, and not by its nature inappropriate for some form of judicial intervention. In turning its attention to this subject, the Court was acting in perfect historical character.

It was to be expected, then, and was, historically speaking, "right" that the Court should focus in the modern period on the relationship between government and the individual's rights. But history also has a precept or two to offer in connection with the question of *how* this comparatively new jurisdiction should be administered. What judicial attitudes, what policies, are most likely to serve the cause the judges have so evidently embraced?

In the first place, the record suggests that the principles of this new jurisprudence cannot be reached by a series of leaps and bounds. The Court's great successes in establishing jurisdiction have never been attained that way. We need only recall by way of example the slow and gingerly steps Marshall took from *Marbury* to *Cohens* v. *Virginia* to confirm the Court's supremacy over the states, or the almost painfully gradual accumulation of precedents that led finally to substantive due process in the late nineteenth century. It is in the nature of courts to feel their way along, and it must not be forgotten that this is a court we are speaking of, albeit a most unusual one.

Moreover—it can hardly be said too often—the Supreme Court, being an American institution, is obliged always to reckon with America and her propensities; and America is a nation that moves hesitantly and changes gradually. In spite of our occasional frenzies, the great alterations in the Republic's development have been the result of long experience and slowly growing conviction. There are those on the modern Court—Justices Black and Douglas are the leading exemplars—who would resolve constitutional uncertainties with large, bold, pioneering strokes of the pen. If this is the proper model for judicial governance, then history is indeed an untrustworthy guide.

Rather similar thoughts are aroused when we apply the historical lens to the question that has plagued the modern Court during the past two decades: granting that civil rights are properly within the judicial purview, and granting (at least for argument's sake) that the structure of the new jurisprudence must be built up gradually, how self-assertive should the Court be in imposing the rules it does devise upon the other branches of government? What are the boundaries of modesty on the one hand and "activism" on the other, even in the civil rights field?

Only a rhetorical purpose is served by answering this query in terms that simply ignore the patterns of history. From time to time it is urged that the Court should carry the virtue of modesty to an extreme, adopting a policy of self-restraint that would leave other branches of government almost entirely immune from constitutional restrictions. Whatever the theoretical merits of such a suggestion, the short answer is that it asks the Court to take leave of its heritage. The Court of history has never assessed itself so modestly, and there is not much reason to expect that the Court of the future will deliberately choose such a policy of renunciation. In fact we might almost think that the argument in its pure form had been foreclosed by the passage of time. As I have earlier suggested, the process of policy formation in America has been handled by a rough division of labor: representation of immediate and sometimes imperative interests has been assigned to the legislative branch; the judiciary has been bequeathed a significant share of the responsibility for taking the longer view. If the Court, after nearly two centuries, should cease to perform its wonted share of this work, there is grave doubt that the shirked task would get done at all.

And surely American democracy would be poorer. An impulsive nation like ours, much given to short-run fads, enthusiasms and rages, can little afford to dispense with the one governmental element that is disposed by its nature to take the long-run into account. To be sure, the record suggests that these popular passions are usually followed in the fullness of time by a cooling-off phase. The basic tendency of American politics is surely not extremist. But unfortunately these impulses, if not countered, are likely to leave behind them a brood of foolish laws and unfair practices that are harder to disown than they were to adopt. In 1960 the "McCarthyist" spirit seemed to have subsided quite thoroughly as an active political factor. But legislative and administrative remnants of that spirit lived on. America needs the Court's advice and control to help mitigate its own extravagances.

Neither, however, should history be ignored in determining how judicial control should be exercised and when it should be brought to bear. Surely the record teaches that no useful purpose is served when the judges seek all the hottest political caldrons of the moment and dive into the middle of them. Nor is there much to be said for the idea that a judicial policy of flat and uncompromising negation will halt a truly dominant political impulse. Grave though the McCarthyist threat was, a discreet judiciary would not assail every manifestation of it that appeared, or hope to reverse the tide unaided. The Court's greatest successes have been achieved when it has operated near the margins rather than in the center of political controversy, when it has nudged and gently tugged the nation, instead of trying to rule it. Consider the success of the Taney Court in its early years, compromising or skirting the areas of greatest controversy, yet developing on the peripheries of those areas a moderate but real national jurisprudence. Or consider the long campaign on behalf of laissez faire from 1905 to 1934, with its pattern of concessions to the principle of regulation, dotted here and there with a warning that the principle could be carried too far. And compare the Court of these times with that of 1858 or 1938 after the urge to dominate had enjoyed two moments of triumphant ascendancy. The Court ruled more in each case when it tried to rule less, and that paradox is one of the clearest morals to be drawn from this history.

It is true that such a judicial policy calls for rather extraordinary talents of character and intelligence. The Court must alter its own perspectives as history's perspectives are altered, yet must not move so fast that the idea of continuity is lost. It must allow government some leeway to act either wisely or foolishly, yet must not become so acquiescent that the concept of constitutional limit is revealed as an illusion. This requires judges who possess what a great poet called "negative capability"—who can resist the natural human tendency to push an idea to what seems its logical extreme, to have done with half-measures and uncertainties. It requires judges who can practice the arts of discrimination without losing the light of reason and getting lost in a welter of *ad hoc*, pragmatic judgments. For it is part of the glory and strength of the American constitutional tradition that it assumes the possibility of being rational about the state and its powers and limits.

This is a challenging bill of particulars, and the Supreme Court in the modern era has not met it in all respects. The Court has adjusted impressively to a new environment, has embraced a new set of interests and values, has shouldered great new responsibilities in the field of civil rights. But here and there—as in the free speech field—it has oscillated between a doctrine of limit too strict for enforcement and a doctrine of permissiveness that bordered on judicial abdication. Here and there—as in the segregation case—it has pressed forward at a rate that seems perilous and perhaps self-defeating. Here and there—as in the cases involving state criminal procedures—it has failed to chart a course that is rationally persuasive or even comprehensible. Here and there—as in the Steel Seizure Case—it has presumed to arbitrate an issue charged with the most explosive and immediate political consequences.

Nevertheless the Court of the modern era, like those of the past, has rendered a service of no small significance. From 1789 to the Civil War, the Court labored to establish a reasoned argument for the cause of union. From the war to 1937 it performed a similar function on behalf of laissez faire. Toward the end of each of those periods, the judges overstepped the practical boundaries of judicial power and endangered the place they had earned in the American governmental system. Since 1937, the Court has striven to evolve a civil rights doctrine that will realize the promise of the American libertarian tradition, yet accord with the imperatives of political reality. Even when criticisms are duly acknowledged, the fact remains that the Court has contributed more to an understanding of this issue than any other agency in American life. It would be a pity if the judges, having done so much, should now once more forget the limits that their own history so compellingly prescribes.

CODA

WHATEVER ELSE can be said about the past thirty years of the Supreme Court's behavior, it certainly does not appear to accord with Robert McCloskey's advice that it proceed by careful incremental steps and avoid "a series of leaps and bounds." Whether the example be *Reynolds* v. *Sims* and the imposition of the one-person, one-vote rule upon the states or *Roe* v. *Wade* and its sweeping aside of the criminal law of almost all of the states in regard to abortion, the Court seemed more than willing to move boldly. The Court appeared to offer as *its* lesson from the past not the merit of cautious, crablike movement, but, rather, that the American public, for all of its grumbling, was quite willing to accept a great deal of political tutelage from it.

Dozens of constitutional amendments were introduced during this period to overturn one or another of the Court's controversial decisions concerning legislative districting, school prayer, the rights of criminal defendants, abortion, flag burning, and busing to achieve desegregation. None of them even got through Congress. One amendment, the Twenty-sixth, did reverse *Oregon* v. *Mitchell,* a 1970 decision of the Court that Congress did not have the power to require states to give eighteen-year-olds the vote in state elections (though the Court found congressional power to require that eighteen-year-olds be allowed to vote in elections for *federal* offices). Though not trivial, the Twenty-sixth Amendment can hardly be described as a major repudiation of the Court. Otherwise, the formal law of the Constitution remained what the Court said it was.

It would be a mistake, though, to describe the Court as exhibiting any great eagerness to be far in front of those it professed to lead. Perhaps the Leninist dictum of two steps forward, one step backward better describes the Court. A number of very bold decisions were followed by more cautious retreats. In few areas—abortion may be one of them—can the contemporary Court be described as truly determined to prevail against legislative opposition. The message of most of the cases is that in fact states and Congress can do what they want. Ironically, when the Court does insist on its own agenda, the objects of its wrath are as likely to be lower-court judges as legislators or executives. Thus the contemporary rampage in behalf of capital punishment is directed primarily at liberal judges viewed by the Court's conservative majority as far too generous to vicious murderers (for it is a result of the Court's earlier jurisprudence of the 1970's that almost everyone now on death row has in fact been convicted of brutal murders) and, concomitantly, too indifferent to the victims of the crimes and the fears of the onlooking public about rampant crime.

Whether the object of the Court's concern is the judge below or the local administrator of a state welfare system, the student must address a question that McCloskey addressed only indirectly: To what extent do the pronouncements of the Court actually affect behavior throughout the society? Anthony G. Amsterdam once compared the Court to the Delphic Oracle. However impressive her emergence from the Temple might be, especially given the smoke and incense surrounding the Oracle, onlookers were left, at the end of the day, scratching their heads, wondering what the message actually was. It was then up to the priests to give actual meaning to the truly "delphic" pronouncements. Whether one views the Court as the Delphic Oracle or as the Wizard of Oz, one can still wonder how many ordinary public officials are even aware of its pronouncements, let alone structure their behavior in accordance with the goals presumably sought by the Court.

The essence of lawyering is the making of distinctions, and it is usually no great feat for a city attorney faced, for example, with a local "affirmative action" ordinance—or, for that matter, one of the judges of what the Constitution labels the "inferior" federal courts reviewing the ordinance—to offer reasons why the particular case at issue differs from the case proffered by the Court to control the issue. This is all the more true insofar as the Court, as is often its wont, offers complex "balancing" tests with multipart items to be weighed.

Though Gerald Rosenberg may have been exaggerating in describing the Court as a "hollow hope" in regard to the desire of activists to use it to promote wide-scale changes not otherwise supported by the ordinary political branches, his McCloskeyan note of caution rings true. For the Court to be effective as an agent of change, it must evoke the loyalties of thousands of relatively low-visibility officials who count as "the Government" for most ordinary citizens. It could, of course, ruthlessly monitor the behavior of these officials, but that is almost impossible; the Court just does not have the resources to do so, even were it to accept far more than the roughly 100–120 cases per year it has recently been taking. It remains substantially true, as Hamilton suggested in *Federalist* 78, that the Court possesses neither "purse nor sword" and must depend, therefore, on the willingness of legislative and executive officials to conform their behavior to the judgments announced by the Court.

One might suggest that the likelihood of such conformity is related to what political scientists sometimes describe as the "diffuse support" accorded the Court, the general propensity of the public to pronounce the Court admirable and thus to expect their public servants to comply with its commands. Interpretation of public opinion is an art akin to decoding delphic pronouncements, but it is hard to believe that the Court enjoys enough diffuse support to be able to rely on relatively unproblematic acquiescence to its more controversial policy goals. Both the American public in general, and the legal culture in particular, seem increasingly fragmented in regard to the great issues of the day, and few can plausibly believe that the Court possesses the moral or political authority to resolve bitter disputes about race, the scope and administration of the welfare state, or crime, to mention only three of the dominant domestic issues of the 1990's.

A signal moment in American legal culture occurred in 1991, when Dean Guido Calebresi of the Yale Law School wrote in the pages of the *New York Times* that "I despise the current Supreme Court and find it aggressive, willful, statist behavior disgusting." To be sure, the Court has never been the object of undivided solicitude. It was the famous New York antislavery newspaper editor Horace Greeley who wrote that he would as soon trust the judgment of his dog as that of Roger Taney, and many other such examples can be found over the past two hundred years. "Impeach Earl Warren" billboards were a standard feature of the roadside throughout the 1950's and 1960's—and not only in the South.

But the Dean of the Yale Law School is not a populist demagogue, or even a fiery newspaper editor. Yale is a special law school, together with Harvard the acknowledged citadel of the American legal elite and regular contributor of alumni to the Supreme Court itself. (Indeed, Calebresi made his statement in a column ostensibly supporting the nomination to the Court of Yale alumnus Clarence Thomas.) For the Dean of that school, in the pages of America's leading newspaper, to express such contempt is a revelation indeed of the inability of the contemporary Court to call even on its traditional allies to make standard speeches about how the Justices are undoubtedly fine persons doing their best to resolve difficult issues and, therefore, how responsible citizens need to rally round the Court regardless of disagreements.

Indirect support for the uncertain status of the contemporary Court is found in its felt need repeatedly to deem itself the "ultimate interpreter" of the Constitution, lest the citizenry believe that the Court's opinions are only one among a set of legitimate interpretations of the Constitution. Indeed, the Court has gone so far as to assert that *Marbury* declared the "basic principle that the federal judiciary is supreme in the exposition of the law of the Constitution, and that principle has ever since been respected by this Court and the Country as a permanent and indispensable feature of our constitutional system." This statement appeared initially in *Cooper* v. *Aaron* (1958), in which the Court dismissed, in no uncertain terms, attempts by the Little Rock, Arkansas school board to argue that it was not covered by the Court's rulings in the earlier school segregation cases that had, after all, arisen elsewhere. In that context, one can easily sympathize with the Court's description of its role. Yet it is really quite preposterous, requiring, for starters, that one ignore the thought of Madison, Jefferson, Jackson, Calhoun, Lincoln, and Franklin Roosevelt. Such claims, both to theoretical ultimacy and, just as significantly, the popular acceptance of same, have the overtone of the scared whistler going past the graveyard.

The extent of division concerning the Court—and the character of its members—was most sharply revealed in the extraordinarily bitter battle over the 1987 nomination by President Reagan of Judge Robert Bork to succeed Lewis Powell on the Court. Bork, a former Yale professor and Solicitor General of the United States before being named to the Court of Appeals for the District of Columbia, was one of the most prominent critics of the Warren Court and of the activism that it stood for. Indeed, he denounced it as basically lawless insofar as judges drifted from what he posited as the one true method of constitutional interpretation, the ascertaining and enforcement of the "original meaning" of the Constitution. Bork was particularly savage in his criticism of the Court's return to substantive due process and the enforcement of "unenumerated rights" in cases like *Griswold* v. *Connecticut* and *Roe* v. *Wade*. In the absence of explicit constitutional prohibitions, according to Bork, political majorities had basically unfettered authority to do what they wished. This is, of course, very close to what Holmes argued in the *Lochner* dissent. That dissent, the anthem of liberals during the run-up to the New Deal and for some two decades after, took on a different hue in the era of the Warren Court, which was far less accepting than was Holmes of the duty to uphold what it deemed "tyrannical" legislation.

If Bork was demonized by his opponents, who sometimes described him as blithely indifferent to oppression, then he was just as surely deified by his supporters, who saw him as a Herculean figure ready and willing to clean out the Augean stables desecrated by the jurisprudence of the last several decades. At the end he was rejected, but the scars of the battle remain vivid. And the debacle concerning Clarence Thomas's nomination in 1991 was even greater, as national attention ultimately focused on whether he had in fact sexually harassed an employee.

Never again will the nomination and confirmation of a judge take eight days, as was the case with Byron White in 1962 or even three weeks, as with John Paul Stevens in 1976. Even more will it be impossible for someone like Sherman Minton, who when nominated in 1949 was a member of the Seventh Circuit Court of Appeals, to refuse to testify before the Senate Judiciary Committee on the grounds that it was improper to direct questions at a sitting judge. Yet, ironically, the new public attention paid to appointment to the Court is evidence that the citizenry expects the Court to play a significant role in defining public policy. It is that expectation that makes it worth the while of various groups to marshal their resources in favor of or against particular nominees.

To the extent that the rejection of Robert Bork was based, among other things, on his unwillingness to endorse the legitimacy of the Court's protecting the citizenry against certain legislative invasions of "privacy," then the Senate, strongly backed by the public, can be viewed as giving its imprimatur to the rebirth of substantive due process following its apparent demise in 1937. Even Clarence Thomas, apparently more conservative than Rehnquist or Scalia, could gain confirmation only by denying to the Senate, truthfully or not, that he had ever thought seriously about *Roe* or had any opinions about the constitutional status of privacy and abortion. To have admitted what quickly became obvious, that he would in fact overrule *Roe,* would have doomed his nomination. Indeed, the Republican Party's failure to mount a serious attack on the 1993 nomination to the Court by President Clinton of Ruth Bader Ginsburg, a strong proponent of judicial protection of reproductive choice, signalled its acquiescence to the constitutionalization of basic abortion rights, even if the struggle would continue about their scope.

It is, then, chimerical to believe that the Court will ever retire from the political arena and simply adopt the role of some kind of "neutral" referee making sure that the active players conform to the rules of the constitutional game. The Court will continue to assess the rules and, on occasion, to rewrite them, quite independently of the wishes of the other players. The members of the Court, therefore, have to decide what role they wish to play. At the same time, those responsible for choosing members of the Court—presidents, senators, ultimately the citizenry—must decide as well what sort of person should be placed on the Court. What attributes should one look for? In particular, how does one try to guarantee the presence of the sound political judgment that, as much as legal "expertise," defines the role of the Supreme Court justice?

One of the most striking differences between the Warren and post-Warren Courts concerns the pre-appointment experiences of the Justices. The 1954 Court that decided *Brown,* for example, was headed by the immensely popular former governor of what was rapidly becoming the second-largest state; Earl Warren had been a candidate on the Republican ticket in 1948, and he continued to be spoken of as a presidential possibility in 1952. His colleagues included three former senators (Hugo Black, Sherman Minton, and Harold Burton); two of the leading legal academics of their time (Felix Frankfurter and William O. Douglas), both of whom had been involved at the highest level of the Roosevelt Administration during the New Deal; two former Solicitors General (Robert Jackson and Stanley Reed); and two former Attorneys General (Jackson and Tom Clark). Only one of them, Minton, had any prior judicial experience. To be sure, the pattern shifted somewhat thereafter. The other four Eisenhower appointees—Brennan, Harlan, Stewart, and Whittaker—all had judicial experience and, perhaps even more to the point, had little or no *non*-judicial experience in public life. Only one of Kennedy's and Johnson's four appointees—Thurgood Marshall—had judicial experience, and no one seriously would focus on that aspect of Marshall's pre-Court career when assessing his fitness for the Court. Far more important was his status as perhaps the leading public lawyer of the age, the central architect of the NAACP attack on segregation. Marshall would have merited a full-scale biography had he been run over by a truck the day before joining the Court. This simply cannot be said of anyone appointed to the Court since Marshall.

The only subsequent Justices about whose pre-Court experiences one might even write a chapter are Lewis Powell, Clarence Thomas, and Ruth

Bader Ginsburg. Powell had actively participated in the desegregation of Richmond, Virginia and was a relatively reformist president of the American Bar Association. Thomas had headed an important federal agency, the Equal Employment Opportunities Commission, while Ginsburg, as a practicing lawyer and professor of law in the 1970's, devised, and advocated before the Court, important arguments relating to discrimination against women. None, though, could truly be compared to Warren, Black, Frankfurter, Douglas, or Marshall—or past figures like John Marshall, Roger Taney, Salmon P. Chase, Louis Brandeis, William Howard Taft, or Charles Evans Hughes. Whatever their important differences, each of these figures *brought* real stature to the Court rather than having it thrust upon them by the fact of appointment. That is the meaning of the "biography test."

Since Lewis Powell's appointment in 1971, every single subsequent nominee to the Court has been serving already as a member of the judiciary; indeed, with the exception of Sandra Day O'Connor, they have been chosen from the federal courts of appeals. Although published press reports indicated that President Clinton was eager to appoint someone with significant political experience, his second nominee, Stephen G. Breyer, like his first, Ruth Bader Ginsburg, was a long-time federal appeals judge devoid of any such background. Few of the nominees particularly stood out; save for the ill-fated Bork, none was promoted by a coterie of public admirers in the way, say, that the case for appointing Benjamin N. Cardozo, by far the most important state-court judge of his time, was pressed upon President Hoover.

Why prior judicial experience is thought so important as a prerequisite for the Supreme Court is a mystery; it is surely not the case that the greatest judges of the past—whether measured by statesmanship, moral sensitivity, or eloquence in behalf of the values we would like to believe undergird the constitutional order—have necessarily had such experience. The best one can say is that it is not a disqualification and that the nine-justice Court probably needs one or two members who can bring the lessons of that experience to Washington. It is certainly not clear, though, that the habits of thought necessary to performing as a judicial underling are those most truly needed on the Supreme Court. Holmes is the great counter-example, though perhaps all one can say is that Holmes possessed such transcendent abilities that he could survive two decades of service on the Massachusetts Supreme Judicial Court without destroying his capacity for greatness.

It would be naive in the extreme to argue that the contempt of court revealed by Dean Calebresi (joined, no doubt, by millions of other Americans of various political stripes) would be assuaged simply by the appointment of at least some political figures who have had their character and judgment tested while running for office or otherwise participating in the brutal battles of public conflict about basic issues. The country may be just too polarized to view any set of appointees as possessing sufficient wisdom to make authoritative decisions in regard to the kind of issues presented the judiciary for resolution. But it is even harder to believe that a Supreme Court composed of relative nonentities, devoid of practical political experience—and devoid as well of public displays of genuine political courage equal even to Lewis Powell's activities in Richmond, let alone Thurgood Marshall's throughout the Deep South in the 1940's and 1950's—will gain the general public respect conducive to achieving compliance with far-reaching decisions.

The Supreme Court of the United States undoubtedly remains the most powerful court of any in the world, and there is no real reason to think that will change in the foreseeable future. However, what we have learned, especially in the past thirty years, is that the possession even of apparently awesome power may not in fact be enough to prevail in an ever-more-complex and fragmented world. After all, the United States— the most powerful country in the world—could not prevail in Vietnam, and nuclear weapons proved irrelevant to keeping the Communist Party in power or, indeed, to prevent the dissolution of the Soviet Union. Deference to established authority seems less and less descriptive of political reality anywhere in the world today, including the United States. The spectre of Oz must inhabit the nightmares of anyone who proclaims his or her power. In an age when incumbent presidents are now regularly defeated—and, indeed, may face primary struggles—and when legislators are increasingly being subjected to term limits for fear that they will somehow become impervious to ordinary electoral challenge, can a lifetime tenured Court be altogether confident that it, too, will not be subjected to similar criticism? Would a single term appointment of, say, eighteen years, which would generate a new justice every two years, really be a blow to the Court's stature or its independence?

Certainly nothing has negated McCloskey's 1960 observation that it gets ever harder to take seriously the image of the judge as the impersonal vessel through whom the Constitution speaks. And even if one could continue to believe such things of the judge, it would still remain open to ask whether that Constitution serves us all that well today. State constitutions enjoy none of the veneration accorded the United States Constitution;

they are not only often amended, but even, with some frequency, replaced with brand new versions. It would require the talents of a claivoyant to predict whether the Supreme Court, powerful though it may be, will continue to escape the storms that seem to be besetting other institutions of government. Yet, as Holmes once wrote, "repose is not the destiny" of humankind. The Supreme Court will remain fascinating, for good or for ill, so long as there is a United States that tries to resolve the tension between popular sovereignty and adherence to fundamental norms even when the majority would prefer to ignore them.

Important Dates

subjects that do not require a uniform national rule—the doctrine of "selective exclusiveness")

1857   *Dred Scott* case (holding the Missouri Compromise invalid)

1862   Justice Samuel F. Miller appointed

1863   Justice Stephen J. Field appointed

1864   Death of Taney

Chief Justice Salmon P. Chase appointed

1865   Thirteenth Amendment ratified

1866   *Ex Parte Milligan* (invalidating wartime military trial of civilians)

1868   Fourteenth Amendment ratified

Thomas M. Cooley's *Constitutional Limitations* published

1870   Fifteenth Amendment ratified

Hepburn v. Griswold (invalidating the Legal Tender Act in certain respects)

1871   *Legal Tender Cases* (upholding the Legal Tender Act in all respects)

1873   *Slaughterhouse Cases* (the Fourteenth Amendment does not forbid a state-granted monopoly)

1874   Chief Justice Morrison R. Waite appointed

1877   *Munn v. Illinois* (rate regulation of grain elevator rates by state is not forbidden by the Fourteenth Amendment)

1888   Chief Justice Melville W. Fuller appointed

1890   Minnesota Commission case (state rate regulation without judicial review denies due process)

1895   *United States v. E. C. Knight Co.* (the Sherman Antitrust Act cannot constitutionally apply to monopolies in manufacturing)

Pollock v. Farmers' Loan and Trust Co. (the Income Tax case)

1896   *Plessy v. Ferguson* (the state may require separate facilities for different races providing that the facilities are equal—the "separate but equal doctrine")

1902   Justice Oliver Wendell Holmes appointed

1904   *McCray v. United States* (the Oleomargarine Tax case)

1905   *Lochner v. New York* (the Fourteenth Amendment forbids general hours regulation)

Swift and Co. v. United States (the Antitrust Act can validly apply to sales monopolies)

1910   Chief Justice Edward D. White appointed

1913   Sixteenth Amendment ratified

1916   Justice Louis D. Brandeis appointed

1918 *Hammer* v. *Dagenhart* (the Child Labor case)

1919 *Schenck* v. *United States* (the "clear and present danger" rule)

1921 Chief Justice William H. Taft appointed

1923 *Adkins* v. *Children's Hospital* (the Washington, D.C., Minimum Wage case)

1934 *Nebbia* v. *New York* (upholding the validity of a state milk control law)

1935 *Schechter Poultry Corp.* v. *United States* (holding the National Industrial Recovery Act unconstitutional)

1936 *United States* v. *Butler* (holding the Agricultural Adjustment Act unconstitutional)

   Carter v. *Carter Coal Co.* (holding the Bituminous Coal Act unconstitutional)

   Morehead v. *Tipaldo* (holding the New York Minimum Wage Law unconstitutional)

   Franklin D. Roosevelt re-elected

1937 The "court-packing" plan submitted to Congress, February 5.

   West Coast Hotel v. *Parrish* (upholding the Minimum Wage Law of the State of Washington), March 29

   The National Labor Relations Act decisions (upholding the N.L.R.A.), April 12

   Steward Machine Co. v. *Davis* (upholding the Social Security Act), May 24

   Justice Willis Van Devanter retires, June 2

   Justice Hugo L. Black appointed, August 17

1941 Justice Harlan F. Stone appointed Chief Justice

   United States v. *Darby Lumber Co.* (upholding the Fair Labor Standards Act)

1944 *Smith* v. *Allwright* (the White Primary case)

1946 Chief Justice Fred M. Vinson appointed

1947 *Adamson* v. *California* (affirming that the procedural protections of the Bill of Rights are not embodied in the Fourteenth Amendment)

1951 *Dennis* v. *United States* (upholding convictions of Communist party leaders under the Smith Act of 1940)

1952 *Youngstown Co.* v. *Sawyer* (the Steel Seizure case)

1953 Chief Justice Earl Warren appointed

1954 *Brown* v. *Board of Education* (the Public School Desegregation case)

1955 *Brown* v. *Board of Education* (the enforcement decision)

1956   *Pennsylvania* v. *Nelson* (invalidating state sedition laws)

1956   Associate Justice William J. Brennan appointed

1958   *Cooper* v. *Aaron* (Court proclaims itself as "ultimate interpreter" of Constitution while enforcing *Brown* against Little Rock, Arkansas, school board)

1961   *Mapp* v. *Ohio* (applying to state criminal proceedings "exclusionary" rule regarding evidence seized in violation of Fourth Amendment)

1962   *Engel* v. *Vitale* (first school prayer decision)

        Baker v. *Carr* (holding justiciable issue of legislative apportionment)

        Justice Felix Frankfurter retires

1963   *Schempp* v. *Abington Township* (second school prayer decision)

        Gideon v. *Wainwright* (indigents entitled to lawyers in criminal trials)

1964   *New York Times* v. *Sullivan* (constitutionalizing law of libel)

        Reynolds v. *Sims* (one person-one vote)

        Katzenbach v. *McClung* (upholding Civil Rights Act of 1964)

        Malloy v. *Hogan* (incorporation against states of Fifth Amendment right against self-incrimination)

1965   *Griswold* v. *Connecticut* (use of contraceptives constitutionally protected)

1966   *Harper* v. *Virginia Board of Elections* (unconstitutionality of poll taxes in state elections)

        Miranda v. *Arizona* (police must inform criminal defendants of their rights, including right to silence and to aid of lawyer)

1968   *Green* v. *New Kent County* (duty to eliminate racially identifiable schools)

1969   *Brandenburg* v. *Ohio* (speech protected unless an incitement to immediate unlawful conduct)

        Shapiro v. *Thompson* (unconstitutional to require year of residence in order to receive welfare)

        Warren Burger appointed Chief Justice

1970   *Goldberg* v. *Kelly* (due process requires pre-termination hearings for welfare recipients)

        Dandridge v. *Williams* (no constitutional right to subsistence level of welfare)

        Justice Harry Blackmun appointed

1971   *Swann* v. *Charlotte-Mecklenburg Board of Education* (upholding busing as a remedy for school segregation)

Reed v. *Reed* (laws discriminating against women subject to special scrutiny)

New York Times v. *United States* (the Pentagon Papers case)

Justices Hugo L. Black and John Marshall Harlan retire

Justices William Rehnquist and Lewis Powell appointed

1972   *Furman* v. *Georgia* (striking down capital punishment)

Wisconsin v. *Yoder* (exemption of Amish from Wisconsin compulsory education law)

1973   *San Antonio Independent School District* v. *Rodriguez* (14th Amendment does not require equal funding of public school districts)

Roe v. *Wade* (the Abortion case)

Committee for Public Education & Liberty v. *Nyquist* (the Parochial School Funding case)

1974   *Nixon* v. *United States* (the Watergate Tapes case)

Bradley v. *Milliken* (lower courts not permitted to consolidate separate school districts in order to achieve desegregation)

1975   Justice Douglas retires

Justice John Paul Stevens appointed

1976   *Buckley* v. Valeo (the Election Funding case)

National League of Cities v. *Usery* (striking down minimum wage laws applied to state and local governments)

Gregg v. *Georgia* (death penalty not unconstitutional per se)

Mathews v. *Eldridge* (limiting *Goldberg*)

1977   *Coker* v. *Georgia* (death penalty for rape unconstitutional)

Maher v. *Roe* (no constitutional duty to fund abortions)

1978   *Bakke* v. *Regents of University of California* (the Affirmative Action case)

1980   *Branti* v. *Finkel* (the Political Patronage case)

1981   Justice Potter Stewart retires

Justice Sandra Day O'Connor appointed

1982   *Plyler* v. *Doe* (right of children of illegel aliens to education)

Mississippi University for Women v. *Hogan* (states must offer "substantial" reasons to justify gender distinctions)

1983   *Immigration and Naturalization Service* v. *Chadha* (the Legislative Veto case)

1985   *Garcia* v. *San Antonio Metropolitan Transit Authority* (overruling *National League of Cities*)

1986   *Bowers* v. *Hardwick* (constitutional to criminalize homosexual conduct)

Batson v. *Kentucky* (race-based peremptory dismissals of potential jurors unconstitutional)

Chief Justice William Rehnquist succeeds Warren Burger

Justice Antonin Scalia appointed

1987 Justice Lewis Powell retires

Nomination of Judge Robert Bork rejected by Senate, 58–42, October 23

Justice Anthony Kennedy appointed

1989 *DeShaney* v. *Winnebago County Department of Social Services* (no constitutional right to state protection against harm)

1990 Justice William J. Brennan retires

Justice David Souter appointed

1991 *Rust* v. *Sullivan* (the Abortion Gag Rule case)

Justice Thurgood Marshall retires

Justice Clarence Thomas appointed

1992 *Planned Parenthood of Southeastern Pennsylvania* v. *Casey* (reaffirmation of constitutionally protected status of abortion)

1993 Justice Ruth Bader Ginsburg appointed

BIBLIOGRAPHICAL ESSAY

"THE BODY OF LITERATURE pertaining to the Supreme Court of the United States and to American constitutional law is enormous." Thus began Robert McCloskey's original bibliographical essay almost thirty-five years ago; the statement is even more true today. What follows, therefore, does no more than try to sketch the tip of an every-growing iceberg, and many fine books—and almost all relevant articles—are simply omitted.

A. Primary Sources

One should certainly make the direct acquaintance of the Supreme Court by reading some of its actual opinions. They appear in three equally authoritative sources—the *United States Reports*, which is the official publication of the government; and the privately published *Supreme Court Reporter* and *Lawyer's Edition*. Differing somewhat in the amount and kind of scholarly material they provide to aid their users, all three print the Court opinions in full. They are cited in any legal publication by volume, abbreviated name (U.S., S.Ct., or L.Ed.), and page. Thus, 325 U.S. 1 means volume 325 of the *United States Reports*, page one. Until 1875, the official reports were identified by the name of the reporter (e.g., 7 *Wallace* 299), though this practice was abandoned with the ninety-first volume, and thereafter the official citation practice is the one just illustrated. This is, incidentally, the standard citation form used by legal academics for scholarly journals as well: Thus 70 *Harvard Law Review* 253 is page 253 of volume 70.

Casebooks (i.e., abridged selections of leading decisions and, increasingly, other relevant materials) also deserve brief mention as "semipri-mary" sources. Because most casebooks are published for use in law schools by fledgling lawyers, their editors are likely to omit cases that are viewed of historical importance alone and no longer binding as prece-dent. The most obvious example is a case like *Dred Scott*. Of contempo-rary law school casebooks, by far the most historically oriented is Paul Brest and Sanford Levinson, *Processes of Constitutional Decision Mak-ing* (3d ed., 1992). Also good, but less saturated in history (though with considerably more coverage than Brest and Levinson of contemporary materials), are Geoffrey Stone et al., *Constitutional Law* (2d ed., 1991); Gerald Gunther, *Constitutional Law* (12th ed., 1991); William Lockhart et al., *Constitutional Law* (7th ed. 1991); and William Cohen and Jona-than Varat, *Constitutional Law* (9th ed., 1993). For years the most widely used casebook within political science departments was Alpheus T. Ma-son and William M. Beaney, *American Constitutional Law: Introductory Essays and Selected Cases,* now in its tenth edition (1993) with Donald Grier Stephenson, Jr., replacing Beaney. It includes excellent historical treatments of doctrinal developments. James Fleming, Will Harris, and Walter Murphy, *American Constitutional Interpretation* (1986) focuses, as suggested by its title, on theoretical problems of constitutional inter-pretation.

Anyone interested, whether because of historical curiosity or a com-mitment to "original intent" as a mode of constitutional interpretation, in the specific background of the 1787 Constitution must consult Max Farrand, *The Records of the Federal Convention of 1787* (4 vols., 1911, 1937) and Jonathan Elliott, *The Debates in the Several State Conventions on the Adoption of the Federal Constitution* (5 vols., 1836). Farrand is available in a Yale University Press paperback edition; Elliott can be found only in libraries, alas. Bernard Bailyn has recently published a marvelous two-volume edition on *The Debate on the Constitution* (1993) that orga-nizes the debate chronologically.

At least as important as these materials are commentaries on the Constitution produced during the ratification struggle. Certainly the pri-mary example is the *Federalist Papers*. Written by James Madison, Alex-ander Hamilton, and John Jay under the pen name "Publius," in order to encourage ratification by the New York convention, the eighty-four essays that comprise them have been too often treated as a disinterested (and privileged) guide to constitutional meaning. They have spawned an exten-sive commentary literature of their own. See, e.g., Garry Wills, *Explaining America: The Federalist* (1981); David F. Epstein, *The Political Theory of*

The Federalist (1984); and Morton White, *Philosophy, The Federalist, and the Constitution* (1987).

For the alternative vision to *The Federalist*, the best source is Herbert J. Storing's seven-volume edition of *The Complete Anti-Federalist* (1981), a collection of the leading oppositional writings to ratification. More modest in its coverage, but also excellent, is a reader by Cecelia Kenyon, ed., *The Antifederalists* (1966), which includes, among other things, good excerpts from the Virginia, New York, and North Carolina ratifying conventions. Also vital for serious students (and their teachers) is the five-volume *The Founders' Constitution,* edited by Philip B. Kurland and Ralph Lerner (1987). Going through the 1787 Constitution and the first twelve amendments clause by clause, Kurland and Lerner reprint some of the key historical material that helps to explain both why given issues were bones of contention and why given solutions were seized upon by the Framers. Somewhat different in orientation is Jefferson Powell, *Languages of Power: A Source Book of Early American Constitutional History* (1991), which imaginatively presents a plethora of materials concerning the controversies that wracked the young republic.

Inevitably, the richest body of easily available primary materials concerns the founding period of 1787–91 (the latter date being the ratification of the Bill of Rights). But, obviously, what happened in the 1860's was certainly of major import. Harold Hyman, ed., *The Radical Republicans and Reconstruction, 1861–1870* (1967), includes many materials that certainly touch on basic constitutional questions, including, of course, the addition of the so-called "Reconstruction Amendments" that are by far the most important textual additions to the Constitution since the Founding period. Daniel A. Farber and Suzanna Sherry, eds., *A History of the American Constitution* (1990) contains a helpful 100-page section on these Amendments.

Several "commentaries" on the Constitution have become primary sources for the historian of American constitutionalism insofar as they capture very well the concerns and thought of a particular time, at least within a segment of the elite bar. James Kent's *Commentaries on American Law* (4 vols., 1830) and Joseph Story's *Commentaries on the Constitution of the United States* (3 vols., 1833, reprinted in a one volume edition with an introduction by Ronald D. Rotunda and John E. Nowak, 1987) affected constitutional development for many years. Story, of course, was a leading member of the Court for three decades. Thomas M. Cooley's *Treatise on the Constitutional Limitations Which Rest Upon the Legislative Power of the States of the American Union* (1868) was enormously influential in shaping the doctrines of constitutional laissez faire that were so important to American public law until 1937. One should also mention Laurence Tribe's *American Constitutional Law* (2d ed., 1988), though it is too early to place it in the same rank as Kent, Story, and Cooley. Nonetheless, Tribe is certainly one of the leading liberal constitutional scholars of this past quarter century, and his treatise has the range and intellectual ambition of Tribe's predecessors. (A less ambitious, but helpful, contemporary treatise is John E. Nowak and Ronald D. Rotunda, *Constitutional Law* [4th ed. 1991].) Students should be aware that both of these modern treatises are basically analyses of the decided case law of the Supreme Court, which leaves out a great deal of material relevant to constitutional development.

B. GENERAL REFERENCE WORKS

One of the most welcome developments since 1960 is the publication of many first-rate reference works on the Court. Extremely helpful to any student is Leonard Levy, Kenneth L. Karst, and Dennis J. Mahoney, eds., *Encyclopedia of the American Constitution* (2 vols., 1986), supplemented by an additional volume of over 500 pages in 1992. The three volumes include essays by a host of distinguished scholars on almost every relevant topic. A selection of the entries, focusing on historical developments, has been published as *American Constitutional History* (1989). Only slightly less ambitious and helpful is Kermit Hall, ed., *The Oxford Companion to the Supreme Court of the United States* (1992), a compendium of both short entries and sometimes quite extensive essays on practically all aspects of the Court and its work. Although both of these works include entries on the members of the Supreme Court, students may also want to consult Leon Friedman, ed., *The Justices of the United States Supreme Court: Their Lives and Major Opinions, 1789–1978* (5 vols., 1980). More recently, the Supreme Court Historical Society has published *The Supreme Court Justices: Illustrated Biographies, 1789–1993* (Clare Cushman ed., 1993), which offers extremely readable and succinct 8–12 page biographies of every Justice save Ruth Ginsburg. Finally, one should mention Kermit L. Hall's five-volume compilation, *A Comprehensive Bibliography of American Constitutional and Legal History, 1890–1979* (1984), described by a leading historian as "an incredibly complete collection of virtually everything written on the subject in the last century."

(1987) will quickly bring the student up to date on many of the major current controversies on this topic. Also useful are Herman Belz et al., *To Form a More Perfect Union: The Critical Ideas of the Constitution* (1992) and Richard Beeman et al., *Beyond Confederation: Origins of the Constitution and American National Identity* (1987). For the politics of the Constitutional Convention see Calvin C. Jillson, *Constitution Making: Conflict and Consensus in the Federal Convention of 1787* (1988). Michael Allen Gillespie and Michael Lienesch have edited a very helpful set of essays examining the state-by-state ratification process, *Ratifying the Constitution* (1989). Many of these books and essays refer, in greater or lesser depth, to the classic controversy provoked by Charles A. Beard, *An Economic Interpretation of the Constitution* (1913), which argued that the Constitution's Founders were actively seeking to serve their own economic interests. Beard's unadorned thesis had been successfully challenged by Robert E. Brown, *Charles Beard and the Constitution* (1954), and by Forrest McDonald, *We the People: The Economic Origins of the Constitution* (1958), but, restated in far more nuanced form, it continues to play a role in scholarly debate.

On the initial fifty years of the Supreme Court see Charles G. Haines, *The Role of the Supreme Court in American Government and Politics, 1789–1835* (1944). Haines, with Foster H. Sherwood, also wrote *The Role of the Supreme Court in American Government and Politics, 1835–1864* (1957). Another study of the same period is Kent Newmyer, *The Supreme Court Under Marshall and Taney* (1968). Harold Hyman is another leading constitutional historian, whose contributions include *A More Perfect Union: The Impact of the Civil War and Reconstruction on the Constitution* (1973) and, with William Wiecek, *Equal Justice Under Law: Constitutional Development 1835–1875* (1982). Other perspectives are provided by Herman Belz, *Emancipation and Equal Rights: Politics and Constitutionalism in the Civil War Era* (1978) and Phillip S. Paludan, *A Covenant with Death: The Constitution, Law, and Equality in the Civil War Era* (1975). An enduring controversy concerns Abraham Lincoln's devotion to the Constitution during the Civil War. James G. Randall, *Constitutional Problems Under Lincoln* (1951) is the standard account, though one will also want to read Mark E. Neely, *The Fate of Liberty: Abraham Lincoln and Civil Liberties* (1991).

One of the most contentious controversies among American historians concerns the "original meaning" of the Fourteenth Amendment. One polar view is well argued in Raoul Berger, *Government by Judiciary* (1977), which presents an extremely restricted view of the Amendment that limits it basically to guaranteeing only "civil rights" (as distinguished from "political or social rights") to the newly freed African-Americans. The other polar view is well presented by Michael Kent Curtis, *No State Shall Abridge: The Fourteenth Amendment and the Bill of Rights* (1986), which argues, in contrast (and, I believe, with more plausibility), in behalf of a very expansive reading, including the view that the privileges or immunities clause of the Amendment was intended to apply the Bill of Rights to the states. Closer to Berger is Earl M. Maltz, *Civil Rights, The Constitution, and Congress, 1863–1869* (1990). Also valuable is William E. Nelson, *The Fourteenth Amendment: From Political Principle to Judicial Doctrine* (1988), which focuses on the libertarian background of the Amendment.

The Constitution is brought into the early twentieth century by Loren P. Beth, *Constitutional History, 1877–1917* (1971) and John E. Semonche, *Charting the Future: The Supreme Court Responds to a Changing Society, 1890–1920* (1978). The late William F. Swindler wrote an ambitious three-volume study on *Court and Constitution in the Twentieth Century* consisting of *The Old Legality, 1889–1932* (1969); *The New Legality, 1932–1968* (1970); and *The Modern Interpretation* (1974). Much of this same period is covered in Paul L. Murphy, *The Constitution in Crisis Times, 1918–1969* (1972). An interesting set of essays can be found in Ellen Frankel Paul and Howard Dickman, eds., *Liberty, Property, and Government: Constitutional Interpretation Before the New Deal* (1989).

The Modern Supreme Court (1972) is a posthumous book of Robert McCloskey's essays on the Vinson and Warren Courts. There is not yet a standard scholarly book on the "Burger Court," but Vicent Blasi edited an interesting collection of essays, *The Burger Court: The Counter-Revolution That Wasn't* (1983). As one might gather from the title, the major theme is that the shift from the liberal Warren Court to the more conservative Burger tribunal brought far less rejection of the earlier precedents than was anticipated (and, of course, with *Roe* as the major example, in some areas went far beyond its predecessor). The "Rehnquist Court" has been analyzed by the journalist David G. Savage, *Turning Right: The Making of the Rehnquist Supreme Court* (1992). It is particularly useful in detailing some of the changes in the law of criminal procedure during the 1980's.

Students should be aware of two recent comprehensive books by professors at the Yale Law School. Bruce Ackerman's *We the People: Foundations* (1991) is the first volume of an ambitious three-volume trilogy that attempts to place all of American constitutional development within a coherent narrative that emphasizes, nonetheless, the occurrence of fundamental constitutional change. Ackerman argues that much constitutional "amendment" has in fact taken place outside of the channels of Article V and has very much involved the President and Congress, in addition to the Court. Robert Burt's *The Constitution in Conflict* (1992) also presents a comprehensive overview that attacks traditional notions of judicial supremacy and instead also emphasizes the important roles played by other branches of government in giving meaning to the Con stitution.

Unfortunately, there is no really good comprehensive presentation of the constitutional law that is made by presidents, congress, administrative agencies, and ordinary citizens in addition to that which is made by the courts. Louis Fisher has written on this important topic in *Constitutional Dialogues: Interpretation as Political Process* (1988). Fisher and Neal Devins have also compiled a very interesting reader, *Political Dynamics of Constitutional Law* (1992).

Finally, mention should be made of William Lasser, *The Limits of Judicial Power: The Supreme Court in American Politics* (1988), which explicitly attempts to counter the thesis enunciated by McCloskey in the original edition of this book. Focusing on *Dred Scott* and its aftermath, the 1937 Revolution, and the Warren and Burger Courts, Lasser argues that the Supreme Court has considerably more latitude for action than was acknowledged by McCloskey, who, Lasser believes, overestimated the likelihood of effective attacks on the Court.

D. JUDICIAL BIOGRAPHIES

One excellent way to learn the history of the Court of a given period is by reading a good biography of a Justice. It must be said that a surprising number of the Justices were quite obscure even in their lifetimes and have received no scholarly treatment since then; indeed, even some relatively well-known Justices have been ignored by biographers, save in such general reference works as those mentioned earlier. Still, as one would expect, many important Justices have been the subject of major biographies, some of them, indeed, of several biographies, and the student will find more than enough to keep her busy. All of the standard reference works cited above include, after their entries on a given justice, citations to biographical materials.

Though it is sometimes difficult to remember, there *was* a Court before John Marshall's arrival in 1801. The first Chief Justice, John Jay, is the subject of *John Jay, the Nation, and the Court* (1967) by the distinguished colonial historian Richard B. Morris. Similarly, James Wilson went from being an especially influential figure at the Philadelphia convention and then the Pennsylvania ratifying convention to the Supreme Court. His life and thought are the subject of an extended introduction to Robert McCloskey, ed., *The Works of James Wilson* (2 vols., 1967).

Still, it is John Marshall who dominates the early history of the Court. United States Senator Albert J. Beveridge, a gifted amateur historian, published a four-volume biography of John Marshall in 1916. Although almost idolatrous in its stance toward Marshall, it offers copious insight into the history and political culture of the time. Two more recent biographies are Leonard Baker, *John Marshall: A Life in the Law* (1974) and Francis N. Stites, *John Marshall, Defender of the Constitution* (1981). Marshall's jurisprudence is analyzed in Robert K. Faulkner, *The Jurisprudence of John Marshall* (1968).

A Federalist colleague of Marshall's who was unsuccessfully threatened with impeachment by angry Jeffersonians was Samuel Chase, about whom James Haw and others have written in *Stormy Patriot: The Life of Samuel Chase* (1981). Another significant member of the Marshall Court was William Johnson, ably profiled in Donald G. Morgan, *Justice William Johnson: The First Dissenter* (1959). But certainly the most important member of that Court save Marshall was the brilliant Joseph Story. The best of several biographies is R. Kent Newmyer, *Supreme Court Justice Joseph Story: Statesman of the Old Republic* (1985).

Marshall's successor, Roger Brooke Taney, was the subject of a 1935 biography by Carl Swisher. Somewhat more recent is Lewis Walker, *Without Fear or Favor: A Biography of Chief Justice Roger Brooke Taney* (1965). One of Taney's great adversaries is profiled in Francis P. Weisenburger, *The Life of John McLean: A Politician on the Supreme Court* (1937). Peter Daniel, more states-rightist and pro-slavery than Taney himself, is the subject of John P. Frank, *Justice Daniel Dissenting: Peter V. Daniel* (1964). The sectional tensions on the Court are also set out in Alexander A. Lawrence, *James Moore Wayne: Southern Unionist* (1970).

Salmon Chase, an extremely important abolitionist leader, Republican activist, and, finally, Taney's successor as Chief Justice, is the subject of Frederick J. Blue, *Salmon P. Chase, A Life in Politics* (1987). Two important colleagues of Chase, Samuel F. Miller and Stephen J. Field, have received full-dress treatment. On the former, see Charles Fairman, *Mr. Justice Miller and the Supreme Court, 1862–1890* (1938). On Field, see

Carl B. Swisher, *Stephen J. Field: Craftsman of the Law* (1930). New Deal-influenced historians tended to see Field as a simple lackey of capitalist businessmen. An important corrective to this view, emphasizing his origins in Jacksonian egalitarianism, is Michael Les Benedict, "Laissez-Faire and Liberty: A Re-Evaluation of the Meaning and Origins of Laissez-Faire Constitutionalism," 3 *Law and History Review* 293 (1985).

The first ex-Confederate to be appointed to the Court is treated in James B. Murphy, *L. Q. C. Lamar: Pragmatic Patriot* (1973). Another former slaveholder was John Marshall Harlan, who stands out as literally unique among the late-nineteenth century Justices for his commitment to racial justice. His life is the subject of Loren Beth, *John Marshall Harlan: The Last Whig Justice* (1992).

To be a Chief Justice, even if obscure, seems to guarantee book-length treatment. Thus available are C. Petter McGrath, *Morrison R. Waite: The Triumph of Character* (1963); Willard L. King, *Melville Weston Fuller: Chief Justice of the United States* (1950); Robert B. Highsaw, *Edward Douglass White: Defender of the Conservative Faith* (1981).

Oliver Wendell Holmes is perhaps the best known of all Associate Justices. Indeed, he is one of the most important single Justices in American history, as evidenced by the fact that he is the subject of no fewer than four biographies since 1989 alone! The best of them is surely G. Edward White's *Justice Oliver Wendell Holmes: Law and the Inner Self* (1993), which is illuminating not only as to Holmes's complex personality, but also in regard to his opinions on the Court. A superb short treatment of Holmes's life is Gary J. Aichele, *Oliver Wendell Holmes, Jr.: Soldier, Scholar, Judge* (1989). Anyone particularly interested in Holmes's early life will want to consult Mark DeWolfe Howe's first two volumes of a multi-volume life that he did not live to complete: *Justice Oliver Wendell Holmes: The Shaping Years* (1957) and *The Proving Years* (1963). Finally, Richard Posner edited a sterling collection of Holmes's writings in *The Essential Holmes: Selections from the Letters, Speeches, Judicial Opinions and Other Writings of Oliver Wendell Holmes, Jr.* (1992).

Holmes's great companion on the Court, Louis D. Brandeis, has also received multiple treatments. Alpheus T. Mason's *Brandeis: A Free Man's Life* (1946), has, inevitably, been supplanted by later scholars with access to more copious sources. The best one-volume study is Philippa Strum, *Louis D. Brandeis: Justice for the People* (1984).

Holmes and Brandeis, of course, served under William Howard Taft, whose Chief Justiceship is the subject of Alpheus P. Mason, *William Howard Taft, Chief Justice* (1965). Yet another of Mason's contributions, and almost certainly his most enduring one, concerns yet another colleague of Holmes, Brandeis, and Taft, Harlan Fiske Stone, who would ultimately become Chief Justice himself. *Harlan Fiske Stone, Pillar of the Law* (1956), drew extensively on Stone's private papers, which were often extremely candid regarding his views of his colleagues. It created a storm when published and continues to repay careful study. Merlo J. Pusey, *Charles Evans Hughes* (1951) is also valuable, in part because it conflicts with some of Mason's judgments about the Court of the 1930's. Joel F. Paschal, *Mr. Justice Sutherland* (1951) is a good starting point for understanding the conservative jurisprudence against which Holmes, Brandeis, and Stone (and, at times, Hughes) so forcefully argued.

The "Roosevelt Court," many of whose members lasted into the 1960's, contained some of the most interesting and vivid personalities in our history. J. Woodford Howard's *Mr. Justice Murphy* (1968) is an invaluable study of this Court. Not only a first-rate study of an interesting life, it is also an unusually fine analysis of the inner workings of the Court during an especially contentious period in which it was seeking its way after the tumult of the New Deal and the great retreat of 1937. Murphy, though, was certainly not one of the "stars" of the Court; he was left behind in the struggle for leadership waged by such titans as Felix Frankfurter, Hugo Black, William O. Douglas, and Robert Jackson. This struggle is depicted in a political science classic, C. Herman Pritchett, *The Roosevelt Court: A Study in Judicial Politics and Values, 1937–1947* (1948).

The pre-court years of Frankfurter's remarkable life are covered in Michael E. Parrish, *Felix Frankfurter and His Times* (1982). A second volume is eagerly awaited. Until then, the student can consult Melvin I. Urofsky, *Felix Frankfurter: Judicial Restraint and Individual Liberties* (1991) or Harry N. Hirsch, *The Enigma of Felix Frankfurter* (1981). Also important is the long biographical essay that Joseph P. Lash wrote to introduce *From the Diaries of Felix Frankfurter* (1975). The diary entries, incidentally, vividly convey Frankfurter's intensity, including what can only be described as his hatred of some of his colleagues on the Court, including Black (with whom he later became quite friendly) and Douglas (whom he despised to his dying day). They are the subject of Howard Ball & Phillip J. Cooper, *Of Power and Right: Hugo Black, William O. Douglas, and America's Constitutional Revolution* (1992). Douglas wrote two volumes of autobiography, *Go East Young Man: The Early Years* (1974), and *The Court Years: 1939–1975* (1980), though, as with any autobiographies, they must be used with some caution. James F. Simon has published a helpful biography, *Independent Journey: The Life of*

William O. Douglas (1980). Serviceable, but no better, alas, is Eugene C. Gerhart, *America's Advocate: Robert H. Jackson* (1958). Jackson, one of the most interesting minds (and eloquent writers) ever to serve on the Court, deserves better.

Earl Warren's life is ably treated in G. Edward White, *Earl Warren: A Public Life* (1982). Bernard Schartz published *Superchief* (1983), a not very well-written study of the Warren Court that nonetheless has a lot of valuable material drawn from interviews with and the private papers of some of the Justices. The Warren Court was full of strong intellects and personalities. The great conservative counterweight to Black, Douglas, and Warren, following Frankfurter's retirement in 1962, was John Marshall Harlan, the subject of Tinsley E. Yarborough, *John Marshall Harlan: Great Dissenter of the Warren Court* (1992). A potentially very important member of the Court whose career was cut short by scandal has received full-scale analysis in Laura Kalman, *Abe Fortas: A Biography* (1990).

No scholarly biography has yet appeared on William J. Brennan, arguably the most important single justice since 1960, though Kim Isaac Eisler, a journalist, has published *A Justice for All: William J. Brennan Jr. and the Decisions that Transformed America* (1993). Brennan's colleague and friend, Thurgood Marshall, has already been the subject of several popular biographies. Mark Tushnet, *Making Civil Rights Law: Thurgood Marshall and the Supreme Court, 1936–1961* (1994) is the first of a two-volume scholarly analysis of Marshall.

E. Judicial Writing on the Judicial Role

One might well be interested in how judges, when stepping back from the specific task of writing opinions, describe their role as constitutional interpreters. A fine collection is Mark W. Cannon and David M. O'Brien, eds., *Views from the Bench: The Judiciary and Constitutional Politics* (1985). Also still helpful is Alan P. Westin, ed., *The Supreme Court: Views from Inside* (1961).

Probably the classic judge-written book remains Benjamin N. Cardozo, *The Nature of the Judicial Process* (1921). Cardozo presents a straight-forward defense of pragmatic decisionmaking; his argument has been picked up and elaborated more recently by Richard Posner, a distinguished University of Chicago law professor who is now the Chief Judge of the Seventh Circuit Court of Appeals, in *The Problems of Jurisprudence* (1990). Justice Brennan delivered an important talk, "The Constitution of the United States: Contemporary Ratification," at Georgetown University, which is reprinted in Sanford Levinson and Steven Mailloux, eds., *Interpreting Law and Literature: A Hermeneutic Reader*, pp. 13–24 (1988). A full-scale attack on such arguments (and any others that ostensibly give too much power to judges) was delivered by Robert Bork, President Reagan's ill-fated nominee for the Supreme Court, in *The Tempting of America: The Political Seduction of the Law* (1990).

Older judge-written books still worth reading are Robert Jackson, *The Supreme Court in the American System of Government* (1955); Hugo Black, *A Constitutional Faith* (1968); and Learned Hand, *The Bill of Rights* (1958). (Hand, the most eminent federal appellate judge of his time, is the subject of an unusually subtle biography by Gerald Gunther, *Learned Hand* (1994).) Also very interesting is Philip Kurland, ed., *Felix Frankfurter on the Supreme Court: Extrajudicial Essays on the Court and the Constitution* (1970), a compendium of Frankfurter's copious writings over a fifty-year period on the general subject. All of these volumes are particularly relevant for the student interested in the endless (and not always illuminating) debate about the Supreme Court's "activism" or "self-restraint."

Finally, there is a very interesting reader coedited by federal circuit judge John T. Noonan and Kenneth I. Winston, *The Responsible Judge: Readings In Judicial Ethics* (1993).

F. GREAT CASES

Another good way to learn about the Court is by reading about some of the "great cases" of constitutional law. See, e.g., John Garraty, *Quarrels that Shaped the Constitution* (rev'd ed., 1987) and Peter Irons, *The Courage of Their Convictions: Sixteen Americans Who Fought Their Way to the Supreme Court* (1988), which focuses on civil liberties cases. Irons also published, with Stephanie Guitton, *May It Please the Court* (1993), edited transcripts and cassette tapes of the arguments in twenty-three cases argued before the Supreme Court between 1958 and 1989. One can, for example, hear Thurgood Marshall present his argument in *Cooper v. Aaron*, the Little Rock school case. No student should miss the opportunity to hear these cases and the interaction between lawyers and Justices captured on the tapes.

Marbury v. *Madison* remains one of the great foci of scholarly interest. Robert Clinton, *Marbury v. Madison and Judicial Review* (1989) offers a fresh look at that old chestnut, as does Sylvia Snowiss, *Judicial*

Review and the Law of the Constitution (1990). Mention should also be made of three unusually fine articles, William Van Alstyne, "A Critical Guide to Marbury," 1969 *Duke Law Journal* 1; James O'Fallon, "*Marbury,*" 44 *Stanford Law Review* 219 (1992); and David E. Engdahl, "John Marshall's 'Jeffersonian' Concept of Judicial Review," 42 *Duke Law Journal* (1992). The last two articles criticize what Engdahl describes as "McCloskey's absurd, romanticized account of Marshall's opinion as a 'masterwork of indirection.' " Incidentally, insofar as *Marbury* invariably raises the question of the framer's intent regarding judicial review, the student should certainly consult Raoul Berger, *Congress v. the Supreme Court* (1969), which demonstrated quite conclusively that at least some degree of judicial review was indeed expected and intended by the Framers.

The notorious Yazoo Land scandal is the subject of C. Peter McGrath, *Yazoo: Law and Politics in the New Republic, The Case of Fletcher v. Peck* (1966). Two other classic Marshall Court cases are treated in Maurice G. Baxter, *The Steamboat Monopoly: Gibbons v. Ogden, 1824* (1972) and Francis N. Stiles, *Private Interest and Public Gain: The Dartmouth College Case, 1819* (1972). The most truly significant of all of Marshall's cases, *McCulloch* v. *Maryland*, still awaits the full-scale treatment it deserves, but a good place to start is Gerald Gunther, ed., *John Marshall's Defense of McCulloch v. Maryland* (1969), which details the fascinating newspaper debates, in which Marshall participated anonymously, that followed the decision in that case. Though not in a strict sense a constitutional case, *The Antelope*, an 1825 slavery case, is immensely illuminating about the Marshall Court's view of its role, and John T. Noonan, Jr., deals with the case in *The Antelope: The Ordeal of the Recaptured Africans in the Administrations of James Monroe and John Quincy Adams* (1977).

Stanley Kutler's *Privilege and Creative Destruction: The Charles River Bridge Case* (rev. ed. 1977), is a fascinating study of a key Taney Court case. Don Fehrenbacher's truly magisterial *The Dred Scott Case* (1978) offers a thorough constitutional history of the entire slavery issue as well as an unmatched treatment of the title case. Paul Finkelman, *An Imperfect Union: Slavery, Federalism, and Comity* (1981) is an excellent study of the tortuous interplay between slavery and federalism.

Two other classic cases are well treated in Charles Lofgren, *The Plessy Case: A Legal-Historical Interpretation* (1987) and Paul Kens, *Judicial Power and Reform Politics: The Anatomy of Lochner v. New York* (1990). In *Fighting Faiths: The Abrams Case, the Supreme Court, and*

Free Speech (1987), Richard Polenberg examines in depth one of the crucial free speech cases of the post-World War I era. *Near v. Minnesota* (1931), in which the Court for the first time announced its opposition to prior restraints, is described in Fred W. Friendly, *Minnesota Rag: The Dramatic Story of the Landmark Supreme Court Case that Gave New Meaning to Freedom of the Press* (1981).

Though not about any specific "great case" as such, Peter Irons, in *The New Deal Lawyers* (1982), closely examines the litigation strategies of the Roosevelt Administration in bringing many such cases before the Court. The book is a useful complement to Benjamin R. Twiss, *Lawyers and the Constitution: How Laissez Faire Came to the Constitution* (1942), a study of the important role played by lawyers in providing the Court with ideas and supporting arguments during the earlier era of laissez-faire constitutionalism.

David R. Mainwaring, *Render Unto Caesar: The Flag Salute Controversy* (1962) sets out the context of the 1940 cases that first revealed the significant split among the Roosevelt appointees in regard to protecting the civil liberties of highly unpopular minorities such as the Jehovah's Witnesses. Surely the most scandalous nonprotection of such a minority involved the Court's basic acquiescence to the incarceration of Japanese-Americans for no other reason than their ethnicity. Peter Irons, *Justice at War: The Story of the Japanese American Internment Cases* (1983) details that episode and the particularly shameful behavior of the Executive Branch. Irons has also edited *Justice Delayed: The Record of the Japanese American Internment Cases* (1989), which includes material relating to the reopening of the cases in the 1980's and ultimate formal legal vindication of Fred Korematsu and other Japanese Americans.

Shelley v. Kramer, in which the Supreme Court declared unenforceable racially restrictive housing covenants, is the subject of Clement Vose, *Caucasians Only: The Supreme Court, the NAACP, and the Restrictive Covenant Cases* (1959). Maeva Marcus, *Truman and the Steel Seizure Case: The Limits of Presidential Power* (1977), treats another significant "Vinson Court" case.

The "Warren Court" is indelibly identified with the most important civil rights case of modern times, *Brown v. Board of Education,* the history of which is marvelously set out in Richard Kluger, *Simple Justice* (1975). New York Times columnist Anthony Lewis writes of two other classic Warren Court cases in *Gideon's Trumpet* (1964), which tells the background of *Gideon v. Wainwright,* the indigent criminal defendant case, and *Make No Law: The Sullivan Case and the First Amendment* (1991).

The most controversial case of the past thirty years is surely *Roe v. Wade,* the subject of David Garrow's *Liberty and Sexuality: The Right to Privacy in the Making of Roe v. Wade* (1994). Barbara Hinkson Craig and David M. O'Brien, in *Abortion and American Politics* (1993), include a lot of helpful information and political analysis of various cases brought to the Court, as well as the partial texts of some of the key opinions. Similarly, Lee Epstein and Joseph F. Kobylka offer, in *The Supreme Court & Legal Change* (1992), in-depth case studies of abortion and death-penalty litigation. The litigation of another extraordinarily controversial case is analyzed in Timothy J. O'Neill, *Bakke & the Politics of Equality: Friends & Foes in the Classroom of Litigation* (1985).

Barbara Hinkson Craig, *Chadha: The Story of an Epic Constitutional Struggle* (1988) details the struggle of an alien plaintiff to challenge the decision of Congress to override, via "legislative veto," an administrative determination that he be allowed to remain in the United States. Though subsequent events make Craig's description of *Chadha* as "epic" overdrawn, Craig presents a good introduction to the tangled constitutional dimensions of congressional-administrative agency relations.

A somewhat different kind of book is William K. Muir, *Prayer in the Public Schools* (1968), which looks not at the "background," but, rather, at the subsequent *impact* of the Court's school prayer decisions on the practice of a local school system. One must always remember that Supreme Court decisions are not self-enforcing; many are the public officials, at all levels of government, who must agree to change their behavior before the Court's decisions can be accurately described as in fact affecting the American political landscape. This point is further elaborated in Theodore Becker and Malcolm Feeley, eds., *The Impact of Supreme Court Decisions* (1973). Gerald Rosenberg, *The Hollow Hope: Can Courts Bring About Social Change?* (1991), caused quite a sensation when published, for it argues very strongly and with great vigor that the answer to its question is basically no, and Rosenberg uses *Brown* and *Roe* as the central examples of his thesis.

G. GENERAL APPROACHES TO THE ROLE OF THE SUPREME COURT

The past quarter century has seen the publication of many important books analyzing (and justifying) various roles of the Supreme Court. The two most important were almost certainly Alexander Bickel, *The Least Dangerous Branch* (1962), and John Hart Ely, *Democracy and Distrust* (1980). Both attempted to defend, against the apostles of "restraint," a fairly strong role for the Court. Bickel focused on the Court's ability to discern certain fundamental values within the American constitutional tradition and to enforce them. Ely, who expressed great skepticism about this, nevertheless defended the Court's actively monitoring the political processes by which public policy is made and striving to "reinforce" the representation of certain groups who were the victims of politically disabling prejudice. Also extremely influential has been the writing of philosopher Ronald Dworkin. See especially *Taking Rights Seriously* (1978) and *Law's Empire* (1986).

Other much discussed books defending a strong judicial role are Charles Black, *The People and the Court* (1960); Jesse Choper, *Judicial Review and the National Political Process: A Functional Reconsideration of the Role of the Supreme Court* (1980); and Michael Perry, *The Constitution, the Courts, and Human Rights* (1982). More recently, Perry has written *The Constitution in the Courts: Law or Politics?* (1994). Cass Sunstein's *The Partial Constitution* (1993), an excellent discussion of post-New Deal constitutionalism, is significant in part because it is the first comprehensive statement of constitutional theory by a member of the "post-Warren Court" generation (Sunstein was born in 1954). Mark Tushnet casts a skeptical eye on all comprehensive theories in *Red, White, and Blue* (1988).

Students should also consult two books by Philip Bobbitt, *Constitutional Fate* (1982) and *Constitutional Interpretation* (1991), that outline what he calls the "modalities" of constitutional interpretation and then go on to criticize the notion that there is one privileged method of interpretation. Bobbitt also criticizes books like McCloskey's that offer basically political explanations for many of the Court's decisions.

Certainly the most influential book taking a strongly antiactivist position is Bork's *The Tempting of American Law* (1990). Similarly skeptical about the Court's capacity for positive influence is Robert Nagel, *Constitutional Cultures: The Mentality and Consequences of Judicial Review* (1989).

One of the virtues of constitutional analysis is that one does not have to be a lawyer to engage in it. Much important writing has always been done by political scientists and others formally untrained in the law. For defenses of a vigorous role by the Supreme Court, see, e.g., Sotirios A. Barber, *On What the Constitution Means* (1984) and *The Constitution* of *Judicial Power* (1993). Rogers Smith, in *Liberalism and American Constitutional Law* (1985) also basically defends moderate judicial activism. Strong critiques of any such role are offered by John Agresto, *The Supreme Court and Constitutional Democracy* (1964); Christopher Wolfe, *The Rise of Modern Judicial Review: From Constitutional Interpretation to Judge-Made Law* (1986) and Eugene W. Hickok and Gary L. McDowell, *Justice vs. Law: Courts and Politics in American Society* (1993). Two recent books from theoretically sophisticated political scientists focus on the importance of the specifiable moral principles that ostensibly underlie the Constitution. See Hadley Arkes, *Beyond the Constitution* (1990) and Graham Walker, *Moral Foundations of Constitutional Thought: Current Problems, Augustinian Prospects* (1990). The same subject is treated in an interesting and imaginative way by Duke law professor Jefferson Powell in *The Moral Tradition of American Constitutionalism* (1993).

Other, more idiosyncratic, books should also be mentioned. William P. Harris's brilliant *The Interpretable Constitution* (1992) is a study of the theoretical foundations of the very idea of constitutionalism as a means of structuring political decision making by a sovereign people, while Sanford Levinson's *Constitutional Faith* (1988) looks at American constitutionalism as a "civil religion" and analyzes enduring constitutional controversies by reference to classical religious conflicts. The debate about the authority of the Court, for example, is analogized to the debate about the institutional authority of the Roman Catholic Church within Christianity. Gary Jacobsohn, *Apples of Gold: Constitutionalism in Israel and the United States* (1993), is a very suggestive comparison of the roles of the respective Supreme Courts in using constitutional norms to help shape their societies. Finally, Lief Carter, in *Contemporary Constitutional Lawmaking* (1985), offers a self-consciously "post-modernist" reading of constitutional interpretation and the role of the Court.

Most of the books named above are normative in their approach. There is also a rich empirical literature focusing on the ability of the Supreme Court, practically speaking, to affect public policy. A classic article is Robert A. Dahl, "Decision-Making in a Democracy: The Role of the Supreme Court as a National Policy-Maker," 6 *Journal of Public Law* 279 (1957). The "impact" studies mentioned in the previous section raise similar issues. Students should also be familiar with Donald L. Horwitz, *The Courts and Social Policy* (1977), a classic critique of the Courts' efforts to make general social policy in regard to empirically complex issues. Also examining the Court's attempt to create new constitutional rights is Stuart A. Scheingold, *The Politics of Rights* (1974). These books should be read along with Martin Shapiro's *Law and Politics in the Supreme Court: New Approaches to Political Jurisprudence* (1964), which, though obviously written many years ago, remains full of relevant insights.

The empirical studies necessarily focus on the Court's interaction with other political institutions and, ultimately, on its ability to shape public opinion (and the extent to which the Court's handiwork is itself shaped by public opinion). Walter Murphy, in *Congress and the Court* (1962), examines the response of Congress to a series of highly controversial decisions viewed by many representatives and senators as too favorable to Communists and criminal defendants. And, of course, Murphy assesses the response of the Court itself to Congress's reaction. A more recent article by Gerald N. Rosenberg, "Judicial Independence and the Reality of Political Power," 54 *Review of Politics* 369 (1992), concludes that the Court defers to Congress under certain specified conditions. In "The Non-Majoritarian Difficulty: Legislative Deference to the Judiciary," 7 *Studies in American Political Development* 35 (1993), Mark A. Graber argues that legislatures have frequently been more than happy to pass political hot potatoes on to the judiciary for resolution (and a willingness to take the heat generated by those who dislike the result).

Murphy is, with Joseaph Tanenhaus and Daniel Kastner, an author of *Public Evaluations of Constitutional Courts: Alternative Explanations* (1973), perhaps the best study of the Court's (in)ability to change public opinion. Thomas R. Marshall, in *Public Opinion and the Supreme Court* (1989), compares public opinion on a broad set of issues with Court opinions dealing with those issues and finds significant congruence.

H. INSTITUTIONAL STUDIES OF THE MODERN COURT

There is, of course, a copious literature on the internal behavior of the Court as an institution. David M. O'Brien, *Storm Center: The Supreme Court in American Politics* (2d ed. 1990) is a serviceable text that should be helpful to any student. Mention should also be made of *The Brethren: Inside the Supreme Court* (1979), the classic (and notorious) book by Robert Woodward and Scott Armstrong. Whatever its excesses, it is a readable and insightful look into the actual worklife of the Justices. Vastly more scholarly but equally readable is Walter P. Murphy, *Elements of Judicial Strategy* (1964), which focuses on the strategic problems and choices facing Justices seeking the approval of a majority of their colleagues for given policy goals.

How do cases get to the Court? See H. W. Perry, *Deciding to Decide: Agenda Setting in the Supreme Court* (1991), which examines the certiorari process by which the modern Court decides what specific cases it wishes to hear and issue opinions about.

How do justices get on the Court? The standard book is Henry J. Abraham, *Justices and Presidents: A Political History of Appointments to the Supreme Court* (3d ed. 1982). Since the publication of Abraham's book, the most important nomination was surely President Reagan's of Robert Bork, which failed. See Ethan Bronner, *Battle for Justice* (1989). David J. Danelski, *A Supreme Court Justice Is Appointed* (1964), focuses on the 1922 appointment by President Harding of Pierce Butler.

There is an important body of work on the relationship between the "attitudes" of Supreme Court Justices and the way they vote. A full review of the literature by two of the major scholars adopting this approach is Jeffrey A. Segal and Harold J. Spaeth, *The Supreme Court and the Attitudinal Model* (1933).

I. SPECIFIC DOCTRINAL STUDIES

It would be truly ludicrous to attempt to list all of the literally hundreds of articles and books relevant to specific topics of constitutional law. All of the general reference works cited above, as well as other works cited throughout this note, include copious leads to further research in their footnotes and bibliographies.

A good way to locate important essays is to look at one of the many fine collections of essays on general constitutional topics or on specific doctrinal areas. For example, an excellent four-volume collection, *Selected Essays in Constitutional Law,* was put together in 1938 by the Association of American Law Schools and supplemented with another volume in 1963. Conyers Read, ed., *The Constitution Reconsidered,* originally published in 1938, was slightly updated in 1968 and has a number of important essays. Robert McCloskey, *Essays in Constitutional Law* (1957), also brings together some classic writings on the subject. Another excellent collection was compiled from and published in 1963 by the *Harvard Law Review.*

More contemporary collections include John H. Garvey and T. Alexander Aleinikoff, eds., *Modern Constitutional Theory: A Reader* (2d ed., 1991) and Michael J. Gerhardt and Thomas D. Rowe, Jr., *Constitutional*

Theory: Arguments and Perspectives (1993). Both respond to the intense interest during the 1980s in explicit constitutional "theory," including constitutional hermeneutics, the positing of specific methods of interpretation. John H. Garvey and Frederick Schauer, eds., *The First Amendment: A Reader* (1992) and Geoffrey R. Stone et al., *The Bill of Rights in the Modern State* (1992) are both worth consulting.

Few topics are more important than war and peace, and few topics have been less illuminated by the Supreme Court. A good casebook is Stephen Dycus, et al., *National Security Law* (1990). Among especially fine recent books on the subject are Harold Hongju Koh, *The National Security Constitution: Sharing Power after the Iran-Contra Affair* (1990); Michael J. Glennon, *Constitutional Diplomacy* (1990); and John Hart Ely, *War and Responsibility: Constitutional Lessons of Vietnam and Its Aftermath* (1993). An interesting collection of essays is Richard H. Kohn, *The United States Military under the Constitution of the United States, 1789–1989* (1991).

The problems of war and peace invariably involve the notion of separation of powers, as suggested by the title of Clinton Rossiter, *The Supreme Court and the Commander in Chief* (2d ed. 1976). But the issues generated by the reality of separate branches of government go well beyond war and peace, as demonstrated in an excellent casebook by Harold H. Bruff and Peter M. Shane, *The Law of Presidential Power* (1988). Joseph M. Bessette and Jeffrey Tulis, eds., *The Presidency in the Constitutional Order* (1981), offers a set of essays on the history and contemporary practice of the presidency. See also the collection of essays in Robert A. Goldwin and Art Kaufman, eds., *Separation of Powers—Does It Still Work?* (1986).

The classic account of the development of free speech doctrine is Zechariah Chafee, *Free Speech in the United States* (1948). Subsequent analysts have acutely pointed to a number of Chafee's own axes that were thoroughly ground in his presentation. An important corrective, for example, is Mark A. Graber, *Transforming Free Speech: The Ambiguous Legacy of Civil Libertarianism* (1991). Harry Kalven was a leading commentator in the decades following Chafee; *A Worthy Tradition: Freedom of Speech in America* (1988), is a collection of his essays.

Another very controversial, albeit essential, book is Leonard Levy, *Legacy of Suppression: Freedom of Speech and Press in Early American History* (1960), revised and reprinted as *Emergence of a Free Press* (1985). Levy argues that the framers of the First Amendment had a quite restricted view of freedom of speech, confined primarily blocking prior restraints (but not, for example, prohibiting subsequent punishment for seditious speech). Levy is criticized in David Anderson, "The Origins of the Press Clause," 30 *U.C.L.A. Law Review* 455 (1983) and "Levy v. Levy," 84 *Michigan Law Review* 777 (1986). Levy is also taken to task in David Rabban, "The Ahistorical Historian: Leonard Levy on Freedom of Expression in Early American History," 37 *Stanford Law Review* 795 (1985). A superb, highly readable, general history of freedom of the press throughout American history is Lucas Powe, *The Fourth Estate and the Constitution* (1991).

Powe also wrote an earlier book, *American Broadcasting and the First Amendment* (1987), focusing on the special (and, he argues, indefensible) regulation accorded the broadcasting industry, in contrast to the unregulated press. Powe accepts the unregulated press as the normative model for electronic and new cable media. Cass Sunstein, on the other hand, accepts the regulated broadcasting industry as the normative model for the press in general in Cass R. Sunstein, *Democracy and the Problem of Free Speech* (1993). Lee Bollinger, on the third hand, argues that the present mixture of regulation and non-regulation is just right in *Images of a Free Press* (1991). All of these topics are also ably examined in Rodney A. Smolla, *Free Speech in an Open Society* (1992).

Mark G. Yudof, *When Government Speaks: Politics, Law, and Government Expression in America* (1983) is a seminal examination of the constitutional problems linked to governmental communication with the citizenry, whether through choosing a curriculum for public schools or engaging in direct propaganda in behalf of governmental policies. Donald Alexander Downs, *The New Politics of Pornography* (1989) is a good examination of that extremely volatile subject. The most prominent academic advocate of extensive regulation of pornography is Catherine A. MacKinnon. A good short summary of her views is MacKinnon, *Only Words* (1993).

Another basic subject of the First Amendment, of course, is religion. On the early history of the topic, see Thomas J. Curry, *The First Freedom: Church and State in America to the Passage of the First Amendment* (1986). A good brief overview of one aspect of religion and the First Amendment is Leonard Levy, *The Establishment Clause: Religion and the First Amendment* (1986), though it is marred by too easy acceptance of the standard liberal view of that clause. A very good collection of essays from *The Supreme Court Review* (an annual publication that treats the most important cases of the preceding term of the Court) is Philip B. Kurland, ed., *Church and State: The Supreme Court and the First Amendment* (1975).

The most litigated single clause of the Constitution prior to the Civil War was the contracts clause, and Benjamin F. Wright, *The Contract Clause of the Constitution* (1938) remains the essential source. In many ways the Clause was the victim of the 1937 revolution, though it has never entirely died. A good analysis of the Court's post-1937 contract clause jurisprudence is Jonathan B. Baker, "Has the Contract Clause Counter-Revolution Halted? Rhetoric, Rights, and Markets in Constitutional Analysis," 12 *Hastings Law Quarterly* 71 (1984).

Also key to pre–Civil War constitutionalism, of course, was the issue of slavery. In addition to the Fehrenbacher and Finkelman books mentioned earlier, one is well advised to read William M. Wiecek, *The Sources of Antislavery Constitutionalism in America: 1760–1848* (1972), which, as the title suggests, focuses on the attempt to use the Constitution as the basis of an attack on, rather than protection of, slavery. Wiecek is also author of *The Guarantee Clause of the U.S. Constitution* (1972), a study of the "republican form of government" clause that was, as a practical matter, eliminated from standard constitutional discourse by the Court's decision in *Luther v. Borden* (1847) that it raised a "political question" not appropriate for judicial review.

Another enduring issue of our constitutional politics has been property and its control by the state. A good survey is James W. Ely Jr., *The Guardian of Every Other Right: A Constitutional History of Property Rights* (1992). Two recent helpful works, from opposite ends of the political spectrum, are Jennifer Nedelsky, *Private Property and the Limits of American Constitutionalism: The Madisonian Framework and Its Legacy* (1990), and Richard A. Epstein, *Takings: Private Property and the Power of Eminent Domain* (1985). Nedelsky argues that the very notion of protected property rights has become incoherent, especially following the demise of *Lochner* in 1937 and the legitimation of the regulatory state. Epstein, on the other hand, argues that the pre-1937 Court was right and the New Deal revolution therefore illegitimate and ripe for overruling. More recently, Epstein has written *Bargaining With the State* (1993), examining the particular constitutional problems of the modern welfare state. Also very interesting is Bruce A. Ackerman, *Private Property and the Constitution* (1977), which focuses, among other things, on the differences between the economist's and the ordinary lawyer's understanding of "property."

A basic problem in constitutional theory is whether legislative power extends only to passing laws in the "public interest" and, more particularly, whether the Supreme Court has the ability to distinguish between such laws and laws that serve only "private interests." An unusually instructive book on this point is Howard Gilman, *The Constitution Besieged: The Rise and Demise of Lochner Era Police Powers Jurisprudence* (1993).

There is no great history of the Commerce Clause. Two older books worth looking at are Edward S. Corwin, *The Commerce Power versus States Rights* (1959) and Felix Frankfurter, *The Commerce Clause under Marshall, Taney, and Waite* (1937). Robert L. Stern wrote a classic article, "The Commerce Clause and the National Economy, 1933–1946," 59 *Harvard Law Review* 645 (1946), but obviously a great deal has taken place even since then in terms of the exercise of basically plenary power by Congress.

There is also no great book on race and the Constitution. A serviceable overview is Donald G. Nieman, *Promises to Keep: African Americans and the Constitutional Order, 1776 to the Present* (1991). Good, also, is Andrew Kull, *The Colorblind Constitution* (1992), a relatively short and well-written book tracing the idea of that concept. He is clearly disappointed that it has not in fact prevailed, but he presents a fair treatment of the issues. Judith A. Baer, *Equality Under the Constitution: Reclaiming the Fourteenth Amendment* (1983) is a helpful overview, coupled with a strong argument as to proper interpretation, of the meaning assigned the equal protection clause by the Court. A very skeptical view of recent developments can be found in Herman Belz, *Equality Transformed: A Quarter-Century of Affirmative Action* (1991). Similarly critical is Lino A. Graglia, *Disaster by Decree: The Supreme Court Decisions on Race and the Schools* (1976), which focuses on the Court's "busing" decisions.

Especially since *Griswold* v. *Connecticut,* the once-forgotten Ninth Amendment has been the subject of interest (and, in some cases, dismay). Randy E. Barnett has edited two excellent collections of materials on the Amendment under the title *The Rights Retained by the People: The History and Meaning of the Ninth Amendment* (Vol. I, 1989, Vol II, 1993).

Finally, mention should be made of two dazzling essays by Akhil Reed Amar, "The Bill of Rights as a Constitution," 100 *Yale Law Journal* 1131 (1991), and "The Bill of Rights and the Fourteenth Amendment," 101 *Yale Law Journal* 1193 (1992), which offer a comprehensive (and controversial) synthesis of the original Bill of Rights and their nationalization in the Fourteenth Amendment.

INDEX